Janice VanCleave's
204
Sticky, Gloppy, Wacky, and Wonderful Experiments

JOSSEY-BASS
A Wiley Imprint
www.josseybass.com

All figures except those for experiments 4, 43, 46, 54, 55, 56, 66, 84, 127, 134, 142, 143, 145, 149, 155, 158, 159 and 160 copyright © 2002 by Laurel Aiello.

Published by Jossey-Bass
A Wiley Imprint
989 Market Street, San Francisco, CA 94103-1741   www.josseybass.com

Published simultaneously in Canada

Design and production by Navta Associates, Inc.

Jossey-Bass books and products are available through most bookstores. To contact Jossey-Bass directly call our Customer Care Department within the U.S. at 800-956-7739, outside the U.S. at 317-572-3986, or fax 317-572-4002.

Jossey-Bass also publishes its books in a variety of electronic formats. Some content that appears in print may not be available in electronic books.

The publisher and the author have made every reasonable effort to ensure that the experiments and activities in the book are safe when conducted as instructed but assume no responsibility for any damage caused or sustained while performing the experiments or activities in this book. Parents, guardians, and/or teachers should supervise young readers who undertake the experiments and activities in this book.

Portions of this book have been reprinted from the books *Janice VanCleave's A+ Projects in Earth Science; Janice VanCleave's Biology for Every Kid; Janice VanCleave's Dinosaurs for Every Kid; Janice VanCleave's Ecology for Every Kid; Janice VanCleave's Food and Nutrition for Every Kid; Janice VanCleave's Geography for Every Kid; Janice VanCleave's The Human Body for Every Kid; Janice VanCleave's Insects and Spiders; Janice VanCleave's Microscopes and Magnifying Lenses; Janice VanCleave's Oceans for Every Kid; Janice VanCleave's Plants; Janice VanCleave's Play and Find Out about Bugs; Janice VanCleave's Rocks and Minerals; Janice VanCleave's Science Around the Year; Janice VanCleave's Solar System; Janice VanCleave's Teaching the Fun of Science; Janice VanCleave's 203 Icy, Freezing, Frosty, Cool and Wild Experiments; Janice VanCleave's Volcanoes; and Janice VanCleave's Weather.*

ISBN 0-471-33101-5

Printed in the United States of America
FIRST EDITION
PB Printing   10 9 8 7 6

Dedication

It is my pleasure to dedicate this book to my grandchildren:

Kimberly and Travis Bolden,
Lauren and Lacey Russell,
David, Davin, and Jennifer VanCleave

Acknowledgments

I wish to express my appreciation to these science specialists for their valuable assistance in providing information and/or assisting me in finding it.

Members of the Central Texas Astronomical Society, including Johnny Barton, Dick Campbell, John W. McAnally, and Paul Derrick. Johnny is an officer of the club and has been an active amateur astronomer for more than twenty years. Dick is an amateur astronomer who is interested in science education. John is also on the staff of the Association of Lunar and Planetary Observers, where he is acting Assistant Coordinator for Transit Timings of the Jupiter Section. Paul is the author of the "Stargazer" column in the *Waco Tribune-Herald*.

Dr. Glenn S. Orton, a senior research scientist at the Jet Propulsion Laboratory of California Institute of Technology. Glenn is an astronomer and space scientist who specializes in investigating the structure and composition of planetary atmospheres. He is best known for his research on Jupiter and Saturn. I have enjoyed exchanging ideas with Glenn about astronomy facts and experiments for modeling astronomy experiments.

Dr. Ben Doughty, head of the department of physics at Texas A & M University—Commerce in Commerce, Texas. Dr. Sexton is an instructor of biology and microbiology at Houston Community College Northwest—Houston, Texas. Robert Fanick, a chemist at Southwest Research Institute in San Antonio, Texas, and Virginia Malone, a science assessment consultant. These special scientists have provided me with answers to my many questions. This valuable information has made this book even more understandable and fun.

A special note of gratitude to these educators who assisted by pretesting the activities and/or by providing scientific information: Holly Harris, China Spring Middle School, China Spring, Texas; Anne Skrabanek, homeschooling consultant, Perry, Texas; Connie Chatmas, Sue Dunham, and Stella Cathey, consultants, Marlin, Texas.

A special note of gratitude to these future educators who have assisted me by pretesting activities and/or by providing scientific information—the elementary education students of Dr. Belinda Anderson, dean of the School of Education, Lambuth University, Jackson, Tennessee: Allison Barger, Melissa Bell, Celia Boone, Brittany Carr, Pam Combs, Beth Harrell, Zena Hunt, Heather Jones, Erin Kaiser, Susan Kuykendall, Orman Meadow, Heather Noble, Sumeeta Parker, Stacey Pruett, Lauren Rosser, and Trecie Williamson.

Contents

Introduction   **1**

I.   Astronomy   **3**

  1.   More or Less   4
  2.   Sunrise-Sunset   4
  3.   Sun Path   5
  4.   Time   5
  5.   Saving Time   6
  6.   Longer   6
  7.   Sun Compass   7
  8.   Radiate   7
  9.   Sun Parts   8
10.   Bong!   8
11.   Sun Block   9
12.   Shadow Size   9
13.   Earth Model   10
14.   North Side   10
15.   Reversed   11
16.   How Fast?   11
17.   Rotate   12
18.   Tilted   12
19.   Equal   13
20.   Together   13
21.   Light and Dark   14
22.   Weighty   14
23.   Best Spot   15
24.   In Front Of   15
25.   Ringed   16
26.   Lineup   16
27.   Brighter   17
28.   Same Face   17
29.   Lunar Calendar   18
30.   Minor Planets   18
31.   Space Rocks   19
32.   Launched   19
33.   Heat Telescope   20
34.   Basic   20
35.   Same Size   21
36.   Bigger or Smaller?   21
37.   Star Locator   22
38.   Mobile Stars   22
39.   Pairs   23
40.   Uneven   23

II.   Biology   **25**

41.   Clusters   26
42.   Many Parts   26
43.   Getting Started   27
44.   Hitchhikers   27
45.   Sprouters   28
46.   Dividers   28
47.   Up and Down   29
48.   Anchors   29
49.   Just Alike   30
50.   Leaf Parts   30
51.   On the Edge   31
52.   Falling Leaves   31
53.   Coverup   32
54.   Breakout   32
55.   Lifters   33
56.   Follow Me   33
57.   Spongy   34
58.   Stickers   34
59.   Hummers   35
60.   Migrating Eye   35
61.   Largest   36
62.   Sniffer   36
63.   Pickup!   37
64.   Signals   37
65.   Locked   38
66.   Nails   38
67.   Backbone   39
68.   Squeezed   39
69.   Stoppers   40
70.   Keep Cool   40
71.   Spotted   41
72.   Sweaty   41
73.   Expanded   42
74.   Wrinkled   42
75.   Smelly   43
76.   Double   43
77.   Vibrating Cords   44
78.   Bigger and Better   44
79.   Light Catchers   45
80.   Twice   45
81.   Big or Little?   46
82.   Extra Money   46
83.   How Near?   47
84.   Who Can?   47

III.   Chemistry   **49**

85.   It Matters   50
86.   Just Enough   50
87.   On Top   51
88.   Floater   51
89.   Builders   52
90.   New Stuff   52
91.   Changes   53
92.   Rusty   53
93.   Inside Out   54
94.   No Leftovers   54
95.   Faster   55
96.   Helper   55
97.   Breakdown   56
98.   Trapped   56
99.   Sweeter   57

100. Gassy   57
101. Shortening   58
102. Uncoiled   58
103. Crystals   59
104. Shiny Cubes   59
105. Linked   60
106. No Leak   60
107. Coded   61
108. Bridges   61
109. Glob   62
110. Glob 2   62
111. Mixture   63
112. Blended   63
113. Separator   64
114. Loser   64
115. More!   65
116. Soaker   65
117. Melting Ice   66
118. Attractive   66
119. Twisted   67
120. Foamy   67
121. Hissssssss!   68
122. Puffer   68
123. Sudsy   69
124. Acid Testing   69

IV. Earth Science   71

125. Around   72
126. Only One   72
127. Time Line   73
128. Drifters   73
129. Normal   74
130. Small Portion   74
131. Soil   75
132. Straight Through   75
133. Splat!   76
134. Mudflow   76
135. Compact   77
136. Cemented   77
137. Recycled Rock   78
138. Fire Rocks   78
139. Hot Spot   79
140. Turn Aside   79
141. Fly Away   80
142. Eye of the Storm   80
143. Cloud Maker   81
144. Raindrops   81
145. Water Cycle   82
146. Open and Closed   82
147. Holder   83
148. Pressed   83
149. Reducer   84
150. Down Under   84
151. Streamers   85
152. Rise and Fall   85
153. Washout   86
154. Overflow?   86

155. Below the Surface   87
156. Coming Up!   87
157. Percolate   88
158. Sinker   88
159. Erupting Volcano   89
160. Magma Flow   89
161. Shaker   90
162. Fill 'Er Up   90
163. Pollution Dilution   91
164. Runoff   91

V. Physics   93

165. Unreal   94
166. Backward   94
167. Outward   95
168. Inward   95
169. To the Point   96
170. Beyond   96
171. Within   97
172. Stored   97
173. Cooling   98
174. Cold Skin   98
175. Thermometer   99
176. Gravity   99
177. Weightless?   100
178. Roller   100
179. Balancing Act   101
180. Equal Arms   101
181. Stable   102
182. Contact   102
183. Bumpy   103
184. Slider   103
185. No Rubbing   104
186. Stand Up   104
187. Twang   105
188. Bounce Back   105
189. Louder   106
190. High or Low?   106
191. Shorter   107
192. Spread Out   107
193. Flipper   108
194. Riser   108
195. Pull Away   109
196. Same Kind   109
197. Thin Skin   110
198. Surface Film   110
199. Wetter   111
200. Spread   111
201. Speedy   112
202. Stop!   112
203. Constant   113
204. Hero's Engine   113

Glossary   114

Index   120

Introduction

This book is a collection of science experiments designed to show you that science is more than a list of facts—science is fun! The 204 experiments in the book take science out of the laboratory and put it into your daily life.

Science is a way of solving problems and discovering why things happen the way they do. What is an eclipse? What conditions are needed for seed germination? Why don't raincoats get soaking wet? You'll find the answers to these and many other questions by doing the experiments in this book.

The experiments cover five different fields of science:

- **Astronomy**   The study of the planets, the stars, and other bodies in space.

- **Biology**   The study of the way living organisms behave and interact.

- **Chemistry**   The study of the way materials are put together and their behavior under different conditions.

- **Earth Science**   The study of Earth.

- **Physics**   The study of energy and matter and their relationships.

The Experiments

Scientists identify a problem, or an event, and seek solutions, or explanations, through research and documentation. A goal of this book is to guide you through the steps necessary to successfully complete a science experiment and to teach you the best method of solving problems and discovering answers.

1. **Purpose:**   The basic goals for the experiment.

2. **Materials:**   A list of necessary supplies.

3. **Procedure.**   Step-by-step instructions on how to perform the experiment.

4. **Results:**   An explanation stating exactly what is expected to happen. This is an immediate learning tool. If the expected results are achieved, the experimenter has an immediate positive reinforcement. An error is also quickly recognized, and the need to start over or make corrections is readily apparent.

5. **Why?**   An explanation of why the results were achieved is described in terms that are understandable to the reader, who may not be familiar with scientific terms. When a new term is introduced and explained, it appears in **bold** type; these terms can also be found in the Glossary.

You will be rewarded with successful experiments if you read each experiment carefully, follow the steps in order, and do not substitute materials.

General Instructions

1. **Read first.** Read each experiment completely before starting.

2. **Collect needed supplies.** You will experience less frustration and more fun if you gather all the necessary materials for the experiments before you begin. You lose your train of thought when you have to stop and search for supplies.

3. **Experiment.** Follow each step very carefully, never skip steps, and do not add your own. Safety is of the utmost importance, and by reading the experiment before starting, then following the instructions exactly, you can feel confident that no unexpected results will occur.

4. **Observe.** If your results are not the same as described in the experiment, carefully read the instructions and start over from the first step.

Measurements

Measuring quantities described in this book are intended to be those commonly used in every kitchen. When specific amounts are given, you need to use a measuring instrument closest to the described amount. The quantities listed are not critical, and a variation of very small amounts more or less will not alter the results. Approximate metric equivalents are given in parentheses.

I
Astronomy

1. More or Less

Purpose To determine how the masses of other planets compare to the mass of Earth.

Materials pen   sheet of white copy paper
ruler   calculator

Procedure

1. Use the pen, ruler, and paper to make a table like the one shown here.

MASS RATIOS OF THE PLANETS TO EARTH

Planet	Mass (trillion trillion kg)	Mass Ratio (planet/Earth)
Mercury	0.33	0.06/1
Venus	4.87	
Earth	5.986	
Mars	0.64	
Jupiter	1,899.0	
Saturn	569.0	
Uranus	86.9	
Neptune	103.0	
Pluto	0.012	

2. Complete the table by calculating each planet's mass ratio, which is the ratio of a planet's mass to the mass of Earth.

NOTE: The mass of planets is measured in trillion trillion kilograms. For example, the mass ratio of Mercury is:

$$\text{mass ratio} = \text{planet's mass} \div \text{Earth's mass}$$
$$= 0.33 \div 5.986$$
$$= 0.06/1$$

Mercury's mass ratio is 0.06/1, which means that Mercury's mass is 0.06 times that of Earth.

Results The mass ratio of each planet to Earth in the solar system is calculated.

Why? **Matter** is anything that takes up space and has mass. **Mass** is the amount of substance in a material. The term **mass ratio,** as used in this book, is a number indicating how many times as massive an object is as compared to another object.

Matter in the **universe** is made up of all the natural objects in space including Earth and other planets. **Planets** are celestial bodies that travel in an **orbit** (curved path of one celestial body about another) around the Sun. **Celestial bodies** are natural objects in the sky, such as stars, suns, moons, and planets. The nine planets listed in the table are part of our **solar system** (a group of celestial bodies that move in a curved path about a star called a sun). The mass ratio of each of the planets in our solar system compared to Earth is calculated by dividing the mass of a planet by the mass of Earth.

2. Sunrise-Sunset

Purpose To model the Sun's apparent daily motion.

Materials marker
scissors
22-by-28-inch (55-by-70-cm) piece of poster board
tree

Procedure

1. Use the marker to draw the largest semicircle possible on the poster board. Cut out the semicircle.
2. Label the left side of the semicircle "Sunrise" and the right side "Sunset."
3. Holding the semicircle, stand with your back near the tree.
4. Walk eight paces away from the tree. Then turn and face the tree.
5. Hold the poster board parallel with the ground so that the center of the straight edge of the board is near but not touching your eyes.
6. Turn so that the tree is in line with the left (sunrise) side of the poster board.
7. Slowly turn your body counterclockwise until the tree is in line with the right (sunset) side of the poster board. As you turn, watch the tree while also observing objects in the background.

Results The tree appears to move from one side of the poster board to the other, but does not move in relation to objects in the background.

Why? The apparent motion of the tree from one side of the paper to the other is due to your body turning. The apparent motion of the Sun is also, like the tree, due to your body turning. But for the Sun's motion, instead of you turning your own body, the Earth you stand on turns, or **rotates,** about its **axis** (an imaginary line through the center of an object), taking your body with it. The Sun's daily path is generally from east to west. **Sunrise** is the apparent rising of the Sun above the eastern **horizon** (an imaginary line where the sky and Earth appear to meet). **Sunset** is the apparent setting of the Sun below the western horizon.

3. Sun Path

Purpose To demonstrate the Sun's apparent motion.

Materials tree

Procedure
1. Stand with your back near the tree.
2. Walk eight paces away from the tree.
3. Turn and slowly walk counterclockwise halfway around the tree.
4. As you walk, watch the tree trunk while also observing objects in the background.

Results The tree appears to move slowly against a background of stationary (unmoving) objects.

Why? Just as the tree appeared to move against objects in the background, to observers on Earth, the Sun appears to move eastward among the stars. The apparent path the sun moves in is called the **ecliptic.** The ecliptic runs through a band of **constellations** (groups of stars that appear to make patterns in the sky). This band is called the **zodiac,** and the constellations along the band are called **zodiac constellations.** In ancient times, sky watchers divided this band into 12 segments, each about 30° wide, with a constellation in each segment. About every 30 days, a different segment appears in the daytime sky.

As seen from Earth, the zodiac constellations are the background against which the Sun apparently moves. At specified times, the Sun is said to be "in" a given constellation. So even during the daytime, when the Sun is too bright for the stars to be visible, the constellations around the Sun are known.

In this experiment, you represent the Earth, the tree represents the Sun, and the objects beyond the tree represent the zodiac constellations. The path you walked represents Earth's orbit. The apparent motion of the tree is due to your motion around it. This is also true for the apparent annual movement of the Sun, which is due to Earth **revolving** (moving about a central point) about the Sun. As Earth revolves about the Sun, the zodiac constellation that appears behind the Sun changes throughout the year.

8 paces

4. Time

Purpose To study the relationship between the apparent motion of the Sun and time.

Materials
scissors	transparent tape
butcher paper	straw
ruler	modeling clay
basketball	flashlight
marking pen	

Procedure
1. Cut a strip of paper 4 inches (10 cm) wide and long enough to wrap around the basketball.
2. Fold the strip into three equal sections. Then fold it in half three times to make 24 equal sections.
3. Unfold the strip and draw a line on each fold.
4. Wrap the strip around the basketball and secure the ends together with a piece of tape.
5. Cut three 2-inch (5-cm) pieces from the straw. Use three dabs of clay to stand the straw pieces on three consecutive sections of the strip.
6. Turn on the flashlight and lay it on the edge of a table with the bulb facing outward.
7. Darken the room. Then stand with the flashlight to your right, holding the basketball so that it is about 6 inches (15 cm) away from the bulb and the first straw points straight toward you.

8. Observe the length of the shadows of the straws on the paper. Continue to observe the shadows as you slowly rotate the ball counterclockwise. Stop when the first straw points directly at the light.

Results Shadows are cast by the straws. Straws closer to the light have shorter shadows.

Why? As the straws get closer to the light, their shadows shorten until no shadow is cast by the straw pointing directly at the light. This is a simulation of Earth rotating on its axis toward the Sun, with each of the 24 sections on the paper representing one time zone. A time zone is any of 24 geographic areas into which the Earth is divided. Clocks within a given time zone are set to the same time. The difference in the shadows indicates a difference in distance from the zone beneath the noonday Sun, when the Sun is at its greatest **altitude** (angular distance above the horizon), and thus a difference in time.

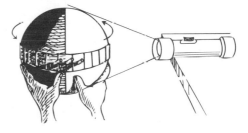

5. Saving Time

Purpose To determine if there is extra sunlight because of daylight saving time.

Materials watch or clock
empty soup can (or can of comparable size)
thin pole, such as a flagpole (a thin tree will work)

Procedure

1. Set the watch to correct standard time, which is 1 hour earlier than daylight saving time. (If you are performing this experiment during daylight saving time, set the watch back 1 hour.)
2. On a sunny day, take the can outdoors about 5 minutes before 10:00 A.M. (or any convenient hour).
3. Locate the shadow of the pole.
4. At 10:00 A.M., push the can into the ground in the center of the pole's shadow.
5. Before the following day, set the watch to daylight saving time (set the watch ahead 1 hour).
6. On the following day, at 10:00 A.M. daylight saving time, observe the pole's shadow. Compare the location of the shadow to the location of the can. Continue to observe the shadow periodically and make note of the time when the can is in the center of the shadow as on the previous day.

Results The can was in the pole's shadow 1 hour later when the watch was set to daylight saving time.

Why? Daylight saving time (DST) is the time from late spring to early autumn when clocks are set forward 1 hour so that there are more usable hours of daylight in the evening. **Standard time (ST)** is the time during the rest of the year. During daylight saving time, nothing changes except the position of the hour hand on the watch. The shadow on the can would have indicated the same standard time of 10:00 A.M. each day. Your watch showed the shadow to be on the can at 11:00 A.M. instead of 10:00 A.M. because you set your watch ahead 1 hour. Dawn and sunset both occur 1 hour later during daylight saving time, so no extra hours of daylight are really available from the time change.

6. Longer

Purpose To determine how the Sun's altitude affects shadow length.

Materials sheet of unruled paper
pen
ruler
grape-size piece of modeling clay
pencil
flashlight

Procedure

1. Lay the paper on a table. Use the pen and ruler to draw two perpendicular lines across the center of the paper.
2. Print the compass directions—N, E, S, W—at the ends of the lines as shown.
3. Use the clay to stand the pencil in the center of the paper where the lines cross.
4. In a darkened room, hold the flashlight on the east side and about 6 inches (15 cm) away from the pencil. The light should be pointed toward the side of the pencil. Observe the length of the shadow.
5. Slowly move the flashlight over the pencil in a semicircle to the west side. Observe the length of the shadow during this movement.

Results The length of the shadow decreases as the flashlight is raised and increases as the flashlight is lowered.

Why? Because of the rotation of the Earth, the Sun appears to move across the sky from east to west. In the morning, when the Sun rises in the east and is at a low altitude, shadows are long. As the altitude of the Sun increases, shadows decrease in length. Shadows are shortest when the Sun is at its highest altitude. This occurs at what is called **solar noon,** which is at or near 12:00 P.M. standard time. After solar noon, the Sun's altitude decreases and shadows increase in length and are longest at sunset. Before solar noon, shadows are cast toward the west, but after solar noon, shadows are cast toward the east.

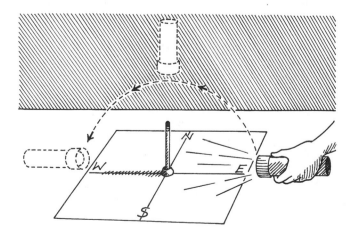

7. Sun Compass

Purpose To find directions without a compass.

Materials   watch or clock
poster board
2 bricks or large rocks
pencil
pen
two 18-inch (45-cm) pieces of string
scissors
helper

Purpose

1. About 1 hour before noon standard time (or about 2 hours before noon daylight saving time), lay the poster board on level ground.
2. Use the bricks to hold the poster board in place.
3. Stick the point of the pencil in the center of the poster board. Adjust the height of the pencil so that the pencil's entire shadow falls across the poster board. The pencil must be perpendicular to the ground (straight up and down).
4. Use the pen to mark a dot at the end of the pencil's shadow. Label the dot "1."
5. Tie one piece of string around the base of the pencil.
6. Stand the pen on the dot. While you hold the pen in place, ask your helper to tie the free end of the string around the pen and to cut away any excess string.
7. Use the attached string and pen to draw a semicircle from the dot, moving clockwise around the pencil.
8. Observe the shadow of the pencil and mark a dot with the pen when the tip of the shadow again touches the semicircle. This will be about 1 hour after noon standard time (or about noon daylight saving time). Label the dot "2."

9. Find the midway point between the dots by laying the second piece of string on the **arc** (section of a circle) between the dots. The string should be as long as the distance between the dots, so cut away excess string. Fold the string in half and mark a dot on the semicircle next to the fold in the string. Label the dot "N."
10. Remove the pen from the original piece of string and stretch the string from the pencil across the N dot and beyond.
11. Stand behind the pencil and note distant landmarks, trees, houses, and so on that the string points toward.

Results You have made a compass. The string points toward the north.

Why? The globe of Earth is divided into imaginary parallel lines called **lines of latitude** that are used to indicate **latitude** (distance in degrees north or south of the equator). The **equator** is at latitude 0° and separates Earth into **Northern** and **Southern Hemispheres.** The north and south ends of Earth's axis, called the **North** and **South Poles,** are at latitudes 90°N and 90°S, respectively. North of latitude 23.5°N, the Sun is never directly overhead, but instead always appears to move across the southern sky a distance from the **zenith** (highest point in the sky). At solar noon, the Sun is at its highest altitude in the southern sky, so the shadow of the pencil is shortest at that time. This short shadow points north.

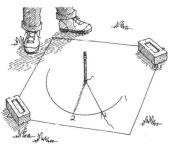

In the Southern Hemisphere, the same experiment could be used to determine which way is south because south of latitude 23.5°S the Sun is never directly overhead and appears to move across the northern sky.

---

8. Radiate

Purpose To demonstrate radiant heat.

Materials   ruler
desk lamp

Procedure

1. Hold one hand about 2 inches (5 cm) under the other.
2. Move your hands so that the top hand is 6 inches (15 cm) below the bulb of the desk lamp.
3. Hold your hands in this position for about 5 seconds. Make note of how warm or cool each hand feels.

Results The top hand, which is closer to the light, feels much warmer than the bottom hand.

Why? The **universe** is made of all the matter and energy in space now and in the past. **Energy** is the ability to cause matter to move. **Radiant energy** is energy that can travel through space. Radiant energy as well as its **transmission** (how it is sent from one place to the other) is called **radiation. Heat** (energy that is transferred from a warm body to a cooler body because of the difference in temperature) transferred by the process of radiation is called **infrared radiation** or **radiant heat.** All objects give off infrared radiation. The hotter the object, the more infrared radiation it emits. The radiant energy from the Sun is called **solar energy.**

In this experiment, since only your top hand feels warmer, this hand is warmed by the infrared radiation given off by the hot lightbulb, not by air touching the skin. The top hand **absorbs** (takes in) the infrared radiation, and the lower hand does not.

9. Sun Parts

Purpose To prepare a model of the Sun's structure.

Materials 2 permanent markers, each a different color
6-inch (15-cm) or larger Styrofoam ball from which one-fourth has been removed
four 1-by-4-inch (2.5-by-10-cm) white labels
4 round toothpicks
pen

Procedure

1. With one of the colored markers, paint an area in the center of the cutaway section of the ball to represent the Sun's core as shown.
2. Use the other colored marker to draw a band inside the cutaway section to represent the convection zone as shown.
3. Prepare flags as shown, following these steps:
   - Put just the ends of the sticky sides of a label together. Do not crease the fold.
   - Carefully press the sticky sides of the label together, leaving a gap near the folded end.
   - Insert one end of a toothpick through the gap and stick the toothpick to the folded end of the label. Press the sides together.
4. Repeat step 3 with the other three toothpicks and labels.

5. Use the pen to write the names of the Sun's layers on the flags: Photosphere, Convection Zone, Radiation Zone, Core.
6. Stick the flags in the model Sun as shown.

Results A model of the layers of the Sun is made.

Why? At the center of the Sun is the **core,** which is the hottest part of the Sun. It is in the core that solar energy is produced by **nuclear fusion,** which is the joining of the **nuclei** (positively charged central parts) of **atoms** (the building blocks of matter). Energy (causes things to move) from the superhot core is slowly transmitted through the area above the core, called the **radiation zone.** From there, gas **expands** (moves farther apart) and rises, then cools, becomes more pressed together, and sinks back. This circulating gas forms the **convection zone.** The next layer, called the **photosphere,** is actually the first layer of the Sun's **atmosphere** (the gaseous area that surrounds some celestial bodies). But from Earth, it appears as the Sun's surface.

---

10. Bong!

Purpose To demonstrate how astronomers use vibrations to determine the nature of the Sun's interior.

Materials stemmed water glass
tap water
metal spoon

Procedure

1. Fill the glass about three-fourths full with water.
2. Gently tap the side of the glass with the spoon and observe the surface of the water.

Results When you tap the glass, repeated raised areas form on the water's surface.

Why? Tapping the glass makes the glass and its contents **vibrate** (move quickly back and forth). The back-and-forth motion of the glass pushes on the water inside the glass, causing **transverse waves** (ripples on a surface following each other at regular intervals) to form on the water's surface.

One back-and-forth motion is called a **vibration,** and the number of vibrations in a specific time period is called **frequency. Astronomers** (scientists who study the Sun and other celestial bodies) use vibrations to study the interior of the Sun. Vibrations pass from the Sun's interior to its gaseous surface, causing it to move up and down.

While the frequency of the vibrations produced by striking the glass is many vibrations in 1 second, the frequency of some solar sounds is only 1 vibration in 5 minutes. You are able to see the waves on the water produced by the vibrating glass. But computers are needed to distinguish between the vibrations produced by the Sun. The study of the interior of the Sun by observing how its surface vibrates is called **helioseismology.**

11. Sun Block

Purpose To model a solar eclipse.

Materials golf ball–size piece of modeling clay
2 pens
4-inch (10-cm) Styrofoam ball
flashlight

Procedure

1. Pull off a grape-size piece of clay and mold it into a ball.
2. Stick the clay ball on the pointed end of one of the pens. The clay ball represents the Moon.
3. Stick the point of the other pen into the Styrofoam ball. This ball represents Earth.
4. Use the remaining clay to stand the model Earth on a table.
5. In a darkened room, turn on the flashlight. Hold it in your left hand, about 12 inches (30 cm) from the model Earth.
6. Hold the model Moon in your right hand, about 1 inch (2.5 cm) from the model Earth. Move the Moon from the back side of the Earth toward the front in a counterclockwise direction.
7. As the Moon moves, notice the shadow it casts on the Earth's surface.

Results The shadow of the Moon moves across the surface of the Earth.

Why? The passing of one body in front of another, cutting off its light, is called an **eclipse.** In this experiment, the Moon eclipses the Sun, which is called a **solar eclipse.** On the celestial sphere, the Moon appears to move across the ecliptic in front of the Sun during a solar eclipse. When the Moon passes directly between the Sun and the Earth, the Moon blocks the Sun's photosphere. If the shadow of the Moon reaches Earth, to observers in part of the shadow the Sun's photosphere is completely blocked, and the Sun seems to disappear. This event is called a **total solar eclipse.**

12. Shadow Size

Purpose To model the size of the Moon's shadow during a total solar eclipse.

Materials sheet of white copy paper
drawing compass
ruler
pencil
penny

Procedure

1. Fold the paper in half, long sides together.
2. Unfold the paper. Draw two arcs centered at opposite ends of the fold. One arc should have a 2-inch (5-cm) diameter and the other a 6-inch (15-cm) diameter. Label the larger arc "Sun" and the smaller arc "Earth."
3. Using the pencil and ruler, draw two lines from where the fold line touches the surface of the Earth to the top and bottom edge of the Sun.
4. Lay the penny between the lines connecting the Earth and the Sun. Move the penny between the lines until you find the place where the penny fits snugly between the two lines.
5. Draw a circle around the penny and label it "Moon."
6. Draw two horizontal lines from the Earth to the Sun so that they touch the top and bottom edges of the Moon.
7. Using the pencil, label the areas between the Moon and the Earth "Penumbra" and "Umbra." Shade the umbra and penumbra as shown.

Results Shaded areas are formed between the Moon and the Earth. Only a small part of the dark shaded area touches the Earth.

Why? A solar eclipse is when the Moon passes between the Sun and Earth. During a total solar eclipse, as demonstrated in this experiment, the Moon's shadow reaches the surface of Earth and the Sun's light is totally blocked for observers in the **umbra** (the inner, darker part of a shadow) of the Moon's shadow, partially blocked for observers in the **penumbra** (the outer, lighter part of a shadow), and not blocked at all for observers outside the shadow. Because the Earth rotates, the Moon's shadow sweeps a narrow path across the Earth's surface.

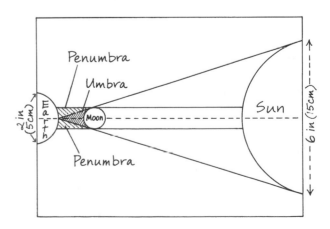

13. Earth Model

Purpose To build a 3-D scale model of the Earth.

Materials drawing compass
metric ruler
8-by-8-inch (20-by-20-cm) square piece of
     poster board, any color
scissors
index card
pen

Procedure

1. The diameter of Earth is 7,973 miles (12,757 km). Using a metric scale of 1 cm = 1,500 km, the diameter of the model Earth can be calculated as follows:

     Earth's diameter ÷ 1,500 km/cm = model's diameter
     12,757 km ÷ 1,500 km/cm = 8.504 cm

     Rounding the number to the closest 0.1 cm, the model's diameter would be 8.5 cm.
2. Use the compass to draw two circles, each with a diameter of 8.5 cm, on the poster board.
3. Cut out the circles. Then cut along a straight line from the edge to the center of each circle.
4. Fit the two circles together at a 90° angle to each other.
5. Prepare a legend showing the scale of the model by folding the index card in half. Write "Earth" and the scale, "1 cm = 1,500 km," on one side of the card. Stand the card alongside the model.

Results You have made a scale model of the Earth.

Why? A **scale model** is a replica made in proportion to the object it represents. Models of objects in the solar system, such as Earth, are valuable because they allow the observer to study these objects separately as well as in comparison to each other. Because celestial bodies are generally very large, models give a view of the entire system so that their shapes, sizes, and distances can be compared.

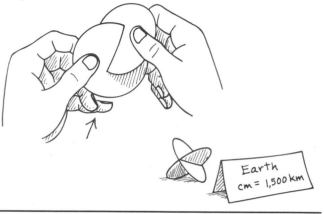

14. North Side

Purpose To demonstrate where the North Pole of Earth is in relation to its orbit.

Materials lemon-size piece of modeling clay
2 pencils
scissors
22-by-28-inch (55-by-70-cm) poster board
large can (such as a coffee can)
protractor

Procedure

1. Break off a walnut-size piece of clay and shape it into a ball around one of the pencils. The pencil should pass through the center of the ball. The clay represents Earth.
2. With the second pencil, draw a circle around the clay ball perpendicular to the pencil in the clay. The circle represents Earth's equator.
3. Cut as large an oval as possible from the poster board. The outside edge of the oval represents Earth's orbital path.
4. Raise the oval above the table's surface by placing the can on the table and centering the oval on top of the can.
5. Shape the remainder of the clay into half a ball. Place this piece flat side down in the center of the poster board, above the can. Use the pencil to write an "N" in the top of the clay. This piece of clay represents the northern hemisphere of the Sun.
6. Holding the eraser end of the first pencil, place the model Earth near but not touching the oval so that the model's equator is in line with the edge of the oval and the pencil is perpendicular to the oval. Tilt the eraser end of the pencil away from the oval so that the model Earth moves a distance of about the width of your thumb. Note which end of the pencil is above the oval.

Results The eraser end of the pencil remains above the oval.

Why? In this experiment the half ball of clay represents the Sun's northern hemisphere. The edge of the oval piece represents Earth's orbit about the Sun. The pencil represents the axis of the model Earth, which is tilted about 23° from perpendicular to its orbit. It was the decision of the International Astronomical Union (IAU) Committee on Nomenclature (nomenclature is the naming of things) that regardless of the tilt of a planet's axis, the end of the axis on the same side of its orbital plane as the Sun's northern hemisphere is called the planet's **north pole.** In this experiment, the eraser end of the pencil represents the **North Pole** (the north end of Earth's axis) of the model Earth.

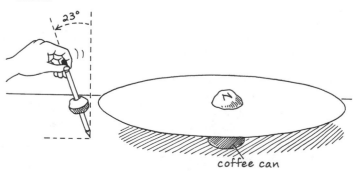

coffee can

15. Reversed

Purpose To demonstrate why the rotation of Venus is reversed from Earth's.

Materials pen
ruler
manila file folder
protractor
model planet from Experiment 14, "North Side"

Procedure

1. Use the pen and ruler to draw two lines perpendicular to each other across the center of one side of the folder. Mark a dot on the folder where the lines cross.
2. Use the pen to label the horizontal line "Orbital Plane."
3. Starting at the dot, use the protractor to measure two angles, 23° and 178°. Draw lines on the folder to indicate each angle and label the angles as shown.
4. Stand the folder on a table.
5. To represent the rotation of Earth, hold the eraser end of the pencil in one hand and the pointed end in the other hand. Hold the pencil vertically and the equator of the model planet in front of the dot on the folder. Keeping the planet in front of the dot, rotate the pencil counterclockwise while you tilt the top of the pencil to the left 23° of the vertical line. The pencil will be in line with the line marked 23°. Note the position of the eraser and the direction of rotation of the ball.
6. To represent the rotation of Venus, repeat step 5, tilting the eraser end of the pencil 178°.

Results The eraser end of model Earth sticks up and the pointed end of model Venus sticks up. The Earth model turns counterclockwise and the Venus model turns clockwise.

Why? In this experiment the horizontal line on the folder represents the orbital plane of the planets around the Sun. The north pole of the models is represented by the end of the pencil sticking up above the orbital plane. (For information about identifying a planet's north pole, see Experiment 14, "North Side.")

The model of Earth and Venus is rotated in the same direction throughout the experiment. When the axis of Venus is tilted 177°, the model turns almost upside down and the opposite end of the pencil sticks up, causing the rotation to be reversed from Earth's.

All planets except for Pluto, Uranus, and Venus have counterclockwise rotations as seen from their north poles. The counterclockwise rotation of the planets is arbitrarily determined to be normal and is called **direct rotation.** Since the axis tilt of Pluto, Uranus, and Venus is more than 90°, they have a clockwise **retrograde** (backward) rotation.

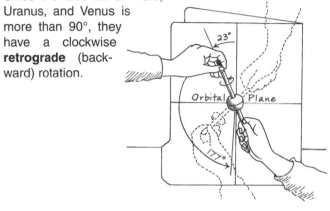

16. How Fast?

Purpose To determine how fast the Earth rotates.

Materials index card
3 pencils
ruler
timer
protractor

Procedure

1. Select an open sunny area outdoors.
2. Lay the index card on the ground.
3. Stick one of the pencils vertically through one end of the card and about 1 inch (2.5 cm) into the ground.
4. Rotate the index card so that the pencil's shadow falls across the center of the card.
5. Repeat step 4, placing the second pencil at the opposite end of the card. This pencil will hold the card in place.
6. Use the remaining pencil to draw a line on the card about 3 inches (7.5 cm) long down one side of the pencil's shadow.
7. Set the timer for 2 hours. At the end of 2 hours, repeat step 6.
8. Use the protractor to measure the angle between the two lines drawn on the card.

Results The shadow moves and the angle between the two lines is about 30°.

Why? As seen from the North Pole, the Earth rotates counterclockwise on its axis toward the east. As it turns, the light from the Sun hits the pencil from a different direction. The angle between the two lines indicates the angular distance Earth turns in 2 hours, which is about 30°. If Earth turns about 30° in 2 hours, then it makes one full rotation of 360° in about 24 hours.

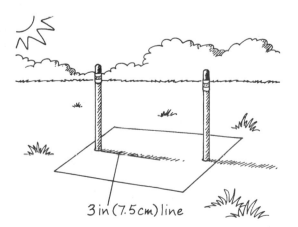

3 in (7.5cm) line

17. Rotate

Purpose To determine why the Sun appears to move across the sky.

Materials   paper clip
model planet from Experiment 14, "North Side"
crayons
2 index cards
ruler
2 grape-size balls of modeling clay
protractor

Procedure

1. Put the paper clip in the clay at a spot above the equator line. The paper clip represents an observer in the Northern Hemisphere of Earth.
2. Use the crayons to draw a symbol of the Sun on one of the index cards.
3. Use the pencil to label the card. Label the right side of the Sun "West" and the left side "East."
4. Draw six or more stars on the other index card.
5. Stand the index cards 12 inches (30 cm) apart in the grape-size balls of clay so that the Sun and the stars face each other.
6. Stand the model Earth between the index cards so that the paper clip observer faces the star card. Use the protractor to tilt the model about 23° toward the Sun, taking care not to move the ball from its location in space.

7. Slowly rotate the model Earth counterclockwise until the paper clip observer faces the right edge (west side) of the Sun card.
8. Continue rotating the model Earth counterclockwise until the paper clip observer faces the left edge (east side) of the Sun card.

Results As the model Earth rotates away from the stars, the paper clip observer on Earth faces the west side of the Sun first and the east side last.

Why? In Earth's Northern Hemisphere, the Sun appears to rise above the eastern horizon, move across the southern sky, and set below the western horizon. If you could view Earth from above the North Pole, you would see Earth, like the model, rotating counterclockwise. The paper clip observer on the clay sphere first sees the western side of the Sun diagram, then the eastern side comes into view as the sphere rotates.

Since we are moving with Earth as it rotates, it appears that the Sun is moving across the sky from east to west, but it is actually Earth that is rotating from west to east.

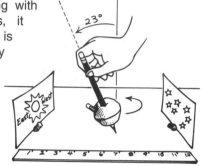

---

18. Tilted

Purpose To determine why seasons are reversed in the Northern and Southern Hemispheres.

Materials   flashlight
model planet from Experiment 14, "North Side"
protractor

Procedure

1. Hold the flashlight about 6 inches (15 cm) from the model. The model represents Earth and the flashlight represents the Sun.
2. Use the protractor to measure as you tilt the eraser end of the pencil (the North Pole) about 23° toward the flashlight. Observe the area of the sphere that is lighted up by the flashlight.
3. Tilt the eraser end of the pencil about 23° away from the flashlight. Observe the area of the sphere that is lighted up.

Results When the top of the sphere is tilted toward the flashlight, more light hits the top half of the sphere than the bottom. The reverse is true when the top of the sphere is tilted away from the flashlight.

Why? Earth's equator is tilted at an angle of 23° to the plane of its orbit around the Sun. Since the Earth's equator is perpendicular to its axis, the angle at which the axis tilts is also 23°. This means that during part of its orbit the North Pole is tilted toward the Sun, and during the other part the North Pole is tilted away from the Sun. The Northern Hemisphere receives the most solar energy when the North Pole is tilted toward the Sun. The day of the year when Earth's North Pole is tilted closest to the Sun is called the **summer solstice** and occurs on or about June 21 in the Northern Hemisphere. The summer season begins on this day. The day when Earth's North Pole is tilted farthest away from the Sun is called the **winter solstice** and occurs on or about December 22. The winter season begins on this day. The dates of the summer and winter solstices are reversed in the Southern Hemisphere.

Perpendicular to Earth's orbit

23°

19. Equal

Purpose To show why Earth has different lengths of daylight and darkness during different seasons.

Materials sharpened pencil
3-inch (7.5-cm) Styrofoam ball
marker
desk lamp
ruler
adult helper

Procedure

1. Ask an adult to insert the pencil through the Styrofoam ball.
2. Use the marker to draw a line around the center of the Styrofoam ball, to represent the equator.
3. In a darkened room, position the desk lamp so that it shines straight down, with its bulb about 6 inches (15 cm) above the table.
4. Position the ball on the table so that the pencil eraser is leaning slightly toward the lamp. Observe how much of the ball is lighted up and how much of the ball above and below the equator is not lighted up.
5. Without changing the tilt of the pencil, move the ball around the lamp in a counterclockwise direction. Notice how much of the ball is lighted up. Observe also any changes in the location of the lighted area above and below the equator as the ball is moved.

Results About half of the ball is lighted up at all times, but the area of the ball that is lighted up changes as the ball moves.

Why? The ball represents Earth. The pencil is Earth's axis. The eraser end represents the North Pole, and the sharpened end represents the South Pole. The lamp represents the Sun. Moving the ball around the lamp represents Earth's revolving about the Sun. Because Earth is a sphere, the Sun **illuminates** (lights up) half of Earth's surface at any one time.

At the vernal and autumnal equinoxes, Earth's axis is not tilted toward or away from the Sun, so Earth's illuminated half is from pole to pole, resulting in equal hours of daylight and dark throughout Earth. The **autumnal equinox** (first day of autumn) and the **vernal equinox** (first day of spring) occur in the Northern Hemisphere on or about September 23 and March 21, respectively. At the winter solstice in the Northern Hemisphere, the North Pole tilts away from the Sun, resulting in less daylight north of the equator and more daylight south of the equator. The opposite is true at the summer solstice.

20. Together

Purpose To show how Earth's shape affects its surface temperature.

Materials 9-inch (22.5-cm) round dark-colored balloon
marker
flashlight

Procedure

1. Inflate the balloon and tie a knot in its opening.
2. Use the marker to draw a line around the center of the balloon.
3. Lay the flashlight on the edge of a table, as shown.
4. In a darkened room, hold the balloon with its center about 4 inches from the light. Note the size and shape of the spot of light on the balloon.
5. Slowly lower the balloon. Observe any change in the size and shape of the spot of light on the balloon's surface.

Results As the balloon is lowered, the spot of light spreads out.

Why? Because Earth is spherical, surface areas facing the Sun are angled away from the Sun by varying amounts. During the vernal and autumnal equinoxes, the angles vary from 0° at the equator to 90° at the poles. In this experiment, the balloon represents Earth, and the line drawn on it the equator. Since the same amount of light left the flashlight regardless of the position of the balloon, the smaller spot of light at the equator indicates a more **concentrated** (gathered closely together) amount of light. Light is a form of energy. Thus, more energy was received in a smaller area when the light hit the equator. This is because the light rays are more direct at the equator and more indirect (at an angle) and thus more spread out at the poles. The Earth's equator receives about two-and-a-half times as much heat during the year as the regions around the poles.

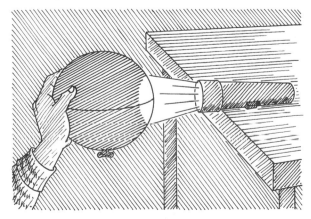

21. Light and Dark

Purpose To model the light and dark areas of Earth during the winter solstice.

Materials marker
2-inch (5-cm) Styrofoam ball
6-inch (15-cm) square of aluminum foil

Procedure

1. Use the marker to make two dots opposite each other on the Styrofoam ball. Label the dots "N" and "S" to represent the North and South Poles, respectively.
2. Draw a circle around the middle of the ball between the poles to represent the equator. Then draw a circle around each pole, making the two circles the same size.
3. Mold the aluminum foil around the ball so that it covers half the ball from pole to pole. Keep the foil loose enough that the ball moves freely. The foil cup represents the half of Earth that is not lighted by the Sun.
4. Holding the foil stationary, tilt the ball so that the North Pole moves under the foil until the upper circle is just under the edge of the foil. Note that the lower circle is now completely outside the foil.

Results The part of the model Earth that is facing the Sun (not covered in foil) changes when you tilt the foil, until all of the circle around the North Pole is covered by the foil and none of the circle around the South Pole is covered.

Why? The half of the ball that is not covered by foil represents the side of Earth that is facing the Sun. The circle around the North Pole represents the **Arctic Circle** (latitude 66.5°N), and the one around the South Pole the **Antarctic Circle** (latitude 66.5°S). Earth's axis is tilted in relation to its orbit and therefore to the Sun. So as Earth orbits the Sun during the course of the year, the North Pole tilts away from the Sun during part of the year. At the point in Earth's orbit where the North Pole is tilted farthest from the Sun—around December 22, the winter solstice— Earth's Northern Hemisphere has longer hours of darkness and the **Arctic region** (area north of the Arctic Circle) is in complete darkness all 24 hours of that day. As Earth continues in its orbit, the North Pole becomes angled more and more toward the Sun, so more and more of the Northern Hemisphere is lighted. Finally, on June 21, the summer solstice, the opposite point in Earth's orbit to the winter solstice, all of the Arctic region is lighted the entire day. The reverse is true for the **Antarctic region** (area south of the Antarctic Circle). On December 22 the Antarctic region is lighted, and on June 21 it is in darkness.

22. Weighty

Purpose To simulate the pull of gravity on some celestial bodies.

Materials pencil
5-ounce (150-mL) paper cup
12-inch (30-cm) string
coins or small rocks (enough to half fill the paper cup)
large bowl
hand scale
tap water

Procedure

1. Use the pencil to punch two pairs of holes in opposite sides of the cup, under the rim.
2. Slip the ends of the string through each pair of holes in the cup and knot each end.
3. Place the coins in the cup and set the cup in the bowl.
4. Hook the string on the hand scale and lift the cup. Note the weight of the cup on the scale.
5. Fill the bowl about three-fourths full with water.
6. With the cup hanging from the scale, lower the cup into the water. The cup should be suspended in the water and not touching the bottom of the bowl. Again, note the weight of the cup on the scale.

Results The cup weighs less when suspended in water.

Why? **Gravity** is the force of attraction that draws objects at or near the surface of a celestial body toward the center of the celestial body. As the mass of a celestial body increases, its gravity increases. **Weight** is a measure of the pull of gravity on an object. Earth has more mass than the Moon and some other celestial bodies. In this experiment, the Earth's gravity pulls down on the cup, causing the spring in the scale to be stretched. Adding water to the bowl decreases the downward pull because the water pushes up on the cup. This upward force of the water cancels some of the downward pull of gravity. The mass of the cup and coins does not change, but their weight changes in the water. The reduced downward pull on the cup and its contents in the water simulates the reduced gravity on some celestial bodies that have less mass than Earth.

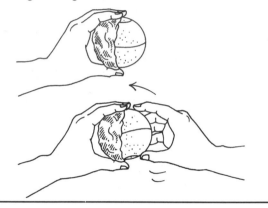

23. Best Spot

Purpose To find the two positions of Venus where it can best be viewed from Earth.

Materials   drawing compass
   ruler
   10-inch (25-cm) square of white poster board
   pen
   penny
   transparent tape
   8-inch (20-cm) string

Procedure

1. Use the compass to draw a circle with a 1-inch (2.5-cm) diameter in the center of the poster board. Label the circle "Sun." Label the sides of the poster board "East" and "West" as shown.
2. Around the Sun, draw two more circles, one with a diameter of 4 inches (10 cm) and the other with a diameter of 6 inches (15 cm). Label the smaller circle "Orbit of Venus" and the larger circle "Orbit of Earth."
3. Place the penny so that its center is at the bottom of the Earth circle, and use the pen to trace around it. Label this circle "Earth."
4. Lay the ruler across the centers of the Earth and Sun circles, and draw a straight line from the center of Earth to the edge of the Sun.
5. Tape one end of the string to the center of the Earth circle.
6. Holding the free end of the string, stretch the string along the line and across Venus's orbit behind the Sun. Then slowly move the string westward, observing the angle between the line and the string. Find the spot

where the string touches Venus's orbit and forms the greatest angle with the line. Mark an X on this spot.

7. Repeat step 6, moving the string to the east.

Results The two best viewing positions of Venus are found.

Why? The angle between the Sun and any planet as viewed from Earth is called the planet's **elongation.** Venus's maximum elongation is about 48°. Venus is an **inferior planet** (a planet whose orbit lies between Earth and the Sun). As it follows its path around the Sun, it appears east of the Sun at times and west at other times. Its greatest eastern elongation is about 48° and its greatest western elongation is also about 48°. When it is at its eastern elongation, Venus is seen in the evening sky. It is seen in the morning sky when at its western elongation. When Venus is between the Sun and Earth or when the elongation angle is small, the Sun's light is too bright for Venus to be seen.

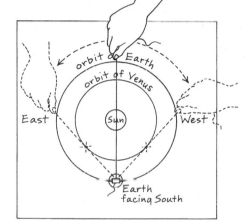

24. In Front Of

Purpose To model the revolution of Venus.

Materials   lamp
   pencil
   4-inch (10-cm) Styrofoam ball

Procedure

1. Set the lamp on a table and remove its shade.
2. Insert the point of the pencil into the Styrofoam ball.
3. Darken the room.
4. Holding the pencil, position the ball slightly below the bulb in front of the lamp.
5. At a slight angle, slowly move the ball counterclockwise halfway around the light, stopping when the ball is behind the bulb. As the ball moves, note the changes in the shape of its lighted side.

Results In front of and behind the lamp, the lighted side of the ball is not visible. As the ball moves from the front to the back of the lamp, the lighted part increases in size.

Why? The ball represents Venus, the bulb the Sun, and you an observer on Earth. Since Venus is closer to the Sun than is Earth, Venus's orbit does not encircle Earth's orbit.

So as the revolution of Venus is viewed from Earth, Venus moves in front of and beyond the Sun. When Venus is between Earth and the Sun, it cannot be seen because its illuminated side faces away from Earth. Also in this position, the brightness of the Sun's light prevents the planet from being seen. As Venus continues its revolution about the Sun, more of its lighted side faces Earth. Venus is said to be **waxing** (growing). When the planet is almost fully sunlit, it moves toward the opposite side of the Sun but not directly behind it, so it is not eclipsed by the Sun. Instead Venus disappears in the brightness of the Sun's light.

25. Ringed

Purpose To model how the rings of Saturn lie around the planet.

Materials   10-inch (25-cm) square of white poster board
drawing compass
ruler
scissors
black marker or crayon
index card
walnut-size piece of modeling clay
wooden skewer
2-inch (5-cm) Styrofoam ball
transparent tape
protractor

Procedure

1. On the white poster board, use the compass and ruler to draw five **concentric** (having the same center point) circles (one inside the other) with these diameters: 2 inches (5 cm), 3 inches (7.5 cm), 7 inches (17.5 cm), 7½ inches (18.75 cm), and 8 inches (20 cm).
2. Working from the outside in, use the black marker to color between the second and third circles and between the fourth and fifth circles. The black areas represent space between the rings of Saturn.
3. Cut out the model of Saturn's rings by cutting around the outside of the largest circle. Then cut away the center circle.

4. Lay the index card on a table and place the clay in its center.
5. Stick the wooden skewer through the center of the Styrofoam ball. Then place the model of Saturn's rings around the ball perpendicular to the skewer. Tape the underside of the rings to the skewer.
6. Stand the free end of the wooden skewer in the clay and tilt the rings toward you. Using the protractor, tilt the skewer about 27° from an imaginary line perpendicular to the index card.

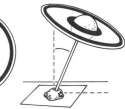

Results A model of Saturn is made showing two rings separated by a dark space.

Why? The rings that you see around Saturn are actually thousands of separate ringlets made up of lots of small chunks of ice orbiting Saturn's equator. In 1675, Giovanni Domenico Cassini (1625–1712), a French-Italian astronomer, observed two rings divided by a dark space, now called **Cassini's division.** Saturn's equator and its rings are always tilted at an angle of about 27° to the plane of Saturn's orbit. The rings and Cassini's division of Saturn's ring, as well as their tilt, are modeled in this experiment.

---

26. Lineup

Purpose To model Jupiter's moons as seen from Earth.

Materials   sheet of white copy paper
drawing compass
ruler
pencil
stiff piece of cardboard about the same size or slightly larger than the copy paper
grape-size piece of red modeling clay
4 different color pea-size pieces of clay

Procedure

1. On the copy paper, use the compass and ruler to draw four concentric circles with these diameters: 2 inches (5 cm), 4 inches (10 cm), 6 inches (15 cm), and 8 inches (20 cm). The circles represent the orbits of Jupiter's moons.
2. Use the pencil to draw dots on the circles in the positions shown.
3. Lay the paper on top of the cardboard.
4. Shape a ball with the red clay. Then tap the ball against a firm surface such as a tabletop to flatten one side of the ball. Place the flattened side of the ball in the center of the circles to represent the Northern Hemisphere of Jupiter. Label edge as shown.
5. Shape balls out of each of the pea-size pieces of clay and place one ball on each dot. These balls represent

Jupiter's moons. Look down on the paper and observe the position of each moon in relation to Jupiter.
6. Raise the cardboard so that it is in front of your eyes and parallel to the floor. Observe the position of each of the moons in relation to Jupiter.

Results From above the paper, the clay balls appear to be randomly placed, but when viewed on the edge, the balls appear to line up in a straight line.

Why? A **natural satellite** is a celestial body revolving around another body, such as a moon around a planet. The four largest satellites (moons) of Jupiter were discovered in 1610 by Galileo Galilei (1564–1642) and are called the **Galilean satellites.** Their names are Io, Europa, Ganymede, and Callisto, from closest to farthest from Jupiter.

These moons have nearly circular orbits in line with Jupiter's equator. So as seen from Earth these moons appear to line up in a straight line with Jupiter's equator. Looking down on the paper shows one possible position of the moons from a view above Jupiter's north pole.

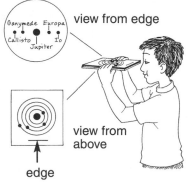

27. Brighter

Purpose To determine why planets and the Moon appear to be so bright in the sky.

Materials transparent tape
sheet of white copy paper
sheet of 9-by-12-inch (22.5-by-30 cm) white
  construction paper
medium-size box with one side at least 9 by
  12 inches (22.5 by 30 cm)
yardstick (meterstick)
3 or 4 books
flashlight

Procedure

1. Tape the copy paper to a wall so that its bottom edge rests on the floor. The paper is your screen.
2. Tape the white construction paper to one side of the box. The paper represents the surface or atmosphere of a planet.
3. Stand the box 12 inches (30 cm) from the screen, with the paper-covered side of the box facing the screen.
4. Set the books near the wall to one side of the screen. Set the flashlight on top of the books so that its bulb is at an angle to the paper on the box and its light shines on the center of the construction paper.
5. Turn the flashlight on, then darken the room. Observe the brightness of the photometer screen.
6. Turn the flashlight off and again observe the brightness of the screen.

Results The screen is bright only when the flashlight is on.

Why? The Sun and other stars are **luminous** (giving off light). But the Moon and planets, even though they shine, are not luminous.

copy paper

9-by-12-inch sheet
of construction paper

These celestial bodies **reflect** (bounce back) light from the Sun to Earth, the same way the construction paper reflects the light from the flashlight to the screen. Without the Sun, the Moon and planets would not shine. An instrument that measures the brightness of light reaching Earth is called a **photometer**. The paper screen acts like a simple photometer.

28. Same Face

Purpose To model the period of rotation of the Moon.

Materials drawing compass
ruler
pencil
sheet of white copy paper
¾-inch (1.9-cm) round color-coding label,
  any color

Procedure

1. Use the compass and ruler to draw an 8-inch (20-cm) circle on the paper.
2. In the center of the circle, use the compass to draw a 1-inch (2.5-cm) circle. Label the small circle "Earth."
3. Stick the round color-coding label on the pencil just above the point. The label represents the Moon.
4. Stand the pencil upright with its point on the outer circle and the Moon facing Earth, as shown.
5. Move the pencil around the circle once. During the revolution, rotate the pencil so that the Moon faces the Earth at all times. Note the number of times the pencil rotates.

Results The pencil rotates one time.

Why? Earth's gravitational pull on the Moon affects the speed of the Moon's rotation. The Moon rotates once during each revolution about the Earth. Therefore, like the label in this experiment, the same side of the Moon faces Earth at all times. The Moon's **period of rotation** (the time it takes to make one turn on its axis) and **period of revolution** (the time it takes to orbit Earth once) are both 27.3 days.

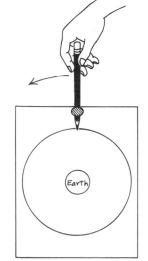

Earth

29. Lunar Calendar

Purpose   To construct a lunar calendar for 1 lunar month.

Materials   sheet of white
copy paper
pen
ruler

Sun.	Mon.	Tues.	Wed.	Thur.	Fri.	Sat.

Procedure

1. Use the paper, pen, and ruler to draw a calendar for 5 weeks as shown.

2. Start the calendar at the first sighting of the waxing crescent moon. This will be several days after the new moon. Use the Moon Phases diagram to identify the shape of the lighted part of the Moon.

3. Record this on your calendar as day 1 and draw the crescent shape on the calendar on this day. Be specific in drawing the size of the crescent. Check the weather report in the newspaper or on television for the time of moonrise.

4. Observe the shape of the Moon until the sighting of the next waxing crescent Moon, of equal size and lighted on the same side as before. This will be about 29 days after the first sighting. (The Moon rises about 50 minutes later each day. This results in the Moon rising half of the lunar month during the day and half at night.)

Results   A lunar calendar for one lunar month is made.

Why?   A **calendar** is a system for showing the length and divisions of a year. The first calendar, a **lunar calendar**, was based on a **lunar month**, which is the time it takes the Moon to pass through its phases—29½ days. (**Phases of the Moon** are the changes in the shape of the sunlit surface of the Moon facing Earth.) The problem of having half a day was solved by having one month with 29 days and the next with 30, followed by one with 29 and so on. The early Babylonians (1800–400 B.C.) began their month with the first sighting of the waxing **crescent moon** (the phase when the lighted area resembles a ring segment with pointed ends—a waxing crescent curves to the right in the Northern Hemisphere). The problem with the lunar calendar is that it does not correspond with the **solar year** (365¼ days), which includes a full cycle of the different seasons. Twelve lunar months last about 354 days (29½ × 12), so that over a period of time, the first day of the year does not start in the same season each year.

The modern calendar used worldwide (except for some religious or other purposes) is the **Gregorian calendar,** which was introduced in 1582 and has 365 days. The average length of a Gregorian year is close to that of the solar year, so that the seasons begin on about the same dates each year. To handle the problem of the quarter day, an extra day is added to the calendar every fourth year. That year is called a **leap year.**

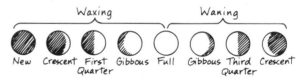

Waxing   Waning

New   Crescent   First Quarter   Gibbous   Full   Gibbous   Third Quarter   Crescent

30. Minor Planets

Purpose   To model the size of Ceres, the largest asteroid in our solar system.

Materials   pencil
ruler
12-inch (30-cm) square of white poster board
14-inch (35-cm) string
scissors
drawing compass
brown construction paper

Procedure

1. Use the pencil and ruler to make a dot in the center of the poster board.

2. Make a second dot 5½ inches (13.75 cm) from the center dot.

3. Tie a loop in one end of the string. Place the pencil point through the loop and stand the point on the second dot. Pull the string outward to stretch it over the center dot. Holding the string on this dot with your thumb, move the pencil around with its point pressed against the paper to draw a circle on the poster board.

4. Cut out the circle and draw a line across its center. Label the line "Moon, 2,200 Miles (3,520 km)."

5. Use the drawing compass to draw a circle with a 1½-inch (3.75-cm) radius on the brown paper. Draw a line across the center of the circle and label it "Ceres, 600 Miles (950 km)."

6. Compare the relative size of the white and brown circles by laying the small brown circle on the larger white circle.

Results   The brown circle covers only a portion of the white circle.

Why?   **Asteroids** are relatively small, irregular, rocky chunks of matter that orbit the Sun. They are also called **minor planets.** The largest asteroid in our solar system, represented by the brown circle, is Ceres, with a diameter of about 600 miles (960 km). This asteroid is large, but not as big as the Moon (the white circle), which has a diameter of about 2,200 miles (3,520 km). In this activity, the scale used for the models is 1 inch (2.5 cm) = 100 miles (160 km). The brown paper is used to indicate that the asteroid is made of material that does not reflect as much light as does the Moon, thus the asteroid is not as bright as the Moon.

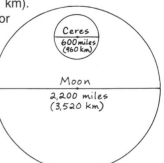

Ceres
600 miles
(960 km)

Moon
2,200 miles
(3,520 km)

31. Space Rocks

Purpose To determine how astronomers identify the shape of an asteroid.

Materials transparent tape
sheet of white copy paper
sheet of brown construction paper
pencil
flashlight

Procedure

1. Tape the white paper to a wall at about shoulder height. This will be your screen.
2. Crumple the brown paper into a loose ball.
3. Tape the ball of brown paper to the pencil.
4. Darken the room and hold the flashlight in one hand to the side of the paper screen with its bulb pointing away from the screen. The screen and the flashlight should be at an angle of about 45°.
5. Holding the pencil in the other hand, position the brown paper ball in front of the flashlight so that light reflects off the ball and onto the screen. Adjust the angle of the flashlight if necessary.

6. Slowly rotate the pencil and observe the light reflected on the screen.

Results The amount of light that is reflected changes as the paper ball rotates.

Why? In the experiment, the brown paper ball represents an asteroid, and the flashlight the Sun. The brightness of the light reflected off the paper ball **fluctuates** (changes continuously). Reflected sunlight bounces in a similar way from an asteroid to Earth. This is because asteroids, like the paper ball, are irregularly shaped and rotate. Different parts of the asteroid reflect different amounts of light. Astronomers study the different amounts of light reflected by an asteroid to determine its shape.

32. Launched

Purpose To determine the forces acting on man-made satellites.

Materials thick book
2 rulers (one with a groove down its center)
towel
marble
tennis ball
masking tape
30-inch (75-cm) string
scissors
helper

Procedure

1. Place the book on a kitchen counter beneath the front edge of an overhead cabinet.
2. Place the bound edge of the book 6 inches (15 cm) from the edge of the counter.
3. Lay the ruler on top of the book so that one end of the ruler is even with the bottom edge of the book.
4. Lay the towel on the counter next to the book as shown.
5. Position the marble at the right end of the ruler. Then position the tennis ball behind the marble.
6. Tape one end of the string to the tennis ball and the other end to the door of the overhead cabinet.
7. Pull the string through the tape on the cabinet so that the tennis ball is raised slightly above the ruler and can swing freely. Cut off and discard any extra string.
8. Ask a helper to pull the ball about 1 inch (2.5 cm) away from the marble and then release the ball while you observe the marble.

Results The tennis ball strikes the marble, which moves off the end of the ruler. The marble's path curves downward after the marble leaves the end of the ruler, until the marble hits the towel on the table.

Why? According to **Newton's first law of motion,** an object at rest tends to remain at rest, and an object in motion tends to remain in motion, unless acted on by an outside force. This tendency is called **inertia.** In this experiment, the marble was at rest until it was struck by the swinging tennis ball. The marble was then pushed forward in a **linear** (having the characteristics of a straight line) direction. Because of inertia, the marble would have continued to move in a straight path until it struck an object. But gravity pulled in a direction perpendicular to the surface of the Earth. The marble's curved path is the result of the two opposing forces: horizontal, due to the linear motion, and vertical, due to the motion caused by gravity. The marble would have continued to move in the curved path, but the table got in the way and stopped it.

In a similar way, Earth gets in the way of falling objects pulled by gravity toward its surface. But if an object has enough forward force, an exact balance between this force and gravity would launch the object into orbit around Earth. **Artificial satellites** are man-made objects that are launched into orbit around Earth.

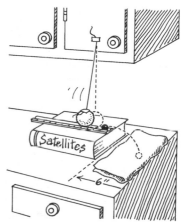

33. Heat Telescope

Purpose To compare the heat radiated from Earth and space.

Materials 12-by-18-inch (30-by-45-cm) piece of heavy-duty aluminum foil
outdoor thermometer

Procedure

1. Place the short sides of the foil together and fold the ends over several times to make a cylinder.
2. Insert the bulb end of the thermometer in one end of the aluminum foil cylinder.
3. Squeeze the foil around the thermometer to form a cone as shown.
4. Adjust the position of the thermometer so that the bulb of the thermometer is at the bottom of the foil cone. A heat telescope is made.
5. On a clear, dry night, stand in an open area outdoors.
6. Point the telescope toward the sky for 1 or more minutes. Note the temperature reading on the thermometer.

7. Point the telescope toward the ground for 1 or more minutes. Again, note the temperature reading.

Results The temperature is lower when the telescope is pointed toward the sky than when it is pointed toward the Earth.

Why? During the day the Sun radiates heat toward Earth and the Earth radiates some of this heat back toward the sky. But at night, when the Sun is not present, the direction of radiation is toward the sky only. When the heat telescope is pointed downward, it catches some of this radiation.

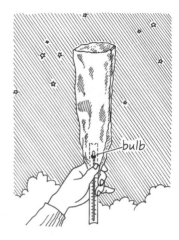

34. Basic

Purpose To determine how a refracting telescope works.

Materials pencil
flashlight
index card
scissors
transparent tape
12-inch (30-cm) square of white poster board
walnut-size piece of modeling clay
2 magnifying lenses
ruler

Procedure

1. Trace around the front (bulb end) of the flashlight on the index card. Cut out the circle.
2. Cut out an arrow shape from the paper circle.
3. Tape the paper circle over the front of the flashlight.
4. Fold the poster board in half and stand it on a table to make a screen.
5. Using the clay as a support, stand one of the magnifying lenses 12 inches (30 cm) from the screen. This will be called the objective lens.
6. Lay the ruler on the table on the side of the objective lens opposite the screen.
7. In a darkened room, turn the flashlight on and with the arrow pointing left, in reference to the screen, hold it above the ruler 4 inches (10 cm) from the objective lens. Observe the blurred patch of light that appears on the screen.
8. Take the second lens, which will be called the eyepiece, and position it between the objective lens and the screen.
9. Move the eyepiece toward and away from the objective lens until a sharp image of the arrow appears on the screen. (The distances set up between the screen

and the objective lens and between the light and the objective lens may have to be adjusted for a clear image to be produced.)

10. Rotate the flashlight so that the paper arrow points to your left. Note the size and direction of the arrow projected on the screen.

Results A large arrow pointing to the right is projected on the screen.

Why? The **image** (likeness of an object formed by a lens or mirror) seen through the two lenses is similar to images viewed through a basic **refracting telescope,** an instrument that uses only lenses to make a distant object such as a star appear closer. (A **lens** is a clear material, often glass, that changes the direction of light passing through it.) The parts of a refracting telescope can be compared to the lenses in this experiment. The lens closest to the light behaves similarly to the **objective lens** on a telescope in that it gathers the light coming from a star. The **eyepiece** is the lens you look through. It magnifies the image of the star and sends this enlarged image to your eye. In this experiment, the screen represents the back of your eye, where images are projected. The image seen through a telescope is reversed, as in this experiment.

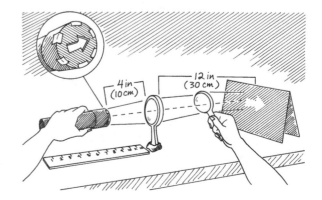

35. Same Size

Purpose To demonstrate the relationship between angular diameter and apparent diameter.

Materials masking tape
36-inch (1-m) strip of adding machine tape
yardstick (meterstick)

Procedure

1. Use the tape to secure the adding machine tape about eye level to a wall, as shown.
2. Stand 10 feet (3 m) from the tape.
3. Close one eye and hold your thumb in front of your open eye.
4. Move your thumb back and forth in front of your eye until it just blocks your view of the tape.

Results At a certain distance from your eye, the width of your thumb appears to be the same as the length of the tape.

Why? The width of your thumb is not the same as the length of the tape, they only appear to be the same. Thus they have the same **apparent diameter** (how large an object's diameter appears to be at a given distance). This is because at the point where your thumb blocks the view of the tape, your thumb and the tape have the same **angu-**lar diameter (angle of the apparent diameter expressed in degrees). In this experiment, the angular diameter of your thumb and the tape is angle A°. When two objects have the same angular diameter, they also have the same apparent diameter. Angular diameters are used to indicate the apparent size of celestial bodies. For example, the Moon's angular diameter from Earth is about 0.5°, which is about half the width of your little finger held at arm's length.

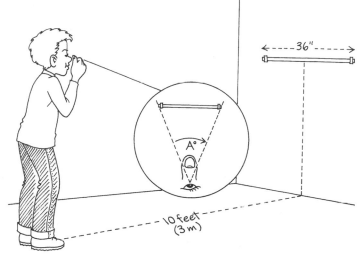

---

36. Bigger or Smaller?

Purpose To determine how distance affects the apparent size of an object.

Materials ruler
sheet of white copy paper
pencil
penny or other coin

Procedure

1. Lay the ruler across the center of the paper.
2. Use the pencil to make three dots on the paper, one at the left edge of the ruler, the second at 4 inches (10 cm), and the third at 8 inches (20 cm). Number the dots.
3. Center the coin on dot 2 and trace around the coin. Remove the coin.
4. Draw two lines extending from dot 1 to either side of the circle to the edge of the paper. Observe the angle made by these two lines.
5. Repeat steps 3 and 4 centering the coin on dot 3. Compare the angle made by these two lines to the angle made by the lines in step 4.

Results The angle made by the lines drawn to the circle that is farther from dot 1 is smaller than the angle made by the lines drawn to the circle that is closer to dot 1.

Why? The **apparent size** of an object is how large it appears to be at a given distance. The circles drawn on the paper are the same actual size, but from dot 1 the closer circle has a greater angular diameter than the farther circle. Thus, the apparent size of an object relates both to its actual size and to its distance. The farther away an object is, the smaller its apparent size.

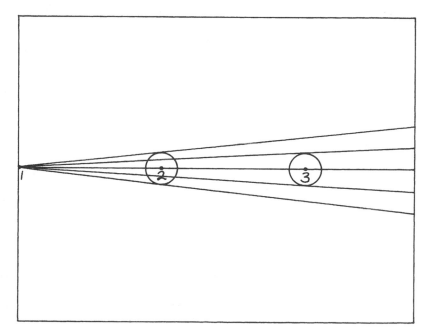

37. Star Locator

Purpose To measure the approximate altitude of Polaris.

Materials your hands

Procedure
1. Your hands can be used as a guide to measure the apparent distance between the stars or their altitude above the horizon. Practice the hand measurements pictured here.
2. During the day, locate a spot outdoors where you can see the northern horizon. Mark this spot or make a mental note of it.

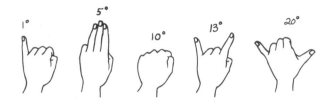

3. On a clear, moonless night, stand at the marked spot facing north.
4. Look for seven stars that form the shape of a large scoop called the Big Dipper. (Note that in the spring and early summer, the dipper will be upside down as shown.)

5. Follow an imaginary line from the two outer stars in the bowl of the Big Dipper to a bright star overhead called Polaris.
6. Use your hands to measure the altitude of Polaris above the horizon. This altitude equals the latitude where you are. For example, if you measure Polaris at four fists above the horizon, this means it is 40° above the horizon, so you are at latitude 40°N.

Results You find Polaris's altitude and your equivalent latitude. Results will vary depending on where you live.

Why? Because of Polaris's position, which is almost directly above the North Pole, its altitude in the sky is the same as your latitude on the globe.

38. Mobile Stars

Purpose To determine how the Earth's revolution makes stars appear to change position.

Materials pencil
1-inch (2.5-cm) square of stiff paper (An index card works well)
scissors
metric ruler
sheet of white copy paper
2 marble-size pieces of modeling clay

Procedure
1. Draw a five-pointed 1-inch (2.5-cm) square star on the stiff paper square. Cut out the star.
2. Use the ruler to draw a straight line from top to bottom down the center of the sheet of paper.
3. Lay the paper on the edge of a table with the line perpendicular to the table's edge.
4. Use one of the clay pieces to stand the ruler on edge parallel to the far edge of the paper with the metric measurements at the top and the 15-cm mark of the ruler at the end of the line on the paper.
5. Stand the star upright in the second piece of clay with the legs of the star in the clay and its top point up.
6. Set the star in the center of the line on the paper.
7. Kneel beside the table with your nose at the end of the line on the paper.

8. Close your right eye and using your left eye observe the position of the star against the ruler behind it. Read the measurement on the ruler behind the star's top point.
9. Without moving your head, open your right eye and close your left eye. With your right eye, again read the measurement on the ruler behind the star's top point.

Results The star appears to move, as indicated by two different measurements read on the ruler behind the star.

Why? In this experiment, the position of each eye represents the different positions of the Earth during its revolution around the Sun. This is much like observing the stars from the Earth at different points along its orbit. Each eye sees the star from a different angle; thus each eye sees a different background behind the star. The apparent change in the position of an object when viewed from two different points is called **parallax.**

39. Pairs

Purpose To model the motion of binary bodies.

Materials transparent tape
2 rulers
one-hole paper punch
½-by-3-inch (1.25-by-7.5-cm) strip of thick
   paper, such as from an index card
18-inch (45-cm) or longer string
food scale
1 pound (454 g) modeling clay
⁵⁄₁₆-by-24-inch (0.79-by-60-cm) wooden
   dowel

Procedure

1. Tape one of the rulers to a table so that the ruler extends about 4 inches (10 cm) over the table's edge.
2. Make a paper sling using the paper punch to make a hole in each end of the paper strip.
3. Bring the holes in the strip together. Thread one end of the string through the holes. Knot the string to hold the holes together.
4. Tie the free end of the string to the outer end of the ruler on the table. Use the second ruler to adjust the length of the string so that the paper sling hangs about 6 inches (15 cm) above the floor.
5. Use the scale to measure two 8-ounce (227-g) pieces of clay. Shape each piece into a ball.
6. Stick one end of the dowel into one of the clay balls to a depth equal to the radius of the ball. The end of the dowel should reach the center of the clay ball.
7. Slide the free end of the dowel through the paper sling.
8. Repeat step 6 sticking the remaining clay ball on the other end of the dowel.

9. Move the dowel back and forth in the sling until it balances. Notice the location of the sling in reference to each clay ball.
10. Gently push one of the balls to start the dowel turning in a counterclockwise direction. Observe the motion of the clay balls from above.

NOTE: Keep this setup for the next experiment.

Results The clay balls revolve around the sling, which is in the center of the dowel.

Why? Binary bodies are two celestial bodies held together by their mutual gravity (the force of attraction between two bodies). Examples of binary bodies are two stars that revolve around each other, or a planet and the Sun, or a planet and its moon. Binary bodies behave as if they were connected by a dowel. The point about which binary bodies revolve is called the **barycenter.** If the masses of the binary bodies are equal, as in this experiment, then the barycenter lies at an equal distance between the bodies.

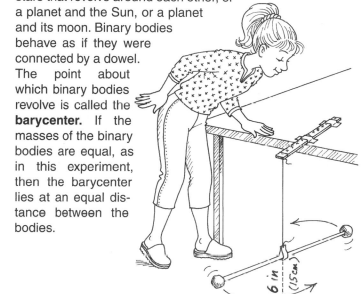

40. Uneven

Purpose To determine the orbital size of binary bodies of unequal masses.

Materials setup from Experiment 39, "Pairs"

Procedure

1. Keeping the dowel in the sling, remove about half of the clay from one end of the dowel.
2. Move the dowel back and forth in the sling until it balances. Notice the location of the sling in reference to each clay ball.
3. Gently push one of the balls to start the dowel turning in a counterclockwise direction. Observe the setup from above to determine the balancing point of the dowel and the size of the curved path of each clay ball.

Results The dowel turns about the sling, which is located closer to the larger clay ball. The smaller ball has the larger curved path.

Why? In this experiment, the balancing point of the clay balls on the dowel represents the barycenter of binary bodies. The barycenter of binary bodies is also their **cen-**

ter of mass, which is the point in an object where its mass seems to be **concentrated** (drawn toward a common center). The center of mass is at the same point as the **center of gravity,** which is the point at which the whole weight of a body may be considered to be concentrated. If the bodies were actually connected, as in this experiment, then they would balance at the point where their center of mass is supported—in this case, the sling. When the binary bodies are not equal in mass, as in this experiment, their center of mass is closer to the larger body. Thus the orbit of the smaller body is larger than the orbit of the larger body.

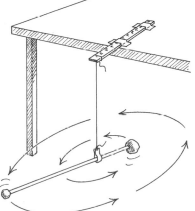

II
Biology

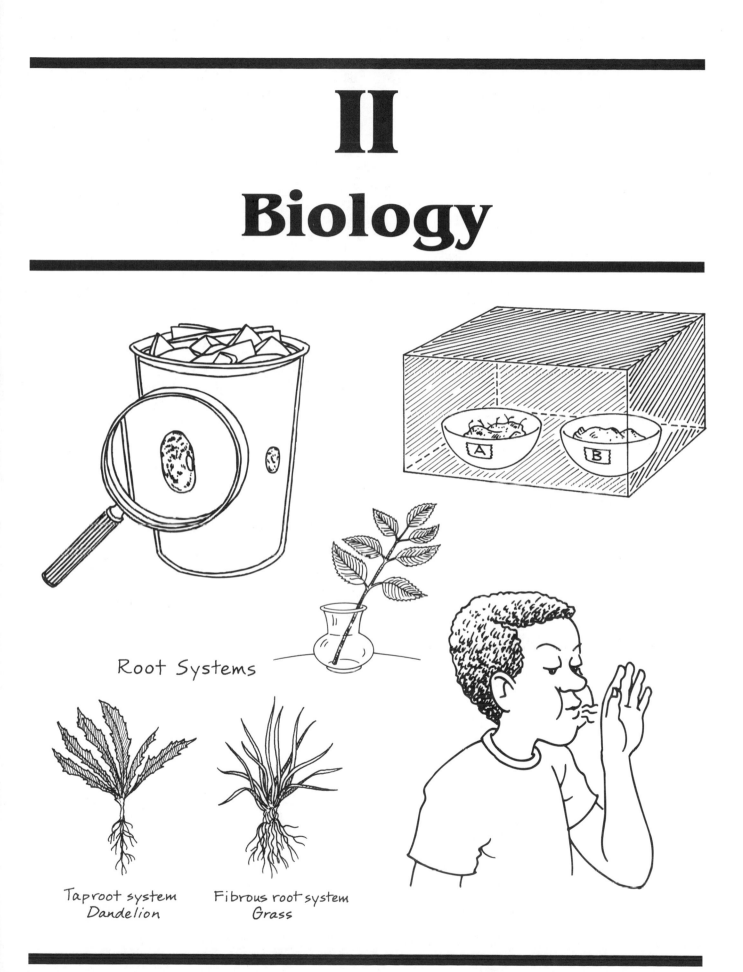

Root Systems

Taproot system
Dandelion

Fibrous root system
Grass

41. Clusters

Purpose   To use pine needles to determine whether a pine tree has soft or hard wood.

Materials   pine needles from one or more pine trees

Procedure
1. Look at the needles from the pine tree.
2. Count the needles in one cluster.
3. Use the figure to determine whether the wood of the pine tree that the needles came from is soft or hard.

Results   One or more pine trees are identified as having hard or soft wood.

Why?   Pine trees are **evergreens,** which are plants that retain some or all of their **leaves** (the main food-producing parts of a plant) throughout the year. The leaves of some evergreens are **broad leaves** (wide, flat leaves), such as those of magnolia and holly trees. But most have **needle leaves** (narrow, needlelike leaves). The needle leaves of pines are grouped in clusters. Each cluster contains a specific number of leaves commonly called **needles,** depending on the type of tree. Pines are divided into two groups, based on the hardness of their wood. The soft pines have needles in bundles of five. White pine is a well-known soft pine. The hard pines have needles in bundles of two or three, such as red pine and pitch pine. Both soft and hard pinewood are used for lumber.

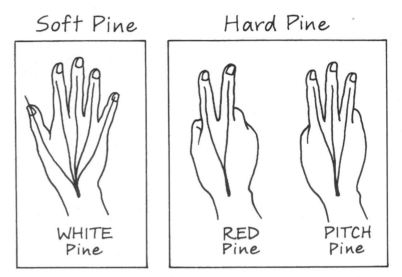

42. Many Parts

Purpose   To identify the parts of a composite flower.

Materials   daisy
magnifying lens

Procedure
1. Use your hands to break the flower head (bloom) in half.
2. Use the magnifying lens to observe the yellow center of one of the halves. Break the center into smaller parts to separate one or more of the tiny flowers that make up the center. Use the diagram to identify the disk flower.
3. Again use the magnifying lens to observe the petal-like parts on the other half of the flower head. Carefully pull out one or more of the "petals" and compare them to the ray flower in the diagram.

Results   The two types of flowers that make up a daisy flower head are identified.

Why?   **Angiosperms** are plants whose flowers produce seeds. About half of the known plants are angiosperms. One of the largest groups of angiosperms is the **composites** (plants with flowers that look like a single flower but are actually a cluster of many separate flowers). The daisy is a composite flower, and the flower cluster as a whole is called a **head.** In some composite flowers, such as the daisy, the head is made up of two types of flowers. The yellow **disk** (center of the head) is made up of tube-shaped flowers called **disk flowers.** The disk flowers of the daisy head, like those in most composite flowers, produce the **seeds** (the part of a flowering plant that is able to grow into a new plant). The parts of the daisy that are commonly believed to be petals are actually **ray flowers.** They are given this name because they radiate from the center of the flower head. The ray flowers help attract insects to pollinate the disk flowers. **Pollination** is the process of plant **fertilization,** which is the joining of special male and female parts to produce seeds.

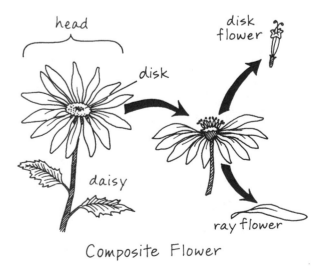

Composite Flower

43. Getting Started

Purpose To determine how long it takes a pinto bean to germinate.

Materials paper towels
10-ounce (300-mL) clear plastic cup
6 pinto beans
tap water
magnifying lens

Procedure
1. Fold a paper towel in half and use it to line the inside of the cup.
2. Crumple several paper towels together and stuff them into the cup. Use enough towels to hold the paper lining firmly in place around the inside of the cup.
3. Place the beans between the cup and the lining, spacing the beans evenly around the **perimeter** (the measurement of a boundary) of the cup.
4. Moisten the paper towels in the cup with water. Keep the paper towels in the cup moist, but not dripping wet, during the entire experiment.
5. Use the magnifying lens to observe the beans two or three times daily until growth is observed. This usually occurs within 4 to 5 days.

Results The first sign of growth occurs when the seed breaks and part of the plant pushes through.

Why? **Organisms** are living things, such as plants and animals. One way that plants **propagate** (produce new organisms) is by seeds. The process by which a seed embryo **sprouts** (begins to grow) or develops is called **germination.** At the start of germination, the **embryo** (the undeveloped organism) inside the seed does not begin life, but rather resumes growth that stopped when the seed matured.

44. Hitchhikers

Purpose To demonstrate how animals affect the spreading around of seeds.

Materials pair of old socks
magnifying lens

NOTE: This experiment gives better results in seasons other than winter.

Procedure
1. Put on the old socks over your shoes.
2. Wear the socks while you walk around in a grassy area of your backyard or on a hiking trail in a park.
3. Remove the socks and use the magnifying lens to observe any seeds stuck to the socks. (Watch out for seeds that have sharp points!)

NOTE: Keep the socks for the next experiment.

Results The socks may have different kinds of seeds stuck to them.

Why? Some seeds have structures that help them to latch on to an animal's fur, a bird's feathers, or even your socks or other clothes. Seed structures that help some seeds to "hitch

a ride" on a passing animal include hooks or barbs, such as those on cockleburs, and sticky substances, such as that on flax. By producing seeds that can stick to a moving animal, the plant is able to spread its seeds over a wider area. Thus more plants have a chance to grow.

45. Sprouters

Purpose To identify the conditions needed for seeds to germinate.

Materials seed-covered socks from Experiment 44, "Hitchhikers"
2 small bowls
masking tape
marker
tap water
box large enough to cover the bowls side by side

Procedure

1. Lay one sock in each bowl with their seed-covered bottoms facing up.
2. Use the tape and marker to label the bowls "A" and "B."
3. Moisten the sock in bowl A with water. The sock should be moist, not soaking wet. Keep the sock in bowl A moist during the remainder of the experiment. Keep the sock in bowl B dry.
4. Place the bowls side by side on a table or floor and cover them with the box. The box covering represents planting.
5. Lift up the box each day for 10 or more days and look for any signs of germination in the seeds on the socks.

Results Some of the seeds on the sock in bowl A probably germinated, but the seeds on the sock in bowl B probably did not.

Why? Seeds remain **dormant** (alive but not growing) during the winter when it is cold and during other seasons when conditions are not right for their growth. Seeds need water, **oxygen** (a gas in the air), and warmth to germinate. The seeds on both socks received oxygen and warmth, but only the seeds on sock A received water. These seeds **absorbed** (soaked up) water, which may have caused changes to occur inside some of the seeds so that they began sprouting. Different kinds of seeds need different amounts of water and warmth, so all of the seeds may not have germinated. If the seeds you collected on your socks did not germinate, you may wish to repeat the experiment walking in a different area and/or sprinkling different purchased flower seeds on the socks.

46. Dividers

Purpose To determine how pinto bean plant stems grow.

Materials 9-ounce (270-mL) paper cup
potting soil
pencil
4 dry pinto beans
ruler
saucer
tap water
marking pen

Procedure

1. Fill the cup about three-fourths full with potting soil.
2. Use the pencil to punch four to six holes around the perimeter of the bottom edge of the cup.
3. Plant the beans in the soil by pushing them into the soil about ½ inch (1.25 cm) below the surface.
4. Place the cup in the saucer and moisten the soil with water.
5. Allow the seeds to germinate and the seedlings to grow to a height of about 6 inches (15 cm) above the rim of the cup. This will take 14 or more days.
6. When the plants have grown 6 inches (15 cm) above the rim of the cup, use the marking pen to mark two equal sections on the stem of each plant between the leaves and the seed leaves as shown.

7. Measure and record the length of the two sections between the marks: section 1, between the true leaves and the center mark, and section 2, between the center mark and the seed leaves.
8. At the same time each day for 14 days, measure and record the length of each section.

Results The only (or greatest) growth occurs in section 1.

Why? Beans are seeds that have two halves called **seed leaves,** which provide food for the growing embryo inside the seed. In time the seed leaves shrink and fall off. As the embryo grows, it develops plant parts, including the first true leaves and a **stem** (the part that supports a plant). The stem grows mainly at its tip, where there are special **cells** (building blocks of organisms) that divide and develop into similar cells. Thus growth is observed in section 1 of each stem.

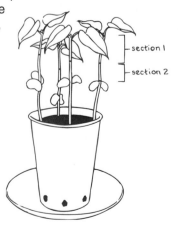

47. Up and Down

Purpose To observe the parts of a root.

Materials magnifying lens
fresh carrot (with green leaves attached if available)

Procedure
1. Use the magnifying lens to study the outer surface of the carrot.
2. Break the carrot in half and observe the cross sections of the broken halves.

Results Tiny hairlike fibers are seen on the outer surface of the carrot. The cross section of the carrot reveals two circles—an inner, dark-orange circle surrounded by a lighter orange circle.

Why? **Roots** are the part of a plant that grow into the ground to anchor the plant. Carrot plants have a **taproot system,** which is made up of one main root, called the **taproot,** that grows straight down and has **rootlets,** small hairlike roots that branch from the taproot. The part of the carrot plant that you eat is the taproot.
  Nutrients (substances needed for the life and growth of organisms) move through tubes in plants as well as the roots. The inner dark circle in the carrot root consists of **xylem tubes,** which carry nutrients from the soil throughout the plant. The lighter circle around the dark center contains **phloem tubes,** which transport nutrients made in the leaves throughout the plant. The phloem and xylem tubes also provide support to the plant.

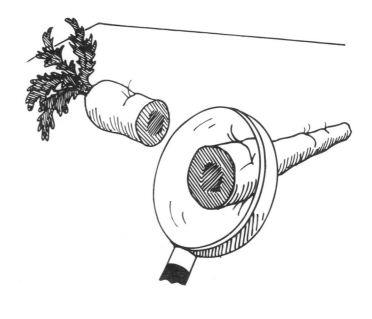

48. Anchors

Purpose To identify the two main kinds of root systems.

Materials plant field guide
bucket
tap water
trowel
backyard or other area where dandelions and grass grow
paper towels

NOTE: Before doing this experiment, obtain permission to dig up the plants.

Procedure
1. Use the field guide to identify dandelions.
2. Fill the bucket with water.
3. Use the trowel to dig up a dandelion plant and a clump of grass. Be sure to get as much of the root system as possible.
4. Dip the roots of each plant up and down in the bucket of water until the roots are free of soil.
5. Lay the wet plants on a paper towel. Blot the plants with another paper towel to absorb any excess water.
6. Examine the roots of each plant and compare them.

Results The dandelion has one large root with other, smaller roots branching off of it. The grass has many roots.

Why? The dandelion and grass represent the two main kinds of root systems: the taproot system and the fibrous root system. The dandelion has a taproot system, which consists of a taproot that grows straight down and rootlets branching from the taproot. The grass has a **fibrous root system,** which consists of a main root that is not easily identified because it is small and all of the many roots branching from it in all directions form a tangled mass that hides the main root.

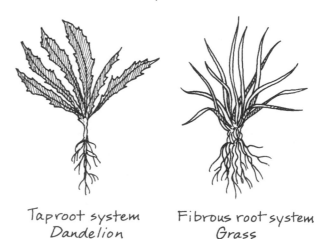

Root Systems

Taproot system
Dandelion

Fibrous root system
Grass

49. Just Alike

Purpose To model flowers that have radial and bilateral symmetry.

Materials two 8-inch (20-cm) squares of white copy
        paper
        ruler
        pen
        sheet of 9-by-12-inch (22.5-
        by-30-cm) red construction
        paper
        scissors
        glue stick or school glue

Procedure

1. Fold one of the white paper squares in half three times—first from top to bottom, then from side to side, and then diagonally.
2. Unfold the paper and use the ruler and pen to trace along the fold lines. Number the lines from 1 to 8 as shown.
3. Fold the red paper in half two times—first from top to bottom and then from side to side.
4. Without unfolding the red paper, use the pen to draw two flower petals on the folded paper. Cut out the petals making sure to cut through all four layers of paper. You will have eight petals.
5. Make a four-petaled flower by gluing four petals on lines 1, 3, 5, and 7. Allow the glue to dry.
6. Fold the square in half along lines 1 and 5 and observe the inside of the folded area, noting whether the fold divides the flower into matching halves.

7. Repeat step 6 three times, folding along lines 2 and 6, 3 and 7, and 4 and 8.
8. Make a three-petaled flower by repeating step 1 and gluing three of the remaining petals on lines 1, 4, and 6. Allow the glue to dry.
9. Repeat step 6 three times, folding along lines 1 and 5, 4 and 8, and 2 and 6.

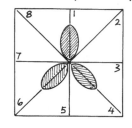

Results The four-petaled flower can be divided into matching halves along any lines, but the three-petaled flower can only be divided into matching halves along lines 1 and 5.

Why? Flowers like the four-petaled flower in this experiment are called **regular flowers** because they have radial symmetry. In **radial symmetry,** the parts branch out from the center in all directions and if folded across the middle from any direction each fold forms a **line of symmetry** (a line that divides a figure into two identical parts that match if folded along the line). Flowers such as the three-petaled flower in this experiment are called **irregular flowers** because they have **bilateral symmetry** (a design with one line of symmetry).

---

50. Leaf Parts

Purpose To model the main parts of the leaf of a broadleaf plant.

Materials 4-inch (10-cm) square of green construction
        paper
        pencil
        scissors
        transparent tape
        sheet of white copy paper
        green marker or crayon

Procedure

1. Fold the green paper in half.
2. Use the pencil to draw the outline of half a leaf on the fold. (See Experiment 51, "On the Edge.")
3. Cut along the line through both layers of paper. Unfold the paper. You will have one leaf.
4. Tape the leaf to the white paper.
5. Use the marker to make a diagram like the one shown. Draw and label the stem, petiole, blade, and veins. Title the paper "Leaf Parts."

Results You have made a model of a broad leaf.

Why? A leaf that is broad and flat is called a broad leaf. Plants with broad leaves are called **broadleaf plants.** Most leaves are broad leaves, but some, such as those of pine and many other evergreens, are needles. Broad leaves, such as the model in this experiment, have two basic parts: the blade and the petiole. The **blade** is the main part of a leaf and is generally green. It is where food in the plant is made. There are **veins** in the leaf, which are phloem and xylem tubes that transport nutrients and provide support for the leaves. The **petiole** is the stalklike structure that attaches the leaf blade to the stem. The petiole also serves as a passageway between the stem and the blade for the transport of water and nutrients. Another job of the petiole is to move the leaf into the best position for receiving sunlight. Most petioles are long, narrow, and cylindrical.

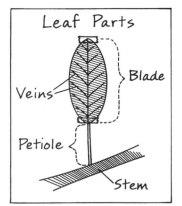

51. On the Edge

Purpose To demonstrate the margin of broad leaves.

Materials sheet of 9-by-12-inch (22.5-by-30-cm) green
　　　　　　construction paper
　　　　　　pencil
　　　　　　scissors
　　　　　　transparent tape
　　　　　　marker

Procedure
1. Fold the green paper in half.
2. Use the pencil to draw the outlines of half of three leaves on the fold as shown.

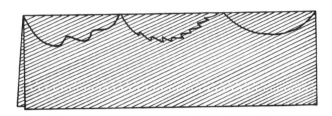

3. Cut along the lines through both layers of paper.
4. Unfold the three leaves and tape them to the white paper.
5. Use the marker to label each leaf as shown. Title the paper "Leaf Margins."

Results You have made a diagram of broadleaf margins.

Why? The edge of a broad leaf is called the **leaf margin.** There are three types of margins: entire, toothed, and lobed. **Entire margins** are smooth and unbroken, as on dogwood and ash trees. **Toothed margins** can be large and blunt, as on beech trees, or small and sharp, as on elm trees. **Lobed margins** have extensions, some of which look like earlobes, hence the name. In identifying leaf margins, first determine whether the leaf is lobed or not lobed. Then determine whether the margins are entire or toothed. Lobed margins can be entire as on sassafras trees or toothed as on sycamore trees. In this model, the lobed leaf is entire.

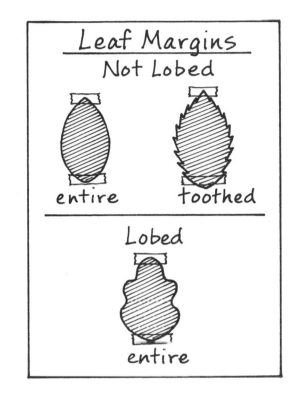

---

52. Falling Leaves

Purpose To demonstrate that the reason leaves fall off stems isn't that they die.

Materials twig with 4 or more green leaves attached
　　　　　　vase

Procedure
1. With adult permission, break a twig with four or more green leaves from a bush or tree.
2. Stand the twig in the vase.
3. Set the vase where it can be observed but not disturbed for 4 or more weeks.
4. Observe the leaves as often as possible, but do not touch them.

Results The green leaves die and turn brown, but do not fall off the stem.

Why? A **deciduous** plant is one that loses its leaves **annually** (each year). The leaves fall off these plants when changes in the plant cause the layer of cells holding the leaf to the stem to break apart. The layer of cells holding the petiole of the leaf to the stem is called the **abscission layer.** These cells have thin walls. Running through the petiole are phloem and xylem tubes carrying nutrients into and out of the leaf. If the stem is broken from the plant before the abscission layer breaks apart, the leaves stay attached to the stem even after they die. The dead leaves may stay on the stem for months, although in time they will crumble.

53. Coverup

Purpose To identify the main external covering of adult insects.

Materials pencil
1-quart (1-L) resealable plastic bag
cricket (Catch it by following the instructions below or purchase one from a pet store or catalog supplier.)
10-ounce (300-mL) clear plastic cup
4-by-6-inch (10-by-15-cm) index card
helper

NOTE: If you caught or purchased the cricket, you should release it outdoors when finished. If it is too cold outdoors or if you wish to keep the cricket for a pet for a few weeks, make a home for it in a jar with holes punched in the lid. Feed it moist fruit and bread. For information about the care of crickets, see Sally Kneidel, Pet Bugs *(New York: Wiley, 1994).*

Procedure

1. Use the point of the pencil to make 15 to 20 small airholes through both layers of the top half of the bag.
2. To catch the cricket, place the cup over it. Then slip the index card under the cup to cover the mouth of the cup.
3. Ask your helper to hold the bag open. Hold the cup and card over the bag.
4. Slowly slide the card away so that the cricket drops into the bag. Have the helper quickly seal the bag.
5. Position the cricket between your thumb and index finger. Then *gently* press the bag against the cricket. With your other hand, *gently* rub the plastic covering over the cricket to feel the texture of the cricket's body.
6. Hold the cricket still by continuing to gently press the bag against its body. Use the magnifying lens to study the cricket's body and legs.

Results The cricket's legs and body are covered with a hard outer covering.

Why? The cricket's body parts and six legs have a jointed outer covering called an **exoskeleton.** This covering is made mostly of a relatively hard but flexible material called **chitin.** The exoskeleton provides support and protection for the insect's body.

54. Breakout

Purpose To determine what happens to the exoskeleton of a growing insect.

Materials 12-inch (30-cm) round balloon
spring-type clothespin
1 tablespoon (15 mL) school glue
1 tablespoon (15 mL) tap water
small bowl
spoon
35 to 40 strips of newspaper, each about 2 by 4 inches (5 by 10 cm)

Procedure

1. Inflate the balloon to about the size of a grapefruit. Twist the end closed and secure it with the clothespin.
2. Put the glue and water in the bowl and mix them by stirring with the spoon.
3. Dip a newspaper strip in the glue mixture and stick the strip on the balloon.
4. Repeat this with a second paper strip, placing it on the balloon so that it overlaps half of the first paper strip.
5. Continue adding strips, overlapping each until most of the balloon is covered with paper. Leave a narrow band around the balloon uncovered.

6. Wait an hour or so until the paper dries.
7. When the paper is dry, hold the closed end of the balloon and remove the clothespin without letting the air out. Gently blow into the balloon, making it slightly larger.

Results A hard paper shell covers all but the band of the balloon. When you inflate the balloon even more, the sections of the paper shell separate on either side of the band. The shell does not expand.

Why? The balloon and hard paper shell represent an insect during the growing stage. The body of the growing insect is covered by an exoskeleton. This exoskeleton does not grow with the insect. As the rest of the insect's body grows, the exoskeleton starts to become too small. A new exoskeleton begins to form under the old one. When the old exoskeleton becomes too small for the growing insect the insect **molts,** meaning the small exoskeleton is shed and a larger one forms.

55. Lifters

Purpose To determine which legs insects lift when they walk.

Materials lemon-size piece of modeling clay
6 round toothpicks

Procedure
1. Shape the clay into a rectangular block.
2. Stick three toothpicks near the edge of each long side of the clay block as shown. The toothpicks should stick out the same amount from the clay. The clay represents an insect's body and the toothpicks its legs.
3. Turn the model insect over and stand it on its six legs. Adjust the length of the legs if the insect wobbles.
4. Take any three toothpick legs out of the clay body, and then try to stand the insect on its three remaining legs. If the insect falls, put the three legs back in.
5. Repeat step 5, taking out three other legs. Keep trying different combinations until the insect can stand on three legs.

Results The insect stands when the front and hind leg on one side and the middle leg on the opposite side are removed.

Why? By lifting the middle leg on one side and the front and hind legs on the opposite side, the center of gravity of the clay insect does not change, or it changes so little that the clay insect balances. When other leg combinations are removed, the center of gravity of the body can change enough to cause the body to be off balance. Insects walk basically by moving the middle leg on one side and the front and hind legs on the opposite side. But unlike the clay insect, real insects can shift their weight so that they can balance on other legs than can the clay model.

---

56. Follow Me

Purpose To determine how ants find food.

Materials 12-by-22-inch (30-by-55-cm) piece of white poster board
anthill with a few ants on the ground around it
4 to 6 rocks or other heavy objects
cracker
binoculars

CAUTION: Do not use fire ants for this activity. Also, be sure not to stand on or too near an anthill as you perform the activity. Take special care not to allow ants to get on your skin. If you are allergic to ant bites or stings, do not perform this activity.

Procedure
1. Lay the poster board on the ground with one end close to the entrance of the anthill.
2. Secure the paper with the rocks.
3. Crumble the cracker on the end of the poster board opposite the entrance of the anthill.
4. From a distance, use the binoculars to watch the ants and cracker crumbs for 5 minutes or more.
5. Return after 1 hour and again observe the ants and cracker crumbs.

Results At first, a few ants examine the cracker crumbs. Some may carry a crumb back to the anthill, but others return without crumbs. After a time, many ants go back and forth, carrying crumbs to the anthill.

Why? You may have noticed that the ants touch their antennae to the ground as they walk. This is because the ants smell through their antennae. The job of some ants is to go out and find food. They use their antennae to find the food, then return to the anthill, some with and some without food. As they return to the anthill, their bodies give off a chemical that leaves a scent on the ground.

The first ants "tell" the rest of the ants about the food. Scientists believe that ants communicate by touching their antennae together. The other ants use their antennae to follow the smell given off by the first ants back to the cracker crumbs.

The scented chemicals that ants and some other animals, especially insects, produce are called **pheromones.** These chemicals are produced inside the insect's body and **secreted** (given off) to the outside of the body. Pheromones are chemical signals used in communication among members of the same **species** (a group of similar organisms).

57. Spongy

Purpose To demonstrate how a fly eats.

Materials spoon
tap water
dishwashing sponge
paper towels

Procedure

1. Pour three spoonsful of water on a table.
2. Place the sponge on the water. Move the sponge around until as much of the water as possible has been removed from the table. (Use the paper towels to dry any water remaining on the table.)

Results Most of the water is soaked up by the sponge.

Why? Some insects, such as flies, have a tubelike mouthpart called a **proboscis.** The sponge end of the proboscis soaks up liquid in much the same way as the sponge soaked up the water. All of the food that flies eat is not in liquid form. They drop a watery liquid called **saliva** on solid food, which quickly **digests** (changes food into smaller parts that the body can use) part of the food, making it liquid. The fly then dabs at the liquefied food with the spongy end of its proboscis, soaking up the liquid. The liquid food moves through the proboscis into the insect's body, where it is further digested, and the nourishing parts are absorbed by the body.

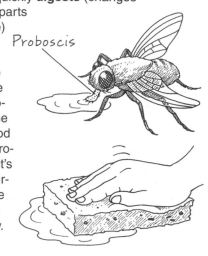

Proboscis

---

58. Stickers

Purpose To demonstrate how spider webs catch flying insects.

Materials 2-inch (5-cm)-wide transparent tape (sticky on one side
20 to 30 cotton balls
plastic container large enough to hold the cotton balls
adult helper

Procedure

1. With adult assistance, run a strip of tape from the center of the top of a doorway to the floor. Then run two strips of tape diagonally between opposite corners of the doorway. The sticky side of all of the pieces of tape should face you and be on the same side of the doorway.
2. Run more strips of tape horizontally and vertically across the doorway. But leave empty spaces between the strips and turn the horizontal strips so that their sticky side faces away from you.
3. Put the cotton balls in the plastic container.
4. Stand about 3 feet (0.9 m) from the sticky side of the vertical and diagonal strips of tape.
5. Throw the cotton balls, one at a time, toward the tape. Count the number of balls that stick to the tape.

Results Most of the cotton balls that hit the tape strips whose sticky side faces you will stick to the tape.

Why? Spiderwebs are constructed by spiders from **silk** (a fine, soft fiber made by some insects) made in their bodies. On the hind end of a spider's body are pointed bumps called **spinnerets.** Liquid from inside the spider flows out of the spinnerets, and the spider spins the liquid silk into strands and weaves the strands into a web. One kind of silk dries in the air and is not sticky (represented by the tape strips whose nonsticky side faces you), and another kind stays sticky (represented by the tape strips whose sticky side faces you). Flying insects (represented by the tossed cotton balls) that hit the sticky side of the tape usually stick. Others fly between the web strands, hit nonsticky strands, or manage to pull away from the sticky strands. Spiders are also able to walk on the nonsticky strands without getting stuck. But they also don't get stuck on the sticky strands, because they have a liquid on their feet that keeps them from sticking.

59. Hummers

Purpose To observe the feeding habits of hummingbirds.

Materials spoon
1 quart (1 L) tap water
1 cup (250 mL) sugar
1-quart (1-L) jar with lid
red food coloring
hummingbird feeder (available at stores that sell pet supplies)
field guide to birds
adult helper

Procedure
1. Mix the water and sugar in the jar.
2. Add 20 drops of food coloring to make the sugar water red. Stir.
3. Fill the bottle of the feeder and secure its feeding base.
4. Ask an adult to hang the feeder near a window where it can be observed from inside your home.
5. Observe the feeder as often as possible for 2 weeks or more. Make note of the behavior of the hummingbirds as they feed. Use a field guide or other book to identify the hummingbirds by their appearance and behavior. Add sugar water as needed, and change the water if it's not used in a few days.

Results Most of the birds remain in the air and hover in front of the feeder as they feed. More young birds are seen feeding on newly hung feeders. Some birds are more cautious and nervous than others.

Why? Some scientists think that all hummingbirds notice the color red more than other colors. Other scientists think that only the young birds take special notice of this color. Either way, red food coloring is often added to hummingbird food to attract the birds. Young birds are very curious and will investigate anything. That may be why they are more attracted to the red feeder.

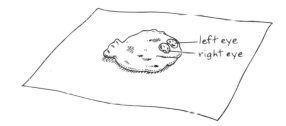

60. Migrating Eye

Purpose To show how an adult flatfish develops to live on the ocean floor.

Materials lemon-size piece of modeling clay
2 pinto beans
sheet of white copy paper

Procedure
1. Model the clay into the shape of a fish with a slightly rounded body.
2. Place a bean on each side of the fish's head.
3. Place the paper on a table and stand the fish belly side down on the paper.
4. Observe the location of the beans and the shape of the fish's body.

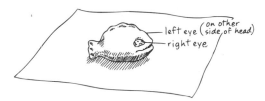

5. Move the left-eye bean to the top of the fish's head.
6. Lean the fish onto its left side and slightly flatten its body and head.
7. Again observe the location of the beans and the shape of the fish's body.

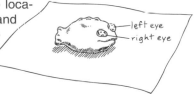

8. Move the left-eye bean again, nearer the right-eye bean.
9. Press the fish's body and head flat as shown.
10. Observe the final location of the beans and the shape of the fish's body.

Results The bean on the left side of the fish's head is moved around the head in stages until both beans are located on one side—the right side—of the head. The fish's body gradually changes from a round form to a flat form.

Why? The beans represent the eyes of a flatfish, such as a flounder. All young flatfish have the general shape of other fish: a rounded body with eyes on either side of their head. The clay model in this experiment does not change in size, but in nature the young flatfish starts to grow larger and its body starts changing. One eye slowly starts to move over the top of the head. At this point, the fish moves to the ocean floor and lies on its blind side. In a short time, the body is greatly flattened from side to side and the two eyes are close together on the upper, sighted side of the head. About three-fourths of flatfish lie on their left side.

61. Largest

Purpose   To show the length of two of the world's largest animals.

Materials   ruler
3 pencils
large, open outdoor area

Procedure

1. Lay the ruler on the floor and stand with one of your feet at one end of the ruler. Take a step that is 1 foot (30 cm) long. Practice several times so that you can take 1-foot (30-cm) steps without the ruler.
2. In the large, open outdoor area, stick one of the pencils into the ground and hold the other two pencils.
3. Stand next to the pencil in the ground, then walk forward 70 feet (21 m) by taking seventy 1-foot (30-cm) steps. Place the second pencil in the ground at the 70-foot (21-m) mark.
4. From the second pencil, walk another 30 feet (9 m) and place the last pencil in the ground at the 100-foot (30-m) mark.

Results   The distances that you have marked are the lengths of two of the world's largest animals.

Why?   The shorter of the two measurements, 70 feet (21 m), is the length of one of the largest dinosaurs, the brachiosaurus. But as big as this dinosaur was, it did not reach the size of the blue whale. The giant blue whale, the world's largest animal, may grow to a length of 100 feet (30 m).

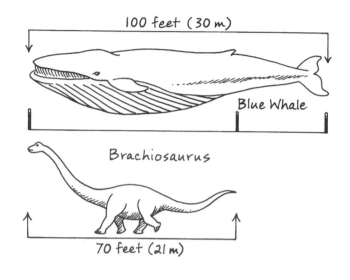

62. Sniffer

Purpose   To model the smelling surfaces of human and dog noses.

Materials   ruler
24-inch (60-cm) strip of 2-inch (5-cm) adding machine tape
pencil
scissors
pen

Procedure

1. Measure 4 inches (10 cm) from one end of the adding machine tape and mark a pencil line across the strip.
2. Cut across the line. Keep both strips of paper.
3. Fold the short strip of paper in half, short ends together.
4. Unfold the paper and use the ruler and pen to mark two lines across the paper 1 inch (1.25 cm) on either side of the fold. Then fold the paper back along each mark into an M shape as shown. This is a model of a human nose.
5. Repeat step 3 with the long strip of paper.
6. Unfold the paper and use the ruler and pen to mark four lines across the paper. Make the first pair of marks 1-inch (2.5 cm) from the fold and the second pair 2 inches (5 cm) from the fold. Then fold the paper back along the 1-inch (2.5-cm) marks. Fold the paper back again along the 2-inch (5-cm) marks.
7. Starting at one end of the long strip, roll the paper into a small, tight roll up to the 2-inch (5-cm) mark as shown. Repeat with the other end. Tuck the rolled ends

inside the M shape so that the outside is the same size as the model of the human nose. This is a model of a dog nose.

Results   The models represent the inside surfaces of a human nose and a dog nose.

Why?   You smell things, such as a hamburger, because molecules leave the object and enter the air. When this air enters your nose, some of these molecules reach special cells in the surface inside your nose. These special smelling cells have hairlike bristles covered with **mucus,** a thick, slimy liquid that coats and protects the inside of the nose and other body parts. First the food molecules **dissolve** (break apart and mix thoroughly with a liquid) in the mucus, then the bristles signal to the brain that food is nearby. A dog can smell things that you cannot because it has about five times the amount of moist surface inside its nose. This is represented by the model made out of a strip of paper 20 inches (50 cm) long, which is five times as long as the human nose modeled out of a 4-inch (10-cm) strip of paper. Since a dog nose is not five times as large as a human nose, the extra smelling surface is folded many times to fit inside the nose.

63. Pickup!

Purpose To demonstrate one of the uses of a primate's thumb.

Materials pencil
coin

Procedure
1. Using your index and second fingers, try to pick up the pencil. Then try to pick up the coin.
2. Repeat step 1 using your index finger and thumb.

Results You can pick up the pencil without your thumb but generally cannot pick up the coin. But it's easier to pick up the objects with your index finger and thumb than with your index and second fingers.

Why? **Mammals** are animals that have hair and feed their young on milk. **Primates** are a category of mammals that includes people, monkeys, apes, and chimpanzees. Most primates have thumbs that are **opposable,** meaning that the thumb can be positioned opposite the fingers, as when you pick up a coin. The thumb and fingers can touch at the tips. Your index and second finger are not oppos-

able, but can be used to lift some things, such as the pencil. Some primates, including chimpanzees, koalas, and lemurs, also have opposable toes. The panda has a wrist bone that acts in the manner of an opposable thumb. With opposable thumbs and toes, animals can more easily pick up small objects.

---

64. Signals

Purpose To demonstrate how tigers "talk" with their tails.

Materials thin, flexible plastic ruler

Procedure
1. Hold the ruler upright and slowly shake it back and forth.

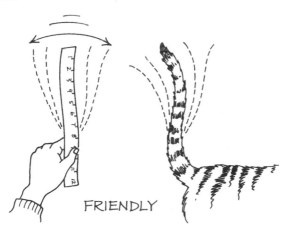

FRIENDLY

2. Hold the ruler sideways and quickly shake it from side to side.

EXCITED

3. Hold the ruler down and at an angle from your body and shake it slightly from side to side.

TENSE

Results You have demonstrated three motions of a tiger's tail that are used to communicate mood.

Why? Animals communicate by sound, such as a tiger's roar. But the roar can mean different things depending on its tone and volume. It could mean a warning to get away, or to come and share the food it has found. Tigers are also known for communicating with their tails. Each position and motion of the tail sends a different message. In this experiment a ruler is used to represent a tiger's tail. In an upright position and slowly shaken back and forth, the ruler represents the motion of a tiger's tail when the animal is sending out the message, "Hi. Want to be friends?" When the ruler is held sideways and shaken quickly from side to side, it represents the motion of the tail when an excited tiger is saying, "Wow! Look at all that food." In the downward position and given a slight shake, the ruler represents the tiger feeling tense, as if to say, "Beware!"

65. Locked

Purpose To demonstrate how dog's teeth lock together.

Materials your hands

Procedure
1. Put your fingers together by overlapping the fingers of one hand on the fingers of the other hand. Press your fingers together, then try to move them apart.
2. Put your hands together by fitting the fingers of one hand between the fingers of the other hand as shown. Now, squeeze your fingers together, then try to move them apart.

Results Your fingers slide apart easily when they overlap, but are more difficult to separate when they fit between each other.

Why? Dogs, as well as other animals, have teeth of different shapes. In people and dogs, the front teeth in the upper and lower jaws, called **incisors,** are relatively flat and have sharp edges used to cut food. These teeth generally overlap, with those on top fitting over the ones on bottom. They easily separate. On either side of the incisors are the **canine teeth,** named for their resemblance to the pointy fangs of dogs. The job of the canines in eating is to tear food. But unlike the canines in people, the canine teeth in dogs are long and lock together much like your fingers lock when they fit between each other. This locking of the teeth, as well as strong jaw muscles, makes it difficult to pull a dog's jaws apart as long as the dog continues to hold them closed. Once the dog closes its mouth around the leg or other body part of another animal, it is almost impossible for the animal to get away.

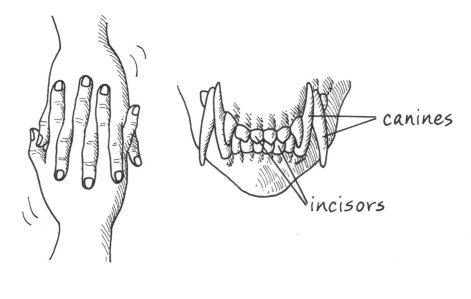

66. Nails

Purpose To identify the different parts of fingernails.

Materials soap
tap water
paper towel
magnifying lens

Procedure
1. Wash your hands with soap and water, then dry them with the paper towel.
2. Use the magnifying lens to examine one of your fingernails.
3. Use the diagram to identify the parts of the nail.

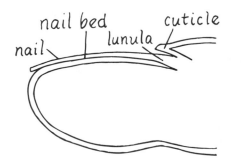

Results The part of the nail that covers the finger is pink; the nail looks white where it extends past the fingertip. There is often a whitish, half-moon-shaped area near the base of the nail. Some nails have white spots. The skin around the nail often looks dry and scaly.

Why? Your fingernails are made up of dead skin cells that have been pressed together tightly to form a thin, rigid plate. These cells contain **keratin,** the tough protein that makes up your hair, nails, and the outer layers of your skin. The **nail bed** is the pink, fleshy area beneath the nail that provides a smooth surface for the growing nail to glide across. Its pink color is caused by the rich supply of blood beneath it. All the growth of a nail takes place beneath the whitish, half-moon-shaped area known as the **lunula.** The lunula is white because this part of the nail is not firmly attached to the nail bed. Ridges and bumps on a nail are due to uneven growth of the nail at its **root** (the area beneath the lunula). White, irregularly shaped flecks in the nail are bubbles of air trapped between the cell layers. The **cuticle** is dead skin around the base and sides of the fingernail.

67. Backbone

Purpose To make a model of the spine.

Materials 6 thread spools
4-by-5-inch (10-by-12.5-cm) piece of poster
   board
pencil
scissors
one-hole paper punch
12-inch (30-cm) piece of string
transparent tape
ruler

Procedure

1. Place the flat end of a thread spool on the poster board.
2. Draw five circles on the poster board by tracing around the end of the spool.
3. Cut out the five circles and use the paper punch to make a hole in the center of each circle.
4. Thread one end of the string through the hole in one of the spools. Then tape the short end of the string to the end of the spool.
5. Stand the spool on end and thread the free end of the string through the hole in one of the poster board circles. Continue to add spools and circles to the string until all are used. Then, tape the end of the string to the top spool.
6. Holding the bottom spool on a table, push the top spool about 2 inches (5 cm) to one side.
7. Push the spool in different directions.

Results The spools are able to bend in different directions.

Why? Your backbone, commonly called the **spine,** is made of separate bones called **vertebrae.** You can bend because your vertebrae, like the spools, are able to separate a little. Thus your spine can bend. A large bundle of **nerves** (fibers that carry messages to and from the brain) called the **spinal cord** runs through holes in the vertebrae. Between each vertebra is a pad, like the circle, called a **disk.** The disks keep the vertebrae from rubbing against each other.

68. Squeezed

Purpose To demonstrate how food is squeezed from the stomach into the small intestine.

Materials tube of toothpaste
3-ounce (90-mL) paper cup

Procedure

1. Hold the tube of toothpaste in your hands.
2. With the cap screwed on tight, position the tube above the paper cup as shown.
3. Moving your fingers along the tube, squeeze the tube in different places.
4. Remove the cap from the tube and squeeze the tube with your fingers.

Results With the cap secured, the toothpaste inside the tube moves around in, but remains inside, the tube. Without the cap, the toothpaste moves out the opening in the tube.

Why? Your **digestive system** is a group of body parts that digest food. The parts of the digestive system represented in this experiment are the **stomach** (where food goes when it is swallowed), the **small intestine** (a long tube where food goes when it leaves the stomach), and the **duodenum** (the upper part of the small intestine closest to the stomach). Your stomach has three layers of muscles contracting in different directions. These squeezing actions, like those of your hands, thoroughly mash the food in your stomach and mix it with liquids that help digest the food, forming a soupy paste. Between your stomach and the duodenum, there is a muscle called the **sphincter.** When the sphincter relaxes, it opens and a small amount of food is squeezed into the duodenum, just as toothpaste moves out of the tube when the cap is off.

After a small amount of food leaves the stomach, the sphincter quickly closes, sealing off the passageway. The rest of the food remains in the stomach until the duodenum is ready to receive it.

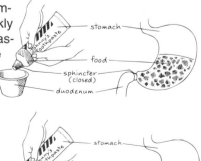

69. Stoppers

Purpose To simulate the formation of blood clots.

Materials scissors
stiff paper (A file folder will work well)
ruler
clear plastic drinking glass
one-hole paper punch
sheet of red construction paper
cotton ball

Procedure

1. Cut out a square piece of stiff paper large enough to rest on top of the glass.
2. Fold the piece of stiff paper in half, and cut a notch in the center of the folded edge. The notch should be about 1 inch (2.5 cm) wide and ½ inch (1.25 cm) long.
3. Unfold the paper and place it across the top of the glass.
4. Use the paper punch to cut 20 or more circles from the red paper.
5. Hold the red circles about 2 inches (5 cm) above the hole in the paper and drop them.
6. Remove the red circles from the glass. Replace the paper cover across the glass. Then pull a small piece from the cotton ball and stretch it across the hole in the paper so that a thin layer of cotton fibers covers the hole.

7. Hold the remaining paper pieces about 2 inches (5 cm) above the covered hole in the paper, and then release them.

Results Without the cotton fibers covering the hole, the paper pieces fall through the hole. With the fibers, the paper pieces stack together on the fibers and do not fall through.

Why? Your **circulatory system** is a group of body parts that carry materials to and from cells. The parts of the circulatory system represented in this experiment are the **blood** (a liquid that circulates in blood vessels, transporting oxygen to cells and removing waste) and the **blood vessels** (pathways in the body through which blood flows). The hole in the paper represents a cut in your skin. A break in the skin usually breaks the wall of one or more blood vessels. The blood flows out the opening, and the body begins an emergency procedure to form a blood clot. A **blood clot** is a solid mass made of **fibrin** (a threadlike fiber) and blood that plugs the hole in the skin. Like the fibers of cotton in this experiment, fibrin covers and plugs the hole, preventing the blood, represented by the red circles, from passing through. Trapped blood in fibrin dries, forming what is called a **scab.**

70. Keep Cool

Purpose To demonstrate the cooling effect of air moving across your skin.

Materials you

Procedure

1. Hold the back of your hand close to, but not touching, your mouth.
2. Open your mouth and blow as hard as possible. Observe how warm or cold your breath makes your hand feel.
3. Repeat steps 1 and 2 pursing your lips.

Results Your hand feels warmer when you blow on it with an open mouth and cooler when you blow on it through pursed lips.

Why? The temperature of your breath is the same whether your mouth is open or your lips are pursed. The

difference in the perceived temperature is that with your mouth open, your warm breath comes out slowly, and gently pushes away the air layer above your hand, and takes its place. Since your breath is warmer than the air layer, your skin feels warmer. But when you purse your lips, the air is forced through a smaller opening and comes out of your mouth more rapidly. The faster-moving air blows away the air layer above your hand, allowing cooler air from the room to move in. This makes your skin feel cooler.

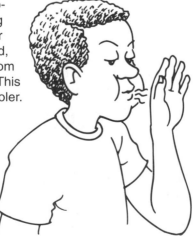

71. Spotted

Purpose To demonstrate how a skin covering protects your skin from the Sun.

Materials   2 sheets of construction paper—1 white, 1 red
one-hole paper punch
4 paper clips
transparent tape

Procedure

1. Fold the white sheet of paper in half twice, placing the long sides together.
2. Use the paper punch to make 30 or more holes in the folded paper.
3. Unfold the paper and place it over the sheet of red paper. Use the paper clips to hold the two sheets together.
4. In the middle of the day, lay the papers white side up on an outdoor table in the sun. Secure the papers with tape.
5. After 2 hours or more, remove the papers from the table and separate them. Observe the color of the red paper.

NOTE: It is not necessary to observe the papers during the 2 hours, but if you remain outdoors, wear protective clothing and sunscreen.

Results The red paper is covered with pink polka dots.

Why? As the red **pigment** (any substance that gives color to a material) combines with oxygen, it **fades** (gets lighter in color). This happens naturally over a period of time, but the process is speeded up in the presence of bright sunlight. The white paper, like most of the clothes you wear, is **opaque** (not allowing light to pass through), so it acts as a sunscreen, preventing sunlight from hitting the red paper that it covers. Cutting holes in the paper allowed the sunlight to hit the red paper beneath, causing these areas to fade to pale red to pink. Sunlight does not fade the color of your skin; instead it causes the production of a pigment called **melanin,** which darkens your skin color.

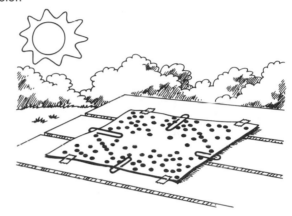

72. Sweaty

Purpose To show how the body loses water through the skin.

Materials   clear plastic bag large enough to cover your foot
rubber band large enough to fit loosely around your ankle
timer

NOTE: During hot weather, perform this experiment indoors, where it is cooler.

Procedure

1. Put the plastic bag over your bare foot.
2. Place the rubber band over the bag and loosely around your ankle.
3. Observe the bag after 10 minutes. Then remove the rubber band.

Results The bag looks cloudy because of tiny drops of water on its inside surface.

Why? The water in the sweat released from the pores of your foot **evaporates** (changes from a liquid to a gas) and **condenses** (changes from a gas to a liquid) on the surface of the bag. For the process of condensation to occur, the gas must be cooled, which means it loses heat. This occurs when the water **vapor** (gas formed from a substance that is usually a solid or a liquid at room tempera-

ture) touches the cool surface of the plastic bag, resulting in the formation of liquid water drops on the bag. For the process of evaporation to occur, the liquid must gain heat. This occurs by the removal of energy from your skin by the water. So as the water evaporates from your skin, your skin loses heat and is cooled. Sweating is one way your body cools itself. The amount of water you lose from sweating is determined by the amount of cooling your body needs.

Warm weather and hard exercise generally cause you to sweat more to keep your body cool. It is not the amount of sweat that makes your body cooler, but the evaporation of the liquid from your skin.

Your entire body sweats, but more sweat is produced on the soles of your feet, palms of your hands, and armpits. Generally, sweat itself is not smelly, but the waste from **bacteria** (microscopic one-celled organisms) that live on moist skin can make sweaty feet smelly.

73. Expanded

Purpose   To determine why the skin around knuckles is more wrinkled on one side.

Materials   flexible drinking straw

Procedure
1. Try to bend the end of the straw that is opposite the flexible end. Note the shape of the bent section of the straw and how difficult it is to bend the straw.
2. Try to bend the straw at the flexible end. Again note the shape of the bent section of the straw and how difficult it is to bend the straw.

Results   The shape of the flexible end is more curved when bent. The straw is easier to bend at the flexible end.

Why?   The straw bends at the flexible section because one side can expand and the other side can squeeze together and contract. The skin on the top side of the knuckles in your fingers is more wrinkled. When your finger is bent, the wrinkled skin on top of your knuckle expands and straightens, while the smooth skin on the underside of the knuckle is squeezed together and contracts.

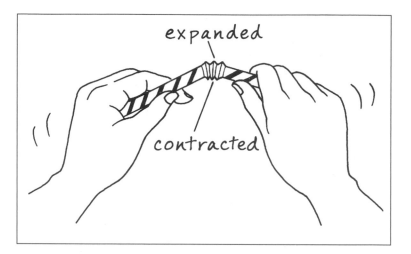

74. Wrinkled

Purpose   To demonstrate why fingers and toes wrinkle in water.

Materials   scissors
ruler
new cellulose kitchen sponge
bowl of tap water
petroleum jelly

Procedure
1. Cut a 1-inch (2.5-cm)- wide strip from the sponge. Keep the strip.
2. Cut a section from the sponge strip as shown so that about half the strip is half as thick.
3. Put the strip in the bowl of water until it's soaked, and then take it out and squeeze out as much water as possible. Allow the sponge to dry thoroughly. This may take several hours.
4. Press the dry sponge strip with your fingers, making it as flat as possible.
5. Thoroughly coat the surface of the thinner section of the sponge strip with petroleum jelly.
6. Dip your finger in the water in the bowl and hold your wet finger above the part of the sponge coated with petroleum jelly. Allow two to three water drops to fall onto the sponge. Observe the surface of the sponge.
7. Repeat step 6, dropping water onto the uncoated, thicker part of the sponge.

Results   The uncoated part of the sponge absorbs water and wrinkles.

Why?   The skin on the tips of your fingers and toes is different from the rest of your skin. It is thicker, and like the uncoated part of the sponge, it is not waterproofed with a coating of oil. That's why your skin soaks up water and wrinkles when you have been in water for a long time.

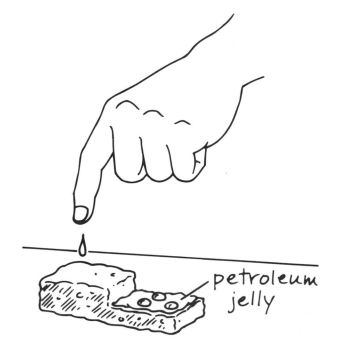

75. Smelly

Purpose To determine the effect of a material's temperature on your sense of smell.

Materials spoon
      scented candle
      1-quart (1-L) resealable plastic bag

Procedure
1. Use the spoon to scrape enough shavings from the candle to cover the palm of your hand.
2. Pour the candle shavings into the plastic bag. Seal the bag.
3. Spread the shavings out in the plastic bag, then lay the bag flat in a freezer.
4. After 30 minutes or more, remove the bag from the freezer and place about half the candle shavings in your hand.
5. Smell the cold candle shavings in your hand and mentally note how strong the scent is.
6. With the candle shavings in your hand, place the palms of your hands together and rub them back and forth for about 10 seconds. You can measure the time by counting to yourself, one thousand one, one thousand two, one thousand three, and so on.
7. At the end of 10 seconds of rubbing your hands, smell the candle shavings in your hand. Then smell the candle shavings remaining in the bag. How does the scent of the warmed shavings compare to the scent of the cold shavings?

Results The warmed shavings have a stronger scent.

Why? Smell happens inside your nose. The scent of the candle comes from molecules that leave the candle and enter the air. When air containing these molecules enters your nose, the molecules are picked up by **smell detectors,** which are special cells in your nose. These detectors send a message to your brain, which then identifies the smell.

    Odor is the property of a substance that **activates** (causes to function) the smell detectors. Materials give off odor when they **vaporize,** which means they change to a vapor. The more vapor that enters the nose at one time, the stronger the smell. The warmer the material, the more it vaporizes and the stronger its odor, because more vapor gets into your nose. Very cold materials vaporize so little that they have little or no odor.

---

76. Double

Purpose To demonstrate that the brain can be tricked.

Materials 2 unsharpened pencils
      helper

Procedure
1. Prepare your helper for this experiment by showing the two pencils and explaining that he or she will be asked to determine the number of pencils used in each part of the experiment.
2. Ask your helper to rest his or her elbow on a table and to separate the index and middle fingers of one hand as wide as possible.
3. With your helper looking away, hold the two pencils together and place them between the separated fingers so that each finger touches one pencil. Tell your helper to gently close the fingers. Move the pencils back and forth between your helper's fingers two or three times. Ask your helper how many pencils are felt.
4. Ask your helper to cross his or her index and middle fingers as shown. With your helper looking away, place one pencil between the two fingers and rub it back and forth two or three times. Again ask your helper how many pencils are felt.

Results At first two pencils feel like one, but with your fingers crossed one pencil feels like two.

Why? With crossed fingers, their outsides (sides normally facing away from each other) touch the pencil at the same time. **Nerves** (fibers that carry messages to and from the brain) from the outside of both fingers send messages to the brain that they are touching a pencil. The brain interprets the messages to mean that two pencils are being touched. With the fingers in their normal side-by-side position, nerves from the inside of the fingers send messages that they are touching a pencil. Usually only one object touches these sides, so the brain interprets the messages to mean one pencil is being touched.

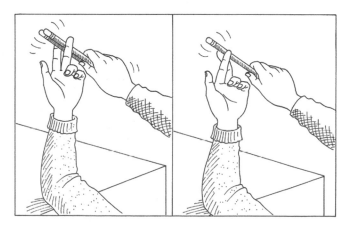

77. Vibrating Cords

Purpose To determine how you make speech sounds.

Materials hand mirror

Procedure
1. Keep your mouth closed while you hum, making the "mmm" sound of the letter *M.*
2. While continuing to hum, open your mouth slightly and note the new sound produced.
3. Make the sounds of the following letters—*D, P, S, A, E, I, O,* and *U*—and look in the mirror to observe the shape of your lips and whether your mouth is open or closed. Also note the position of your tongue as you produce each sound.

Results The "mmm" sound changes to an "ahh" sound when the mouth is opened. The tongue and lips are in different positions for each of the other letter sounds. Only the humming sound of the letter *M* requires the mouth to be closed.

Why? **Vocal cords** are made of **tissues** (groups of cells that perform a special job) stretched across your **windpipe** (a breathing tube from the mouth to the lungs) that vibrate when air from your lungs flows past them. Your lips, tongue, cheeks, roof of your mouth, teeth, nasal cavity, and nose help to change, or "shape," the sounds produced by your vibrating vocal cords. The "mmm" sound made with your mouth closed changes to an "ahh" sound because the path of air flowing out of your head changes when you open your mouth. With your mouth closed, there is little room between your tongue and the roof of your mouth. Opening your mouth moves the tongue down.

The *D* sound requires that the tongue be placed against the front part of the roof of the mouth, called the **hard palate.** In this position the airflow is blocked. The *P* sound is also produced by suddenly stopping the flow of air leaving the mouth, but your lips, not your tongue, stop the airflow.

The *S* sound is made by placing the tongue against the roof of the mouth and forcing air through the narrow opening between the tongue and the hard palate.

The shape of your cheeks and lips allow you to form the vowel sounds of *A, E, I, O,* and *U.* The shape of your mouth is also changed by moving the lower jaw up and down.

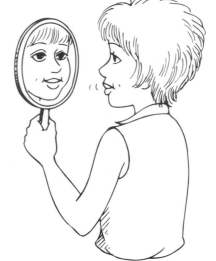

78. Bigger and Better

Purpose To determine if the size of the outer ear affects hearing.

Materials radio
yardstick (meterstick)

Procedure
1. Turn the radio on and set it on medium volume.
2. Stand about 1 yard (1 m) in front of the radio.
3. Turn your left ear toward the radio and note the noise level of the sounds from the radio.
4. Turn your back toward the radio and note the noise level of the sounds from the radio.
5. Cup your left hand and place it over your left ear, with your thumb and index finger touching your ear.
6. Again, note the noise level of the sounds from the radio as you stand first with your left ear toward the radio and then with your back toward the radio.

Results The sounds from the radio are louder with your ear turned toward the radio. The noise level is further increased by placing your cupped hand over your ear.

Why? Your two outer ears act as sound receivers that funnel sounds into your ear canal. The **ear canal** is the passage from the outer ear to the **eardrum** (a thin, tight skin stretched inside the ear that vibrates when sound hits it). Placing your hand over your ear and turning the ear toward the radio causes more of the sounds from the radio to be received and directed inside your ear. This is not to say that having a larger outer ear would make you hear sounds better. In fact, your cupped hand blocks some of the sound waves coming from behind you when your back is toward the radio. If you could move your ears around to "look for" sounds, as some animals do, then a larger ear would help you to receive sounds from different directions.

79. Light Catchers

Purpose To determine why some animals see better at night.

Materials plastic food tray
twelve 3-ounce (90-mL) paper cups
ruler
2 cups (500 mL) of rice
colander
1-cup (250-mL) measuring cup

Procedure
1. Set the tray outdoors on the ground.
2. Place three of the paper cups about 1 inch (1.25 cm) apart in a row across the center of the tray.
3. Hold the colander about 12 inches (30 cm) above the cups.
4. As you pour 1 cup (250 mL) of the rice into the colander, gently shake the colander.
5. Pour the rice collected in the three cups into the measuring cup and note the total amount collected.
6. Repeat steps 2 to 5, placing 12 paper cups in the tray. Compare the total amount of rice collected by 3 cups versus the amount collected by 12 cups.

Results More rice is collected when more cups are used.

Why? The **retina** is the back innermost layer of an animal's eye. In the retina are light-sensitive cells called **rods** and **cones.** Rods are more sensitive to light and work better in dim light than do cones. Both rods and cones contain pigment that makes them sensitive to light. When light strikes these cells, a visual message is sent along the **optic nerve,** which is the main nerve connecting the eye to the brain. Rods send black-and-white messages and cones send color messages. If the light is not bright enough, cones do not work at all. So at night rods are generally the only light-sensitive cells working. Owls, cats, and many other night animals (those that hunt for food at night) have more rods in their eyes than people do. In this experiment, the rice represented light and the cups rods. The more cups used, the more rice they caught. In a similar way, when there are more rods in an animal's eyes, they receive more light. That's why these animals see better in the dark.

80. Twice

Purpose To determine why a night animal's glowing eyes give it better night vision.

Materials walnut-size piece of modeling clay
mirror
flashlight

Procedure
1. Use the clay to stand the mirror upright.
2. In a dimly lit room, turn on the flashlight.
3. Spread your fingers in front of the flashlight with the palm side of your hand facing the light. Observe how illuminated the palm side of your fingers is.
4. Position your hand and the flashlight at an angle to the mirror so that you can see the top side of your fingers in the mirror but the light does not hit the mirror. Looking into the mirror, observe how illuminated the top side of your fingers is.
5. Repeat steps 3 and 4 with your hand in front of the mirror, but this time let some of the light hit the mirror.

Results Only the side of the fingers facing the light is illuminated when the light does not hit the mirror. Both sides of the fingers are illuminated when the light does hit the mirror.

Why? Animals that hunt at night have special eyes which allow them to see in dim light. This ability is called **night vision.** The eyes of these animals are similar to yours, but they have more special light-catching cells called rods, as well as a special mirrorlike reflective surface called a **tapetum.** The mirror in this experiment represents the tapetum of an animal's eye and your fingers represent rods. When light hits the rods of an eye without a tapetum, the rods react to the light once. This was demonstrated by holding your hand at an angle to the mirror so that the light did not hit the mirror. But when light hits an eye with a tapetum, it hits the rods once, then it bounces off the tapetum and hits the rods again. So the rods are hit twice by the same light. This was demonstrated by some of the light hitting one side of your fingers and some bouncing off the mirror and hitting the opposite side of your fingers. The additional reflected light helps the animal to see better at night.

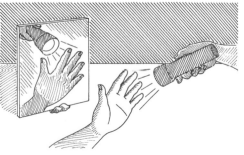

81. Big or Little?

Purpose To demonstrate an optical illusion.

Materials 3 sheets of copy paper—2 white, 1 any color
pencil
scissors
ruler

Procedure

1. Lay one sheet of white paper on top of the sheet of colored paper.
2. On the white paper, use the pencil to draw the curved design shown here. Make the shape as large as possible.
3. Cut out the curved design by cutting through both layers of paper.
4. Use the pencil and ruler to draw a solid line across the remaining white sheet of copy paper.
5. Lay the curved designs side-by-side on the edge of a table with the white paper to the left, as shown, with the bottom corner of the designs on the solid line, as shown.

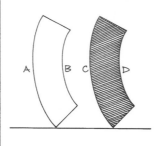

6. Compare the sizes of the paper cutouts. Does one appear to be larger than the other?
7. Switch the positions of the cutouts placing the white paper on the right. Then repeat step 6.

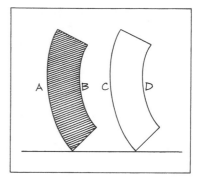

Results The paper on the right-hand side, no matter what its color, appears to be larger.

Why? What seems to be a trick is an **optical illusion** (something that appears to be different from what is really there). In each diagram, curve C on the cutout on the right is longer and extends lower than curve B on the left cutout. Because your eye compares two curves that are next to each other, the cutout on the right will always appear larger.

82. Extra Money

Purpose To demonstrate persistence of vision.

Materials 2 coins of the same value

Procedure

1. Hold the coins together between your thumb and index finger.
2. Quickly rub the coins against each other so that they slide back and forth. Observe the coins and count the number of coins that you seem to see.

Results You seem to see three coins.

Why? When you look at an object, an image of the object is projected on the retina (the back inner wall) of your eyes. Even if the object has moved or is removed, its image remains on the retina for a fraction of a second. This is called **persistence of vision.** Thus, an extra coin seems to appear between the coins.

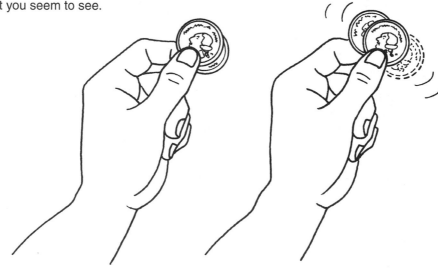

83. How Near?

Purpose To find the closest point where your eye can form a clear image of an object.

Materials ruler
helper

Procedure
1. Hold this book open and as close to your face as possible without touching your face.
2. Slowly move the book away from your face. Stop when the print on the page is as unclear as possible. Move the book back and forth until you find the closest distance it can be from your eyes and have sharp, clear print. (If you wear reading glasses, do the experiment twice, first with and then without your glasses.)
3. Ask a helper to measure the distance the book is from your eyes by holding the ruler near but not touching the face.

CAUTION: Be careful when holding the the ruler near the eye so that you do not touch the eye.

Results The distance will vary, but generally the book is about 10 inches (25 cm) from your face.

Why? As the print is moved, the image of the print formed by the lens of your eye also moves. Eventually, a point is reached at which the image of the print forms on the retina of your eye. If this image is behind or in front of the retina, a blurred image is seen. The average distance for clear distinct vision for people without vision problems is about 10 inches (25 cm) from the eye. "Average" means that most people will measure this distance but some will be have a longer or shorter distance. This distance of distinct vision is called the **near point.**

84. Who Can?

Purpose To demonstrate how the body's center of gravity affects balance.

Materials low stool
helper

Procedure
1. Stand with the tips of your shoes touching a wall. Place one foot behind the other and take three steps back from the wall.
2. Have someone place a stool between you and the wall.
3. Lean over and place the top of your head against the wall. Your legs should be at about a 45° angle to your body.
4. Holding the edge of the seat of the stool, pick it up and hold the seat against your chest.
5. Keeping the stool against your chest, try to stand up.

Results Some people can do this with little or no effort, while others cannot do it at all.

Why? The center of gravity of a body is the point at which its weight seems to be concentrated. If an object is supported beneath its center of gravity, it will balance. Holding the stool next to your chest adds weight to your upper body. This changes your center of gravity, making it higher, or closer to the chest. The higher the center of gravity, the more difficult it is to stand while holding the stool. For those whose body has a low center of gravity, the weight of the stool will not keep them from standing up. But for those whose body has a high center of gravity, the weight of the stool will keep them from standing.

III
Chemistry

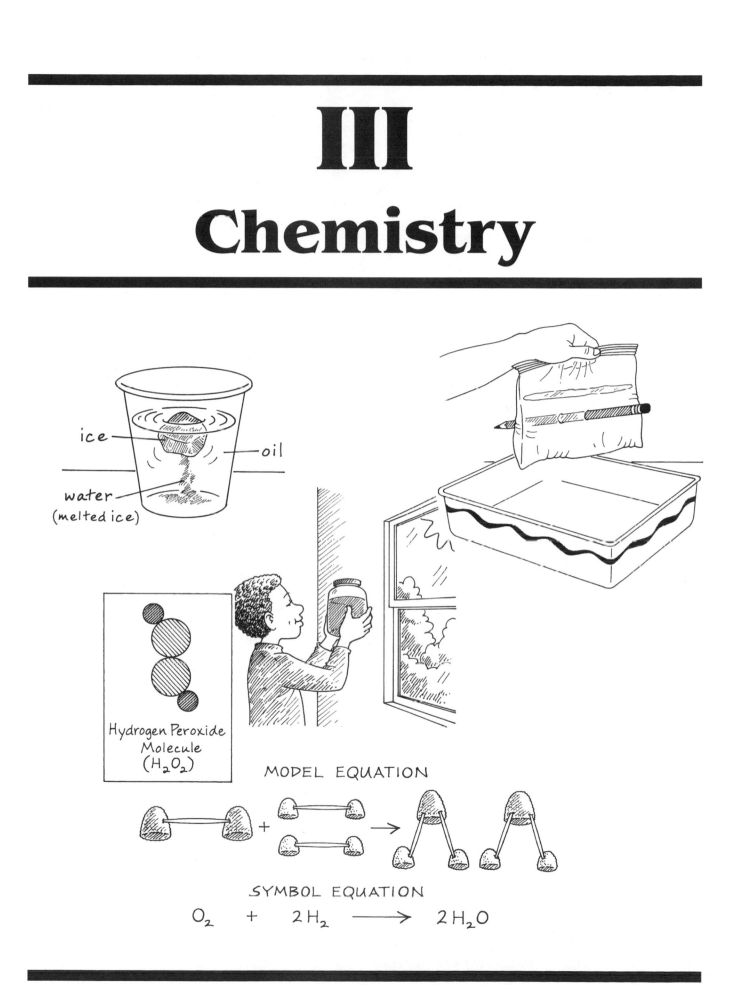

ice

oil

water
(melted ice)

Hydrogen Peroxide
Molecule
(H_2O_2)

MODEL EQUATION

SYMBOL EQUATION

$$O_2 \quad + \quad 2H_2 \quad \longrightarrow \quad 2H_2O$$

85. It Matters

Purpose To demonstrate that gas has volume.

Materials 9-inch (22.5-cm) or larger round balloon
2 or more books

Procedure

1. Blow into the balloon to inflate it, and then let the air out. Repeat this twice to make the balloon more flexible and easier to inflate.
2. Place the balloon on a table and stack the books on the closed end of the balloon. Leave about half of the open end of the balloon extending from beneath the bottom book in the stack. Observe the position of the books in relation to the table.
3. Kneel beside the table and slightly inflate the balloon by blowing into it. Again observe the position of the books in relation to the table.
4. Blow more air into the balloon so that it is about twice as large as it was when you inflated it in step 3. How does the increased amount of gas in the balloon affect the position of the books?

Results The more the balloon is inflated, the higher the books are lifted above the table.

Why? **Chemistry** is the study of the composition, structure, properties, and interactions of matter. Matter exists in three basic forms: gas, liquid, and solid. These forms are called **phases of matter.** Matter has mass and **volume** (an amount of occupied space). In this experiment it was demonstrated that gas has volume, shown by the lifting of the books as your breath inflated the balloon. The confined gas inside the balloon took up space and thus **displaced** (pushed out of place) the books. Exhaled breath is a mixture of gases, including oxygen and carbon dioxide.

86. Just Enough

Purpose To determine how much water is needed to make an ice cube float.

Materials masking tape
marker
two 10-ounce (300-mL) clear plastic cups
tap water
ice cube

Procedure

1. Use the tape and marker to label the cups "A" and "B."
2. Fill cup A about three-fourths full with water.
3. Place the ice cube in the cup of water and observe how much of the ice is below the water's surface.
4. Remove the ice and place it in cup B.
5. Slowly pour the water from cup A into cup B. Add only enough water to make the ice lift from the bottom of the cup and float in the water.

Results When the ice cube was added to cup A, you could see that when the ice floated, most of the cube was below the water level. When you poured the water from cup A into cup B, the ice cube in cup B floated when enough water was added to surround most of the ice cube.

Why? Even though ice and liquid water are both made of water molecules (H_2O), they have different densities. **Density** is the mass of a substance divided by its volume. Normally the density of a substance increases as it gets colder, because as the temperature drops, the molecules in the substance move closer together, so they have the same mass in a smaller volume. But water is an unusual substance because it actually becomes less dense when frozen. The density of water is 1 g/mL (meaning 1 gram of water has a volume of 1 mL), and the density of ice is about 0.9 g/mL. Objects that have a density less than that of water will float in water. The ice cube in this experiment floated as soon as most of it was surrounded by water. The amount of the object that remains beneath the surface of the water will depend on the density of the object. The closer the density of the object to the density of water, the lower the object will float in water.

87. On Top

Purpose To determine which has a lower density, ice or oil.

Materials 1-quart (1-L) jar
tap water
blue food coloring
spoon
ice cube tray
10-ounce (300-mL) clear plastic cup
cooking oil

Procedure
1. Fill the jar with water.
2. Add 20 or more drops of food coloring and stir. The water should be dark blue.
3. Pour the colored water into the ice cube tray and place the tray in a freezer until the water turns to ice. This should take 2 or more hours.
4. Fill the cup about three-fourths full with oil.
5. Remove one ice cube from the tray and place it in the cup of oil. (If the materials used in making the ice were clean, the extra colored ice can be saved and used to cool a drink.)
6. Observe the position of the ice in the oil.
7. Continue to observe what happens as the ice cube melts.

Results The ice floats in the oil with most of the ice below the surface of the oil. The colored water (melted ice) moves down through the oil and collects on the bottom of the cup.

Why? Ice floats in oil, so ice's density is slightly less than that of oil. But oil and ice both will float in water because their density is less than that of water. So as the ice cube melted, the denser liquid water sank through the oil and collected on the bottom of the cup.

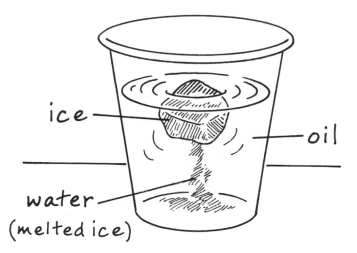

88. Floater

Purpose To determine whether an apple's density is greater or less than that of water.

Materials bowl about twice as deep as an apple
tap water
small apple

Procedure
1. Fill the bowl about three-fourths full with water.
2. Push the apple to the bottom of the bowl of water and release it.

Results The apple rises and floats on the surface of the water.

Why? Density is a measure of the mass of a given volume of a material. If the density of a material is less than the density of water, which is 1 g/mL, the substance will float in water. Since the apple floats, you know that its density is less than 1 g/mL. Objects that sink in water have a density greater than 1 g/mL.

89. Builders

Purpose   To make models of molecules.

Materials   3 round toothpicks
2 large gumdrops (of one color)
2 small gumdrops (of another color)

Procedure

1. Insert a toothpick in one of the large gumdrops, then place the second large gumdrop on the other end of the toothpick.
2. Repeat step 1 twice using the small gumdrops.

NOTE: Keep the three models for the next experiment.

Results   You have made three model molecules, two of which are alike.

Why?   The building blocks of matter are called atoms. The individual gumdrops represent atoms. In this experiment, the large gumdrops represent a different kind of atom than the small ones. The gumdrop models represent **molecules,** which are substances made up of two or more atoms. The atoms in the molecules are linked by **bonds,** or forces that link atoms together, represented by the toothpicks in your models. In this experiment, the two linked large gumdrops represent an oxygen (O_2) molecule and each of the two linked small gumdrops represents a

hydrogen (H_2) molecule. The symbol for an oxygen atom is O, and the symbol for a molecule of oxygen containing two atoms of oxygen is O_2. The symbol for a hydrogen atom is H, and the symbol for a molecule of hydrogen containing two hydrogen atoms is H_2. A number in front of the symbol tells how many molecules are present. For example, $2H_2$ means that there are two molecules of hydrogen.

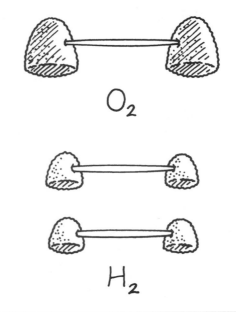

90. New Stuff

Purpose   To model a chemical reaction.

Materials   3 model molecules from Experiment 89, "Builders"
1 round toothpick

Procedure

1. Pull one gumdrop off of each model, leaving the toothpick in the remaining gumdrop.
2. Recombine the gumdrops using the extra toothpick, so that there are two small gumdrops connected by toothpicks at an angle to each other.

Results   The three original models are broken apart and recombined, forming two new models. The new models represent water molecules (H_2O) with two smaller hydrogen atoms and one large oxygen atom.

Why?   A **chemical reaction,** also called a **chemical change,** is a process of forming one or more new chemicals. The diagram gives two types of equations that show what happens in a chemical reaction: a model equation and a symbol equation. Each equation shows the **reactants** (starting materials) in the reaction and the **products** (final materials) of the reaction. When two or more molecules combine to

form one or more different molecules, the change is called a **combination chemical reaction.**

In this experiment reactants of the combination chemical reaction were the oxygen and hydrogen molecules, and the product was two water molecules. The reactants contain a total of six atoms: two large gumdrops (oxygen) and four small gumdrops (hydrogen). The product consisting of two water molecules contains the same number of total atoms as well as the same number of each kind of atom: two large gumdrops (oxygen) and four small gumdrops (hydrogen). The **law of conservation of matter** states that during a chemical reaction, matter is neither created nor destroyed, but remains constant. The model of the chemical reaction in this experiment demonstrates this law.

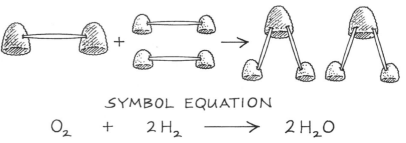

MODEL EQUATION

SYMBOL EQUATION

$$O_2 \; + \; 2H_2 \; \longrightarrow \; 2H_2O$$

91. Changes

Purpose To demonstrate a chemical reaction.

Materials 2 paper towels
saucer
1 teaspoon (5 mL) Epsom salts (available at pharmacies)
2 teaspoons (10 mL) tap water
5-ounce (150-mL) paper cup
spoon
1 tablespoon (15 mL) school glue

Procedure

1. Lay the paper towels together, one on top of the other. Then fold the towels in half twice and place the folded towels in the saucer.
2. Mix the Epsom salts and water together in the cup. Stir this mixture until as much Epsom salts as possible dissolves in the water. There may be a few undissolved salt crystals on the bottom of the cup.
3. Add the glue to the cup and stir thoroughly.
4. Pour the contents of the cup in the center of the folded towels in the saucer.
5. Fold the towels over the mixture and press down with your fingers to squeeze out the extra liquid. Rinse your hands in water afterwards to remove any Epsom salt on them.
6. Unfold the towels and use your fingers to peel the material off the paper. Observe the appearance of the material, then roll it into a ball and try to bounce it.

NOTE: Discard the material in the trash when the experiment is completed.

Results The combination of white solid crystals of Epsom salts, transparent liquid water, and opaque white liquid glue produces a bouncy white solid.

Why? Sometimes when two or more substances are combined, each substance keeps its own physical characteristics. The resulting product is called a **mixture.** If a chemical reaction occurs when substances are mixed together, then one or more new substances are produced. Unlike in a mixture, this new substance has different characteristics from any of the substances that were combined to make it. The product produced in this experiment is so different in appearance and form from the reactants that you can assume that a chemical reaction occurred.

92. Rusty

Purpose To demonstrate a chemical reaction.

Materials coarse steel-wool pad (available where paint supplies are sold)
10-ounce (300-mL) plastic glass
1 tablespoon (15 mL) vinegar

Procedure

1. Place the steel wool in the glass.
2. Pour the vinegar over the steel wool.
3. Observe the color of the steel wool immediately and then periodically for 2 or more hours.

Results The steel wool is silvery in color at the beginning of the experiment. As time passes, parts of the steel wool have a reddish brown color.

Why? The vinegar removed any protective surface from the steel wool so that the iron in the steel could rust. **Rusting** is a chemical reaction in which a material combines with oxygen. The combination of oxygen with other materials is an example of a chemical reaction called **oxidation.**

The term *rusting* is usually used to mean iron combining with oxygen to form a reddish brown chemical called iron oxide. Iron oxide is commonly called **rust.**

93. Inside Out

Purpose To demonstrate that rusting is an oxidation reaction.

Materials coarse steel-wool pad (available where paint supplies are sold)
10-ounce (300-mL) plastic glass
1 tablespoon (15 mL) vinegar
rubber dishwashing gloves
pencil
empty plastic 1-L soda bottle
9-inch (23.5-cm) round balloon

Procedure

1. Place the steel wool in the glass.
2. Pour the vinegar over the steel wool.
3. Wearing the gloves to protect your hands, pull the steel wool into threads and use the pencil to push the threads into the bottle.
4. Attach the balloon to the mouth of the bottle.
5. Watch the balloon for 4 or more hours.

Results The balloon slowly turns inside out as it moves into the bottle and then inflates inside the bottle.

Why? At first the bottle is filled with air containing oxygen and other gases. The **force** (the push or pull on things) of the gas molecules in the air from both inside and outside the bottle on the balloon is the same. But when the steel wool rusts, oxygen from the air inside the bottle is combined with iron in the steel wool. Thus a chemical reaction called oxidation occurs. As a result of this reaction, in which some of the oxygen is combined with the iron in the steel wool, there are fewer gas molecules in the air inside the bottle pushing on the balloon. The greater force of the gas molecules in the air outside the balloon pushes the balloon into the bottle.

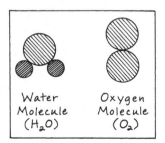

94. No Leftovers

Purpose To model a decomposition reaction.

Materials 2 sheets of different colored construction paper
protractor
scissors
poster board

Hydrogen Peroxide Molecule (H_2O_2)

Procedure

1. Fold one of the sheets of paper in half twice, first from top to bottom and then from side to side.
2. Draw as large a circle as possible on the outside of the paper.
3. Use the scissors to cut out the circle, cutting through all four layers.
4. Repeat steps 1 to 3 on the other sheet of paper, drawing a circle about half as large.
5. Use the large and small circles to form two hydrogen peroxide (H_2O_2) molecules as in the diagram.
6. Break the hydrogen peroxide molecules apart and, on the poster board, recombine the atoms to form as many water (H_2O) and oxygen (O_2) molecules as possible.

Results Two hydrogen peroxide molecules are broken apart to form two water (H_2O) molecules and one oxygen (O_2) molecule.

Why? When chemicals such as hydrogen peroxide **decompose** (break apart into basic substances), they recombine to form new substances. This type of chemical reaction is called a **decomposition reaction** (a chemical reaction in which a substance decomposes). During a decomposition reaction, all of the atoms in the reactant are used to form the products.

Water Molecule (H_2O)

Oxygen Molecule (O_2)

As in this demonstration, it may take more than one molecule of reactant to have enough atoms to combine and form the products with no leftover atoms.

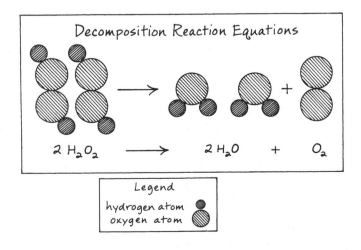

Decomposition Reaction Equations

$$2 H_2O_2 \longrightarrow 2 H_2O + O_2$$

Legend
hydrogen atom
oxygen atom

95. Faster

Purpose To demonstrate a decomposition reaction.

Materials 1 teaspoon (5 mL) soil
10-ounce (300-mL) plastic glass
1 tablespoon (15 mL) 3% hydrogen peroxide
(available where first-aid supplies are sold)

Procedure
1. Place the soil in the glass.
2. Pour the hydrogen peroxide into the glass.
3. Observe the contents of the glass periodically for 1 or more hours.

Results Within seconds, bubbles form. In time the bubbles stop forming.

Why? A **catalyst** is a substance that changes the speed of a chemical reaction without being changed itself. An **enzyme** is a catalyst found in living organisms. Soil contains dirt as well as parts of decayed leaves and other organisms. The remains of organisms contain an enzyme called catalase. Hydrogen peroxide is a chemical that on its own will slowly decompose into water and oxygen. In the presence of catalase, this change occurs quickly. The bubbles seen on the surface of the soil are oxygen. When the bubbles break, the oxygen in the bubbles mixes with the air. The process by which a chemical decomposes, with or without the presence of an enzyme, is called a **decomposition reaction.**

96. Helper

Purpose To model the action of a catalyst.

Materials 2-by-8-inch (5-by-20-cm) piece of paper
2 metal paper clips with different colored plastic coatings

Procedure
1. Place the two paper clips in your hands and shake them around. Do they combine or join together?
2. Fold the paper in thirds as shown.
3. Clip the paper clips over only two layers of the folded paper, one at each end as shown.
4. Holding the two ends of the folded paper, slowly pull in opposite directions until the paper is stretched out.

Results The paper clips generally do not combine when shaken in your hands, but when they come off the paper, they are attached to each other.

Why? Shaking the paper clips allows them to hit against each other, but they usually do not combine as a result of this action. If you shake a large number of paper clips, over time some of them will eventually combine. This represents a random or chance combination of chemicals. The folded paper represents a catalyst that increases the possibility that two chemicals (represented by the paper clips) will combine. The attached paper clips represent a new chemical product. The catalyst is actively involved in the chemical reaction (combination of the paper clips) but is not a reactant or part of the product. The catalyst can be used over and over again.

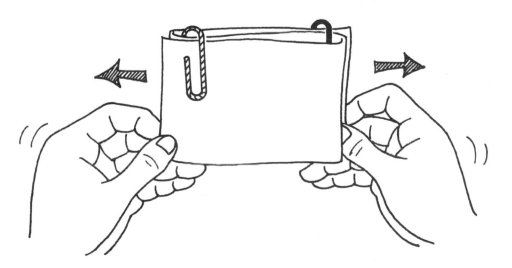

97. Breakdown

Purpose   To observe the effect of enzymes on gelatin.

Materials   6-ounce (170-g) package of gelatin dessert
mix, any flavor
two 1-pint (500-mL) bowls
masking tape
pen
½ cup (125 mL) canned pineapple chunks
spoon
½ cup (125 mL) fresh pineapple chunks
timer
adult helper

Procedure

1. Ask an adult to prepare the gelatin dessert mix according to the instructions on the box, pouring equal portions of the liquid into the 2 bowls.
2. Use the tape and pen to label the bowls "1" and "2."
3. Add the canned pineapple chunks to the gelatin in bowl 1 and stir.
4. Ask an adult to cut ½ cup (125 mL) of fresh pineapple chunks.
5. Add the fresh pineapple chunks to the gelatin in bowl 2 and stir.
6. Place the bowls in the refrigerator for 3 or more hours.
7. Remove the bowls from the refrigerator and observe the gelatin in each bowl. Tilt the bowls slightly and compare their firmness.

Results   The gelatin in bowl 1 with the canned pineapple becomes firm, but the gelatin in bowl 2 with the fresh pineapple is less firm or more watery.

Why?   **Gelatin** is a gummy protein obtained from animal tissues that is used in making jellylike desserts. (**Proteins** are large molecules necessary for life and growth.) Pineapples contain the enzyme **bromelin,** which digests the gelatin. If you put raw pineapples in a gelatin dessert, the bromelin in the fruit prevents or inhibits the gelatin's firming. Canned pineapples have been cooked, which **deactivates** (causes it not to function) the enzyme. This is why gelatin will get firm if mixed with canned pineapples.

98. Trapped

Purpose   To discover a method of speeding up the ripening of a banana.

Materials   pencil
paper
2 unripe bananas
paper lunch bag

Procedure

1. Observe and record the color of both bananas on day 1 (starting day).
2. Place one banana in the bag. Close the bag and place it on a table or kitchen counter.
3. Lay the other banana next to the bag.
4. Observe and record the color of the bananas each day at about the same time for 3 more days. Note how much the appearance of each banana changes—for example, "mostly green with yellow areas" or "about half yellow."

Results   The covered banana in the bag changed from green to yellow more quickly than did the uncovered banana.

Why?   Bananas change from green to yellow as they ripen because they lose their green **chlorophyll** (a green pigment that enables plants to use solar energy to make food). Bananas and other fruits produce ethylene gas, an enzyme that speeds up the ripening process. As the fruit ripens, it produces even more ethylene gas. The ethylene gas produced by the banana in the bag was trapped, causing the banana to ripen even faster. Most of the gas produced by the uncovered banana **diffused** (spread freely and scattered) in the air around it before it could affect the banana. Other fruits can be ripened using this method.

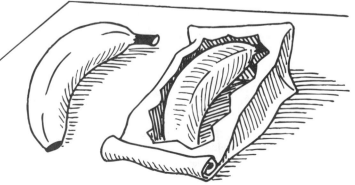

99. Sweeter

Purpose To show how ripeness affects the taste of fruits.

Materials unripe banana
glass of water
overripe banana

Procedure

1. Take a small bite of the unripe banana. Chew the banana and make note of its sweetness.
2. Drink some water to wash the banana taste from your mouth.
3. Take a small bite of the overripe banana. Chew the banana as before, comparing its sweetness to that of the unripe banana.

Results The overripe banana tastes sweeter.

Why? **Physical properties** are characteristics of a material, such as how it looks, feels, or tastes, its size, and its phase of matter. A common physical property of sugar molecules is their sweet taste. **Starch** is a nutrient. Molecules of starch are made up of many smaller sugar molecules bonded together in a long chain. Even though starch is made of sugar, it does not taste sweet. Most fruits, including bananas, include starch molecules that break apart into sugar molecules as the fruit ripens. This change is called ripening and results in the fruit tasting sweeter.

100. Gassy

Purpose To study the results of combining the leavening agents baking powder and baking soda with liquids.

Materials marker
eight 3-ounce (90-mL) paper cups
measuring spoons
2 teaspoons (10 mL) baking powder
2 teaspoons (10 mL) baking soda
4 tablespoons (60 mL) vinegar
4 tablespoons (60 mL) tap water
timer
paper
pen or pencil
helper

Procedure

1. Use the marker to label four of the cups "BP," "BS," "V," and "W." Repeat with the other four cups.
2. Add 1 teaspoon (5 mL) of baking powder to the two BP cups. Add 1 teaspoon (5 mL) of baking soda to the two BS cups.
3. Pour 2 tablespoons (30 mL) of vinegar in the two V cups. Pour 2 tablespoons (30 mL) of water in the two W cups.
4. Group the cups into two sets of four cups as follows:
   Set 1: BP, BP, V, W
   Set 2: BS, BS, V, W
5. Ask your helper to pour the liquids from the cups in set 1 into the cups containing baking powder (BP) at the same time that you pour the liquids in set 2 into the cups of baking soda (BS). Pour the vinegar into the V cup and the water into the W cup in each set. Do not mix.
6. Observe and record the contents of the cups immediately, then after 30 seconds, and again in 5 minutes.

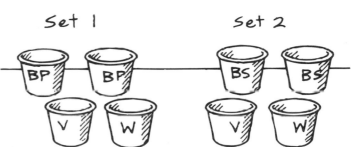

Results

TEST RESULTS OF LEAVENING AGENTS + LIQUIDS

Leavening Agent + Liquid	Immediately	After 30 Seconds	After 5 Minutes
1. BP + V	many bubbles	some bubbles	same
2. BP + W	some bubbles	same	same
3. BS + V	many bubles	no bubbles	same
4. BS + W	no bubbles	same	same

Why? Breads are made from baking **dough,** which is a mixture of flour and a liquid.

A special ingredient called a **leavening agent** is added to the dough to make it less dense when baked. When mixed with the dough, the leavening agent produces a gas. This causes an increase in volume, thus decreasing the density of the dough. An **acid,** such as vinegar, is a substance that reacts with baking soda to produce bubbles of carbon dioxide gas. The leavening agent baking powder is a mixture of baking soda and a dry acid. The addition of water to baking powder allows the baking soda and acid to chemically react, producing carbon dioxide gas. The addition of water to baking soda alone produces no reaction.

101. Shortening

Purpose   To determine how a molecule can be shortened.

Materials   2 small bowls
spoon
measuring spoons
4 tablespoons (60 mL) all-purpose flour
tap water
fork
1 tablespoon (15 mL) shortening
ruler

Procedure

1. In one bowl, mix 2 tablespoons (30 mL) of flour with enough water to make a soft ball. You will need about 2 tablespoons (30 mL) of water.
2. In the other bowl, use the fork to blend together the shortening and the remaining 2 tablespoons (30 mL) of flour.
3. Add drops of water to the flour-and-shortening mixture until you can make a soft ball.
4. With your hands, shape each ball into a tube-shaped roll about 3 inches (7.5 cm) long.
5. Holding the ends of the flour-and-shortening roll, pull outward to stretch it. Observe the ease with which the roll stretches or breaks.
6. Repeat step 5 with the flour-and-water roll.

Results   The flour-and-water mixture was stretchier than the flour-and-shortening mixture.

Why?   The combination of flour and water produces a dough containing a tough, elastic protein called **gluten.** Gluten gives dough firmness but also allows the dough to stretch. When a leavening agent is added to the dough, the gluten in the dough is stretched by the carbon dioxide produced by the leavening agent. Once the gluten has been dried by baking, it gives the food firmness. Fats in the dough break the gluten strands and thus shorten the gluten molecules. Because fat shortens the gluten molecules in dough, fats commonly used for baking are often called **shortening.** The shortened gluten molecules cause the dough to easily break. The more shortened gluten in the baked product, the less firm it is.

102. Uncoiled

Purpose   To determine how beating affects egg whites.

Materials   3 egg whites (Ask an adult to separate the whites from the yolks)
deep 1-quart (1-L) bowl
timer
fork
wire whisk (or an electric mixer used with adult assistance)
adult helper

CAUTION: Wash your hands and utensils well when working with raw eggs, as they can contain harmful bacteria.

Procedure

1. Place the egg whites in the bowl and let them stand at room temperature for about 10 minutes.
2. Using the fork, lift the egg whites and observe their appearance.
3. Using the whisk, beat the egg whites until they are stiff. You should be able to make peaks that stand upright on the surface of the mixture when you lift the whisk from the beaten egg whites.
4. Using the fork again, lift the egg whites and observe their appearance.
5. Discard the egg whites.

Results   Before beating, the egg whites are a clear, slightly yellow, thick liquid. After beating, the egg whites are white, thick, and foamy.

Why?   The kind of proteins in egg whites called **globular proteins,** are made up of chains of molecules coiled into compact balls, much like tiny balls of yarn. When the bonds between the molecules are broken by beating the egg whites, the protein uncoils. This process of changing protein from its natural form is called **denaturing.**

   In their natural state, the egg whites are a **viscous** (having a relatively high resistance to flow) pale yellow liquid. You see the yellow color because of the way light passes through the clear liquid. Beating the egg whites not only uncoils the protein in them, but forces bubbles of air to be mixed with the uncoiled protein, forming a thick, stiff, white foam. The denatured foamy mass scatters the light in a way that makes the beaten egg whites look white.

103. Crystals

Purpose To model the axis of a cubic crystal.

Materials scissors
ruler
3 different-colored drinking straws
lemon-size piece of modeling clay
sheet of white copy paper

Procedure

1. Cut three 1-inch (2.5-cm) sections from each of the three colored straws.
2. Divide the clay to form two balls, one a walnut-size straw holder and the other a support stand.
3. Insert six straw sections, two of each color, into the clay holder at 90° to each other, as shown. Letters A, B, and C represent the three axes: A, *a*-axis; B, *y*-axis; and C, *z*-axis. Use the remaining three straw sections to make a legend on the sheet of paper.
4. Set the clay support stand on the paper and insert one end of either straw B section into it.

Results You have made a model of the axis of a cubic crystal.

Why? A **crystal** is a solid made up of atoms arranged in an orderly, regular pattern of flat **faces** (sides). It has a

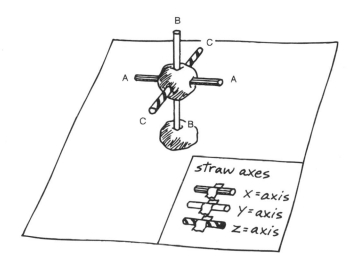

recognizable shape that results from the repetition of the same combination of atomic particles. All crystals are **three-dimensional,** meaning they have length, width, and depth. In this experiment, a model of a cubic crystal is made. Cubic crystals have three axes that are the same length and are at 90° to each other. (An **axis** is a line about which a three-dimensional structure is symmetrical.) Table salt is a substance that has cubic crystals.

104. Shiny Cubes

Purpose To grow cubic crystals.

Materials scissors
sheet of black construction paper
plate
3-ounce (90-mL) paper cup
tap water
2 tablespoons (60 mL) table salt
spoon
magnifying lens

Procedure

1. Cut as large a circle as possible from the paper to fit in the plate.
2. Fill the cup about three-fourths full with water.
3. Add the salt to the cup of water and stir well.
4. Place the plate on a table where it will not be disturbed. Then pour the salt solution over the black paper.
5. Allow the paper to dry. This may take 2 or more days depending on temperature and how dry the air is.
6. After the paper dries, use the magnifying lens to observe the crystals on the paper.

Results Small, individual, shiny cubes can be seen on the paper.

Why? Table salt is the common name for the chemical sodium chloride. The atoms of sodium and chlorine, which make up sodium chloride, are too small to see even with most microscopes. But when many hundreds of thousands of these atoms stack together, they bond to form a cube shape. The size of the crystals depends on the number of atoms bonded together. When salt is mixed with water, the bonds between the atoms of salt break apart and the atoms separate. As the water evaporates, there is a smaller amount of water and the separated atoms of salt get closer together. As the water continues to evaporate, eventually the atoms recombine and stack together into visible crystals.

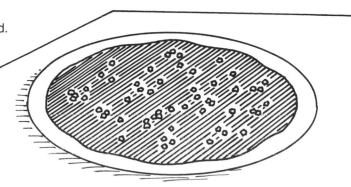

105. Linked

Purpose To model a polymer.

Materials modeling clay (any color)
scissors
12-inch (30-cm) pipe cleaner (available
where craft supplies are sold)

Procedure

1. Divide the clay into nine equal pieces. Shape each piece of clay into a ball.
2. Cut the pipe cleaner in half three times so that you have eight pieces.
3. Stick about one-third of one pipe cleaner piece into one of the clay balls. Stick a clay ball on the free end of this pipe cleaner.

4. Continue using pipe cleaner pieces and clay balls to make a single chain.

Results A chain of similar clay balls is made.

Why? A **polymer** is a very long chainlike molecule. *Poly* means "many" and *mer* means "unit." A polymer is made by bonding many small molecules called **monomers** (molecules that can combine to form polymers). Polymers can be made up of different kinds of monomers, and they can be bonded in different ways. In this experiment, the model has one type of monomer, represented by identical clay balls. The model could represent a short segment of a polyethylene polymer, which is used to make things such as plastic bags, milk jugs, and lids. An actual molecule of polyethylene is made up of thousands of ethylene monomers.

106. No Leak

Purpose To demonstrate that the physical property of a material depends on how its chemicals are organized.

Materials baking pan
clear plastic sandwich bag
water
pencil

Procedure

1. Place the baking pan on a table and fill the plastic sandwich bag three-fourths full with water.
2. Position the bag over the baking pan. Holding the bag at the top, push the pointed end of the pencil through one side of the bag and out the other side.
3. Leave the pencil in place and observe any leakage around the pencil.
4. Remove the pencil and observe any leakage.
5. Note the size and shape of the hole made by the pencil in the plastic bag.

Results The plastic bag does not leak when the pencil is pushed through it. Removal of the pencil shows that the hole left by the pencil appears stretched around the edges (not torn) and is slightly smaller in diameter than that of the pencil. Water is able to stream out of this hole.

Why? The plastic bag is made of polyethylene, which is a polymer. Ethylene is the monomer used to make polyethylene. The physical organization of polyethylene is like a ball of fuzzy yarn with fibers intertwined and sticking out in all directions.

When the pencil enters the plastic bag, the polyethylene molecules move out of the way, but they remain entangled and pull together around the pencil. The plastic is prevented from leaking as long as the pencil remains in place.

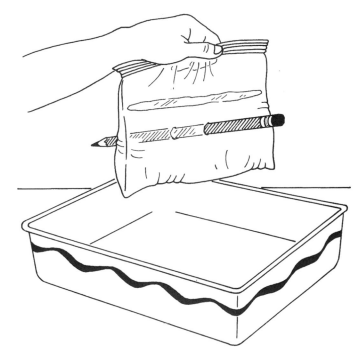

107. Coded

Purpose To identify polymer types.

Materials plastic containers (available around your home)

Procedure
1. Find the recycling code on the bottom of each plastic container. This code consists of a triangle of three arrows with a number in the center.
2. Use the Recycling Codes table to identify the different types of plastic that each container is made of. How many types of plastic did you find?

Results The author found all the types of plastic in her kitchen.

Why? Plastics make up about 20 percent of the solid waste in a typical U.S. city. Since plastic products do not break down for many years, it is important that they are recycled instead of thrown away. Not only is it important to recycle plastic to reduce the amount of solid waste in landfills, but plastic is a petroleum product and petroleum is a nonrenewable resource. This means that there is a limited amount of petroleum, so it should be **conserved** (not wasted) when possible. One way that plastic is recycled is by breaking the polyethylene terephthalate (PETE) in products such as soda bottles into its monomers and then rebuilding the polymer. In this way, new soda bottles can be made from used ones.

RECYCLING CODES

Recycling Symbol		Name of Polymer
1	PETE	polyethylene terephthalate
2	HEPE	high-density polyethylene
3	V	vinyl
4	LDPE	low-density polyethylene
5	PP	polyproylene
6	PS	polystyrene
7	other	all other polymers

108. Bridges

Purpose To model the cross-links in polymers.

Materials scissors
ruler
sheet of white copy paper
index card (any color)
transparent tape

Procedure
1. Cut four strips, each about ½ inch (1.25 cm) wide, down the length of the white paper.
2. Lay the strips one on top of the other. Place them tightly against the edge of the table. Keeping the papers taut, slide the strips across the table edge to curl the strips.
3. Then release the strips. Separate the strips and observe how difficult or easy this is.
4. Cut two ½-by-1-inch (1.25-by-2.5-cm) pieces from the index card.
5. Place two of the white paper strips side by side and about ½ inch (1.25 cm) apart on a table. Lay one of the index card pieces across the paper strips at one end and secure it with tape. Repeat, placing the second card piece at the opposite end.
6. Hold the strips in your hands and try to separate them without breaking the paper.

Results When the strips are not connected, the single coiled strips move apart easily but do pull on each other when they are separated. The connected strips are less coiled and spread out, but do not separate when pulled on.

Why? The strips represent individual molecules of a polymer, such as the polyvinyl acetate molecules found in most brands of white school glue. A bottle of glue contains millions of these separate molecules. These molecules can slip and slide freely over one another, but like the curled paper strips, they coil together and interfere with the motion of one another. This interference causes glue to have a high **viscosity** (measure of a substance's resistance to flow).

The connecting card pieces represent cross-links formed when glue is mixed with certain chemicals, such as borax. The borax forms bridges linking the polymer molecules, much like rungs linking the two sides of a ladder. The cross-links between the polymer molecules increase the viscosity of the material. (See the next experiment for a recipe for a cross-linked polymer.)

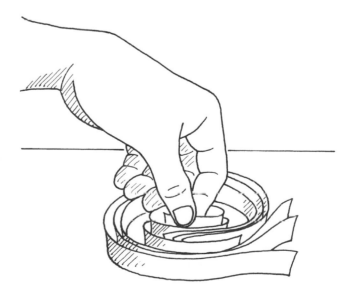

109. Glob

Purpose To make a cross-linked polymer.

Materials 4-ounce (120-mL) bottle of white school glue
1-pint (500-mL) jar
tap water
green food coloring
spoon
1-cup (250-mL) measuring cup
1 teaspoon (5 mL) borax (a laundry aid, available in supermarkets)
2-quart (2-L) bowl
1-quart (1-L) resealable plastic bag

CAUTION: Do not eat borax or the glob produced. Follow the precautions printed on the borax container.

Procedure

NOTE: The glob made in this experiment can stain furniture and stick to cloth or carpet. Keep it off furniture and clean it off cloth or carpet with hair conditioner or 2 tablespoons (30 mL) of vinegar in 1 cup (250 mL) of water.

1. Pour the glue into the jar.
2. Fill the empty glue bottle with water and pour the water into the jar containing the glue. Add 10 drops of food coloring and stir well.
3. Put 1 cup (250 mL) of water and the borax into the bowl. Stir until the borax dissolves.
4. Slowly pour the colored glue into the bowl containing the borax. Stir as you pour. A thick wet glob will form.
5. Take the glob out of the bowl and place it on top of the plastic bag.

6. Allow the glob to air dry on the plastic for about 1 minute, then pick up the glob with your hands and knead it for several minutes until it is smooth and dry.
7. Try these investigations, observing what happens to the glob each time.
   - Roll the glob into a ball and bounce it on a smooth surface.
   - Hold it in your hands and quickly pull the ends in opposite directions.
   - Hold it in your hands and slowly pull the ends in opposite directions.

NOTE: Put the glob in the plastic bag and keep it for the next experiment. To prevent the glob from getting moldy, store it in the refrigerator.

Results You have made a soft, flexible material that bounces slightly when dropped, breaks apart if pulled quickly, and stretches if pulled slowly.

Why? The glob is a cross-linked polymer. It is also called a **non-Newtonian fluid** because its behavior is different from the way the English scientist Sir Isaac Newton (1642–1727) described the behavior of **fluids** (liquids or gases). One particular difference is that when **pressure** (a force spread over an area) is quickly applied to glob, instead of spreading out like other fluids, glob acts more like a solid and breaks.

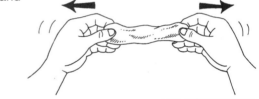

---

110. Glob 2

Purpose To determine how an increase in cross-linking affects the viscosity of a polymer.

Materials 4-ounce (120-mL) bottle of white school glue
1-pint (500-mL) jar
tap water
red food coloring
spoon
1-cup (250-mL) measuring cup
2 teaspoons (10 mL) borax
2-quart (2-L) bowl
1-quart (1-L) resealable plastic bag
glob from Experiment 109, "Glob"

CAUTION: Do not eat borax or the glob produced. Follow the precautions printed on the borax container.

Procedure

1. Repeat steps 1 to 7 of Experiment 109, "Glob," with the new materials listed here. You have made glob 2. The glob made in Experiment 109 will be called glob 1.
2. Compare glob 1 and glob 2 using the investigations in step 7 of Experiment 109.

Results Glob 2 is not as slimy or stretchy as glob 1, and glob 2 is more bouncy.

Why? A **solution** is a mixture of a **solute** (a substance that dissolves in a solution) and a **solvent** (a substance that dissolves a solute). Dissolving is the breaking of a solid solute into small particles that move throughout a solvent. In this experiment, the borax is the solute and the water the solvent. By increasing the amount of borax without changing the amount of water, the **concentration** (the amount of one substance in another substance, such as the amount of dissolved solute in a solution) of the borax solution increases. This means that there is more borax to react with the glue in the glue solution. The borax forms cross-links between the glue molecules, which can be visualized as steps on a ladder. With more borax present, there are more cross-links making the product less flexible and therefore more viscous.

111. Mixture

Purpose To make a heterogeneous mixture.

Materials 1 teaspoon (5 mL) unsweetened grape-
flavored powdered drink mix
1 teaspoon (5 mL) sugar
1-pint (500-mL) resealable plastic bag
spoon
sheet of graph paper
magnifying lens

Procedure
1. Put the powdered drink and sugar in the bag.
2. Shake the bag vigorously to thoroughly mix the powdered drink and sugar.
3. Pour one spoonful of the mixture in the bag onto the
graph paper. Spread the material out as evenly as possible.
4. Use the magnifying lens to study the mixture covering
four or more squares on the paper. Determine if the
mixture in every part of each square has the same
number of drink mix and sugar particles.

NOTE: Keep the mixture for the next experiment.

Results The amount of sugar and powdered drink particles varies from one square to the next.

Why? One or more substances combined with another
substance to form a mixture. Generally, when solid particles are mixed together, the particles do not evenly blend
together, so the mixture is called a **heterogeneous mixture** (a mixture that is not the same throughout). In this
experiment, the number of particles of powdered drink and
sugar is not the same throughout, so the mixture is heterogeneous.

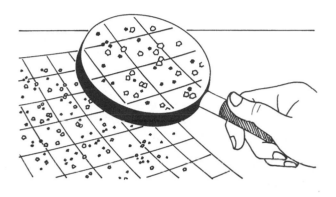

112. Blended

Purpose To make a homogeneous mixture.

Materials 1-quart (1-L) glass jar with lid
tap water
½-teaspoon (2.5-mL) measuring
spoon
mixture from Experiment 111,
"Mixture"

Procedure
1. Fill the jar about three-fourths full with water.
2. Pour ½ teaspoon (2.5 mL) of the mixture into
the water in the jar. Close the jar with the lid.
3. Shake the jar vigorously to thoroughly mix its
contents.
4. Hold the jar in front of a window with direct
sunlight or in front of a desk lamp. Determine
if the color of the liquid appears the same
throughout.

Results The color of the liquid appears the
same in every part of the jar.

Why? A mixture that is the same throughout is
called a **homogeneous mixture.** Some solids
when mixed with a liquid dissolve and form a
solution. A solution is an example of a homogeneous mixture.

113. Separator

Purpose   To demonstrate how fat is broken into globules.

Materials   pen
2 index cards
2 small cereal bowls
tap water
measuring spoons
2 teaspoons (10 mL) cooking oil
desk lamp
spoon
timer
1 teaspoon (5 mL) dishwashing liquid

Procedure

1. Use the pen to label the cards "A" and "B."
2. Fill the bowls half full with water.
3. Add 1 teaspoon (5 mL) of cooking oil to each bowl.
4. Set the bowls under the desk lamp, each bowl on one of the cards. Observe the contents of the bowls.
5. Vigorously stir the contents of bowl A with the spoon.
6. Observe the bowl's contents immediately, then again after 5 minutes.
7. Add the dishwashing liquid to bowl B.
8. Repeat steps 5 and 6 with bowl B.

Results   Before the contents of the bowls were stirred, the oil formed a thin layer over the surface of the water in each bowl. After the contents were stirred, the oil in both bowls mixed with the water. After standing, the oil in bowl A separated into globules (small drops) that floated to the surface. Only some of the oil in bowl B separated, while some remained mixed with the water.

Why?   Stirring a mixture of two liquids that do not dissolve in each other, such as oil and water, causes one of the liquids (oil) to be suspended (hung) in globules throughout the other liquid (water). The result is called an **emulsion.** If allowed to stand, the liquids in an emulsion separate like the oil and water in bowl A. If an **emulsifier** (substance that prevents an emulsion from separating) such as dishwashing liquid is used, the emulsion does not separate, as in bowl B.

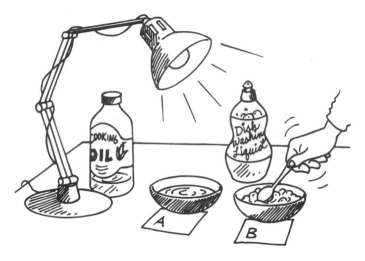

114. Loser

Purpose   To determine why some chemicals dry out.

Materials   1 tablespoon (15 mL) Epsom salts
sheet of black construction paper
magnifying lens

Procedure

1. Place the Epsom salts on the paper and spread the crystals out as much as possible.
2. Use the magnifying lens to observe the surface of the crystals.

Results   Some of the crystals have a shiny, glassy look, while others look more white and powdery.

Why?   Epsom salts are a **hydrate** (a crystalline substance that contains water). When exposed to air, some or all of the water in the soda crystals is lost and a white powder is left. This loss of water from a hydrate is called **efflorescence.**

115. More!

Purpose To determine why salt gets wet when exposed to air.

Materials ¼ teaspoon (1.25 mL) table salt
saucer
magnifying lens

Procedure
1. Place the salt on the saucer.
2. Set the saucer in the kitchen or bathroom where it can be observed but not disturbed.
3. Use the magnifying lens to observe the salt crystals periodically during the day for 2 or more days.

Results The salt becomes moist and may totally dissolve.

Why? Salt is **hygroscopic** (absorbing water vapor from the air). If a hygroscopic material absorbs enough water that it dissolves and passes into a solution, then it is called **deliquescent.** Table salt (sodium chloride) contains an impurity called magnesium chloride, which makes table salt a deliquescent material. Table salt absorbs water from the air and becomes moist or even dissolves. Rice is more hygroscopic than salt, but is not deliquescent. That is why rice is often added to salt shakers. It absorbs water, so the salt stays dry and easy to pour.

116. Soaker

Purpose To determine the sugar content of foods.

Materials marker
3 small resealable plastic sandwich bags
slice of bread
hard cookie

Procedure
1. Use the marker to label the three bags "1," "2," and "3."
2. Feel the bread slice and the cookie. Note how firm they are.
3. Break the bread and the cookie in half.
4. Place a bread half and a cookie half in bag 1. Seal the bag.
5. Place the remaining bread half in bag 2 and the cookie half in bag 3. Seal each bag.
6. After 1 or more days, open the bags. Compare the firmness of the bread in bags 1 and 2. Then compare the firmness of the cookies in bags 1 and 3.

Results The bread and cookie halves placed in separate bags had little or no change. But the bread in the bag with the cookie is firmer and the cookie is softer.

Why? Sugar is a hygroscopic chemical, which means it will absorb water from the air. There is sugar in both the bread and the cookie. Both also contain moisture, which evaporates and enters the air. When the food is placed in separate bags, some of its moisture leaves the food but most is absorbed again, so the firmness of each food changes little or not at all. Cookies generally contain more sugar than bread, so when the cookie and bread halves are placed together in a bag, the moisture lost by the bread is more readily absorbed by the cookie. So the bread dries out and becomes firmer and the cookie becomes softer.

117. Melting Ice

Purpose To demonstrate the effects of salt and sand on ice.

Materials masking tape
marker
2 saucers
2 ice cubes
½ teaspoon (2.5 mL) sand
½ teaspoon (2.5 mL) salt
timer

Procedure

1. Use the tape and marker to label one saucer "Salt" and the other "Sand."
2. Place one ice cube in each saucer.
3. Place the sand on the ice in the saucer marked "Sand."
4. Place the salt on the ice in the saucer marked "Salt."
5. Place both saucers in a freezer.
6. Observe the contents of the saucers every 10 minutes for 30 minutes or more.

Results The ice covered with salt begins to melt, but the ice covered with sand does not melt.

Why? A solution of salt water has a lower freezing point than water alone. The **freezing point** of a liquid is the temperature at which it **freezes** (changes to a solid). The greater the concentration of the salt water, the lower its freezing point. So when salt is sprinkled on the surface of ice, the salt dissolves in the watery surface layer of the ice and causes the ice to melt. Even though the solution is at or slightly below the freezing point of water, the salt water does not refreeze.

At very low temperatures, it is difficult to melt ice with salt because the ice has a dry surface and salt cannot dissolve in the tightly bound surface ice. So the ice doesn't melt.

Sand is used to create a nonslippery barrier between objects and the ice. Since sand doesn't dissolve in water, it just sits on the ice. If pressed, due to **friction** (a force that tends to stop the motion of objects that are moving against each other), sand can break the ice into tiny pieces that melt more easily.

118. Attractive

Purpose To demonstrate how to separate a mixture.

Materials colored hard candies, such as M&Ms
scissors
ruler   ruler
2 round coffee filters   small bowl
2 soda cans   tap water
large shallow cooking pan   transparent tape

Procedure

1. For each candy color, cut one 1-by-6-inch (2.5-by-15-cm) strip from the coffee filters.
2. Set the soda cans in the pan as far apart as possible so that the ends of the ruler rest on the can tops.
3. Fill the bowl half-full with water.
4. Place one candy in the bowl of water. When the candy starts to color the water, lift the candy and shake as much water as possible off of it.
5. On one strip of paper, rub the wet candy about 1 inch (2.5 cm) from one end of the paper.
6. Tape the uncolored end of the paper to the ruler. The free, colored end should touch the bottom of the pan.
7. Repeat steps 4 to 6 for each of the other candy colors.
8. Allow the paper strips to dry. This should take 5 to 10 minutes.
9. Pour just enough water into the pan so that the end of each paper strip touches the water.
10. Observe the paper strips for 20 minutes or more.

Results The colors move up the paper strip. Some of the colors separate into other colors.

Why? The method of using paper to separate the colors in a dye is called **chromatography** (a method of separating a mixture into its different substances). In this experiment, the candy colors are first dissolved in water to form a solution called a dye. The dye is used to stain the paper strips. After the strips dry, only the **colorants** (pigments) in the dye are left in the fibers of the paper. As the water moves through the hanging paper, the colorants dissolve in the water and move with it. The color that has the least attraction to the paper moves fastest and farthest up the paper. The other colors move slower and a shorter distance, and the one with the greatest attraction moves the slowest and the least. Some of the dyes have only one colorant and some have more. For example, green has blue and yellow colorants.

119. Twisted

Purpose To make paste.

Materials 2 tablespoons (30 mL) flour
3-ounce (90-mL) paper cup
1-teaspoon (5-mL) measuring spoon
craft stick
tap water
sheet of copy paper

Procedure

1. Put the flour in the paper cup.
2. Add 1 teaspoon (5 mL) of water to the cup and stir its contents with the craft stick. Continue to add water 1 teaspoon (5 mL) at a time until a thick paste forms. It will take about 3 teaspoons (15 mL) of water. If the paste is too thin, add a little flour. If it is too thick, add a little water.
3. Fold the paper in half.
4. Unfold the paper and use the craft stick to spread a thin layer of flour paste on one half of the paper below the fold line. You don't have to cover the entire surface.
5. Refold the paper and press the halves together with your fingers.
6. Allow the paste to dry, then try to separate the layers of paper without tearing them.

Results The layers of paper stick together and will not separate without tearing.

Why? Flour is made of large molecules of starch (a nutrient found in some plants, such as wheat). When water is mixed with the flour, the starch molecules get twisted together much like long strings of spaghetti in a bowl. When spread on the paper, the starch molecules fill up microscopic depressions in the paper. When the water evaporates, the dry starch molecules are left behind. Some of the dried, intertwined starch molecules stick to one sheet of paper and some stick to the other sheet. Thus the two sheets of paper become stuck together.

120. Foamy

Purpose To make simulated plastic foam.

Materials 1 cup (250 mL) cold tap water
2-quart (2-L) bowl
2 tablespoons (30 mL) dishwashing liquid
whisk
mixing spoon
1-cup (250-mL) measuring cup
timer
1-tablespoon (15-mL) measuring spoon

Procedure

1. Pour the water into the bowl.
2. Add the dishwashing liquid to the water in the bowl.
3. Use the whisk to beat the liquid until you have made a big mound of foam.
4. Use the mixing spoon to fill the measuring cup with foam. Be careful not to transfer any liquid to the cup.
5. Put the cup where it will not be disturbed.
6. Observe the foam as often as possible for 4 hours.
7. After 4 hours, or when all the foam has changed to a liquid, use the measuring spoon to measure the liquid in the cup.

Results When the mixture is foamy, bubbles fill the cup. After the bubbles have popped, the cupful of foam changes to about 2 tablespoons (30 mL) of liquid.

Why? Beating the liquid produces bubbles filled with air. The foam is mostly air. When the cup is allowed to sit, the bubbles break, the air escapes, and the foam turns back to a soapy liquid. Like the soap foam, plastic foam such as Styrofoam is full of air. But unlike the soap foam, plastic foam bubbles don't break unless pressure is applied, so plastic foam stays the same size. Because plastic foam is mostly air, large materials made with this plastic are very lightweight and easy to transport. Air is a good **insulator** (a material that does not easily transfer heat). So air-filled plastic is also a good insulator. However, such plastics take up large amounts of space in landfills, which is bad.

121. Hissssssss!

Purpose   To determine the effect of volume on the pressure of gases.

Materials   plastic soda bottle one-fourth filled with soda

NOTE: It is recommended that this experiment be performed outdoors in case the soda spews out of the bottle.

Procedure

1. Standing outdoors, hold your thumb tightly over the mouth of the bottle. Point the mouth of the bottle away from yourself or anyone else. Keep your thumb securely in place until step 5.
2. Shake the bottle vigorously 10 or more times. Then look at the contents of the bottle and observe the bubble formation in the liquid.
3. When the bubbling stops, repeat step 2.
4. Repeat steps 2 and 3 three times for a total of six shakes.
5. After the last shaking, allow the bubbling to stop. Then while observing the bottle's contents, slowly lift your thumb. Listen for any sound.

Results   During the first shaking, many bubbles form and rise to the surface of the liquid, forming foam which quickly goes away. Fewer bubbles form with each repeated shaking. When your thumb is lifted, a hissing sound is heard and many bubbles again form.

Why?   Soda contains dissolved carbon dioxide gas. When the bottle of soda is shaken, the gas molecules collect and are visible as bubbles in the liquid. These bubbles are lighter than the liquid and rise to the surface of the liquid. Bubbles beneath the surface of the liquid are pockets of carbon dioxide surrounded by the liquid in the bottle. Bubbles above the surface of the liquid are made of carbon dioxide gas surrounded by a thin liquid skin that forms as the gas escapes from the liquid. When this skin breaks, its liquid contents fall to the surface of the liquid and the escaped gas mixes with the air above the surface. As more gas collects above the surface of the liquid, the pressure of the gas on the surface increases. As the pressure increases, it reduces the number of bubbles that can form. Opening the bottle reduces the pressure above the liquid, and more bubbles immediately form. The pressure is reduced because the gas is able to expand to the volume of the bottle plus the outdoor area the bottle is in. When the mouth is opened, the trapped gas in the bottle quickly escapes through the opening, as indicated by the hissing sound.

122. Puffer

Purpose   To demonstrate fermentation.

Materials   permanent black marker
three 9-ounce (270-mL) plastic glasses
2 spoons
1-teaspoon (5-mL) and 1 tablespoon (15-mL) measuring spoons
4 tablespoons (60 mL) flour
4 tablespoons (60 mL) granulated sugar
1 teaspoon (5 mL) active dry yeast
warm tap water

Procedure

1. Use the marker to label the glasses "1," "2," and "3."
2. In glass 1, use one of the spoons to thoroughly mix together 2 tablespoons (30 mL) each of flour and sugar.
3. In glass 2, use the other spoon to thoroughly mix together the yeast and 2 tablespoons (30 mL) each of flour and sugar.
4. Fill glass 3 about half-full with warm water.
5. Add 2 tablespoons (30 mL) of warm water to glasses 1 and 2 and thoroughly mix.

6. Observe the contents of glasses 1 and 2 periodically for 1 or more hours.

Results   The contents of glass 1 did not change, but the contents of glass 2 increased in volume.

Why?   A chemical reaction called **fermentation** occurred in glass 2, the glass with the flour, sugar, water, and yeast. Fermentation is the breaking down of **glucose** (a type of sugar) into simpler substances, one being carbon dioxide gas. This process occurs through the action of enzymes in the yeast. It is the carbon dioxide gas that causes the mixture in glass 2 to puff up. Glass 1 had no yeast, thus no fermentation occurred so no carbon dioxide formed.

123. Sudsy

Purpose To determine the effect of hard water on soap.

Materials 2 large bowls
distilled water
1 tablespoon (15 mL) Epsom salts (available
  at pharmacies)
bar of soap
towel

Procedure

1. Fill the bowls half full with water.
2. Add the salts to one of the bowls.
3. Dip your hands into the bowl of plain water.
4. Hold the bar of soap in your wet hands and move the soap around to make as many suds as possible. Dip your hands in the water if more water is needed.
5. Observe the amount of suds that were made, then rinse your hands under a faucet and dry them on the towel.
6. Repeat steps 3 to 5 using the bowl of salt water.

Results In the salt water, the soap made few suds, but many suds were made in the plain water.

Why? **Minerals** are solid substances that were never an animal or a plant and that were formed in the earth by nature. Water that is rich in the minerals calcium, magnesium, and/or iron is called **hard water.** Calcium is gener-

ally the more abundant mineral in hard water, but the greater the amount of any one of these minerals, the harder the water. Water that has little if any of these minerals is called **soft water.** It is difficult to make suds in hard water because the minerals combine with the soap and form **soap scum** (a waxy material that doesn't dissolve in water). In this experiment, the soft water (distilled water) was made hard by adding Epsom salts, which contain magnesium.

124. Acid Testing

Purpose To use baking soda to test for the presence of acids in liquid foods.

Materials 1-tablespoon (15-mL) and ½-teaspoon (2.5-mL) measuring spoons
food samples: 2 tablespoons (30 mL) each of orange juice, apple cider, and milk
three 3-ounce (90-mL) paper cups
baking soda

Procedure

1. Pour 2 tablespoons (30 mL) of orange juice into one of the cups.
2. Add ½ teaspoon (2.5 mL) of baking soda to the cup. Observe the contents of the cup for the presence of bubbles.
3. Repeat steps 1 and 2 for each food sample used.

Results The liquid in each of the cups began to bubble when the baking soda was added.

Why? Baking soda can be used to test for the presence of acids in liquid foods. This is because bubbles appear when baking soda is combined with an acid. The baking soda dissolves in the liquid and reacts with the acid, producing carbon dioxide bubbles.

IV
Earth Science

Prime Meridian
90° W
North Pole
180°
0°
90° E

Prime Meridian
90° W
180°
0°
90° E

Western Hemisphere
Eastern Hemisphere

125. Around

Purpose To model meridians on a globe.

Materials orange
two 12-inch (30-cm) pieces of string

Procedure
1. Tie one piece of string around the middle of the orange.
2. Tie the other piece of string around the orange perpendicular to the first string.
3. Hold the orange so that the strings cross at the top and bottom. Observe the position of the strings and the distances between them (1) at the ends where the lines cross, and (2) in the center of the orange midway between the ends.

Results The lines approach and cross each other at the top and bottom of the orange and are farthest apart around the center of the orange.

Why? **Meridians** are imaginary great circles around the Earth from the North Pole to the South Pole. (A **great circle** has the same center point as the sphere it surrounds.) The east-west distance between the meridians on Earth, like the distance between the strings on the orange, is greatest at the middle and decreases toward the Poles.

Meridians are also called **lines of longitude** because they indicate **longitude** (distance in degrees east or west of the prime meridian). The **prime meridian** is located at 0° longitude, which runs through Greenwich, England. Longitudes 0° and 180° form a **great circle** (circle with the same center point as the sphere it surrounds) and divide the Earth into the Eastern and Western Hemispheres. The **Eastern Hemisphere** includes the meridians from the prime meridian east to 180°. The halfway point is longitude 90°E. The **Western Hemisphere** includes the meridians from the prime meridian west to 180°. The halfway point is longitude 90°W.

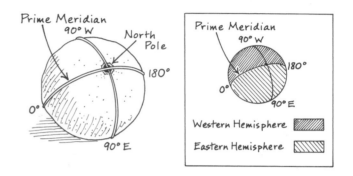

126. Only One

Purpose To make a model of Earth's equator.

Materials pencil
large lid
sheet of copy paper
scissors
pen
ruler

Procedure
1. Use the pencil to trace around the lid on the paper. Cut out the circle.
2. Fold the circle in half twice, once from top to bottom and then from side to side.
3. Use the pen and ruler to trace the fold lines.
4. Use the pen to label the meridian and the equator, as well as the Northern and Southern Hemispheres.

Results You have made a model of Earth's equator.

Why? Imaginary circles around Earth that run parallel to each other and perpendicular to the meridians are called **parallels.** The parallel that runs around the center of the globe, equidistant from the Poles and perpendicular to any meridian, is called the equator. The equator is the only parallel that is a great circle. Parallels are also called lines of latitude. The equator divides the globe into the Northern and Southern Hemispheres. The latitude in each hemisphere ranges from 0° at the equator to 90° at the Poles. Latitudes are labeled "N" in the Northern Hemisphere and "S" in the Southern Hemisphere.

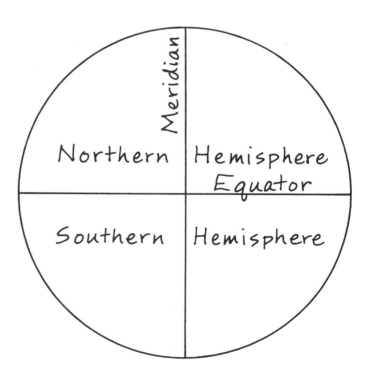

127. Time Line

Purpose To construct a scale model of the Earth's geologic eras.

Materials meterstick   masking tape
scissors   pencil
adding machine tape

Procedure

1. Measure and cut a 460-cm piece of adding machine tape.
2. Stretch the paper strip out on an uncarpeted floor and use tape to secure the ends.
3. Draw a line across the tape 5 cm from the top. Write the label "Present" above this line.
4. Draw a second line 6.5 cm from the first line. Label this line "65 million" and write "(65)" vertically on the right side of the tape in this section.
5. Draw a third line 16 cm from the second line. Label the line "225 million" and write "(160)" on the right side as in the previous step.
6. Draw a fourth line 37.5 cm below the third line. Label the line "600 million" and write "(375)" on the right side as before.
7. Write "Beginning" at the bottom of the tape. Write "4,500 million" above the word and "(3,900)" on the right side.
8. Use the diagram to label these eras on the tape: "Cenozoic," "Mesozoic," "Paleozoic," and "Precambrian."

Results A time line comparing the length of time of the four different geologic eras of the Earth's history is constructed.

Why? The paper scale uses length to compare the differences in time between the Earth's four geologic eras. The length of the eras can be compared at a glance by studying the size of each section. A more accurate length of time for each era appears in the numbers along the side. The shortest section and the youngest era is the Cenozoic era, which so far has lasted about 65 million years. The era of the dinosaurs is second in age and lasted for about 160 million years. The eras preceding the Mesozoic era increase in length of age, with the Precambrian era being the largest section, the longest era, and the oldest era.

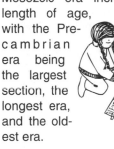

Present	
Cenozoic 65 million	(65)
Mesozoic 225 million	(160)
Paleozoic 600 million	(375)
Precambrian 4,500 million Beginning	(3,900)

128. Drifters

Purpose To demonstrate how the continents may have drifted apart.

Materials large shallow baking pan
tap water
9 round toothpicks
dishwashing liquid

Procedure

1. Cover the bottom of the pan with water.
2. Place eight of the toothpicks side by side on the surface of the center of the water.
3. Wet one end of the ninth toothpick with dishwashing liquid and put the wet end in the center of the floating toothpicks.
4. Wet the toothpick again with dishwashing liquid, and put the wet end in the center of each group of floating toothpicks.
5. Repeat step 4, wetting the toothpick each time before you put it in the center of a group.

Results When you put the toothpick with the dishwashing liquid between the eight floating toothpicks, they separate, forming two groups with four toothpicks in each group. When you put the toothpick

with dishwashing liquid in the center of the two groups, the toothpicks divide into four groups. Touching the toothpick with dishwashing liquid between the remaining groups results in toothpicks quickly moving away from each other.

Why? The group of eight toothpicks represents the single landmass called **Pangaea** (the name given to the large, single landmass believed to have existed before it broke apart into separate landmasses), and the water in the pan represents the single ocean called **Panthalassa** (the name given to the large, single ocean believed to have existed before Pangaea broke apart). The first separation of the toothpicks can be compared to the breaking apart of Pangaea into a northern landmass called Laurasia and a southern landmass called Gondwanaland. While not exact, the remaining separations of the toothpicks can be compared to the formation of present-day landmasses, or **continents** (the seven major landmasses of the Earth: North America, South America, Africa, Australia, Antarctica, Europe, and Asia). Laurasia is believed to have separated into the continents of North America, Europe, and Asia. Gondwanaland is believed to have separated into the continents of Australia, Africa, South America, and Antarctica. The eighth toothpick represents the country of India, which broke off of Gondwanaland and, over time, moved and became attached to Asia.

129. Normal

Purpose To determine the distinguishing characteristics of a normal fault.

Materials two lemon-size pieces of clay of different
 colors
 ruler
 plastic knife
 2 round toothpicks

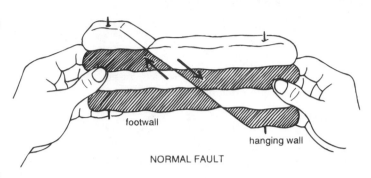

footwall

hanging wall

NORMAL FAULT

Procedure
1. Break each piece of clay in half.
2. Shape each clay half into a roll about 4 inches (10 cm) long.
3. Lay the clay rolls together, one on top of the other, alternating the colors.
4. Press the rolls together into one large clay piece. Flatten the sides of the clay piece by tapping them against a hard surface, such as a table.
5. Use the table knife to cut the clay piece into two parts diagonally.
6. Secure the layers in each part together by inserting a toothpick through the layers, top to bottom.
7. Hold the parts together so that the colored layers match up, then move the left part up and the right part down, as shown.

Results The clay is cut and shifted so that the layers of colored clay in the two parts no longer form continuous horizontal lines.

Why? Each clay color represents a layer of rock. The knife cut in the layers represents a **fracture** (a break in rock layers). If there is movement on either side of the fracture line, the fracture is called a **fault**. The fracture line of a fault is called a **fault plane**. The model in this experiment represents a **normal fault** in which the movement is up and down. The **footwall** (the side below the fault plane) moves up and the **hanging wall** (the side above the fault plane) moves down.

130. Small Portion

Purpose To demonstrate the amount of land available for agriculture.

Materials apple-size piece of red clay
 lemon-size piece of blue clay
 walnut-size piece each of yellow and green
  clay
 plastic knife

Procedure
1. Shape the piece of red clay into a ball.
2. Cut a quarter section from the ball.
3. Cover the curved surface of the three-quarter section with blue clay.
4. Cover the curved surface of the quarter section with yellow clay.
5. Cut the quarter section in half lengthwise to make two eighth sections.
6. Cut one of the eighth sections into four equal parts to make four thirty-second sections.
7. Cover the curved surface of the thirty-second sections with green clay.

Results The red clay ball is cut into six separate pieces and the curved surfaces are covered with different colors of clay. One curved surface is blue, four are yellow, and one is green. All the flat surfaces remain red.

Why? The red ball represents the Earth. The three-fourth section covered in blue represents the area of the Earth covered by oceans. The yellow one-eighth section represents land areas such as the Antarctic, deserts, mountains, and swamps, where no crops can be grown. The three yellow one-thirty-second sections represent land areas that are too wet, too hot, or too rocky, or that have soil that is too poor for agriculture. The last thirty-second section, covered in green, represents the land area.

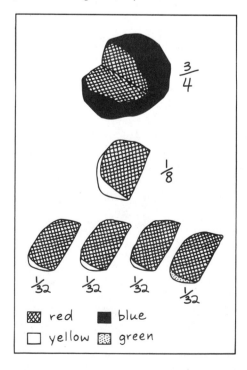

$\frac{3}{4}$

$\frac{1}{8}$

$\frac{1}{32}$ $\frac{1}{32}$ $\frac{1}{32}$ $\frac{1}{32}$

red blue
yellow green

131. Soil

Purpose To determine the texture of soil.

Materials 1 quart (1 L) soil
garden trowel
1-quart (1-L) bowl
marker
masking tape
3 identical 1-pint (500-mL) transparent jars
newspaper
colander with large holes
large fine-mouth mesh strainer

Procedure

1. Select a spot with soil, such as near a tree or where plants are growing. A bare soil area in a garden is also acceptable. Ask for permission to remove about 1 quart (1 L) of soil.
2. Use the trowel to fill the bowl with soil.
3. Use the marker and tape to number the jars "1," "2," and "3."
4. Lay the newspaper on a table.
5. Spread the soil on the newspaper and use the trowel to pick up live or dead organisms and transfer them to where the soil was collected.
6. Pour the soil into the colander and shake the colander over the newspaper until no more particles fall through the holes in the colander.

7. Put the particles left in the colander into jar 1.
8. Pour the particles on the newspaper into the strainer. Shake the strainer over the paper until no particles fall through.
9. Put the particles in the strainer into jar 2 and the particles on the newspaper into jar 3.
10. Compare the amount of material in each jar.

Results The soil is separated into three sizes of particles—large, medium, and small. The amount of material in each jar will vary with different soil samples.

Why? **Soil** is a mixture of particles of rock, **humus** (decayed animal and plant matter), air, and water. All soils are not alike. The rock particles come from different kinds of rocks, and the amount and composition of humus vary. Most soil contains particles of varying size. In this experiment, you separated the particles. Coarse-grained particles, as in jar 1, are larger than medium-grained particles, as in jar 2. Fine-grained particles, as in jar 3, are smaller than the other two particle types. The **texture** (how large the grain is) of soil depends on which type of particles predominates in the soil. For example, if there are more particles in jar 3, then the texture of the soil sample would be considered fine-grained.

132. Straight Through

Purpose To compare the permeability of soil, sand, and cat litter.

Materials 2 pencils
three 9-ounce (270-mL) paper cups
paper towel
marker
scissors
¼ cup (63 mL) soil
¼ cup (63 mL) sand
¼ cup (63 mL) fresh cat litter
plate
transparent tape
3-ounce (90-mL) paper cup
tap water
timer
helper

Procedure

1. Use the point of one pencil to make six equal-size holes in the bottom of each 9-ounce (270-mL) cup.
2. Fold the paper towel in half twice. Set one of the cups from step 1 on the paper towel and use the marker to trace around its bottom. Cut out the circle, cutting through all of the layers and cutting on the inside of the lines to make the cutouts slightly smaller than the bottom of the cup.
3. Place one paper cutout in the bottom of each cup and discard the extra cutout.

4. Pour the soil, sand, and cat litter in the cups. Label the cups "Soil," "Sand," and "Cat Litter."
5. Lay the two pencils parallel to each other across the plate. Secure with tape.
6. Set the cup containing soil on the pencils, making sure that the pencils do not cover the holes in the cup.
7. Fill the 3-ounce (90-mL) cup with water.
8. As you pour the water into the cup of soil, have a helper time how long it takes for all of the water to drain through the cup and onto the plate. Stop timing when no more water drains from the cup.
9. Repeat steps 6 to 8 using the cups of sand and cat litter.

Results The water drains fastest through the sand and slowest through the cat litter.

Why? **Permeability** is a measure of how easily water flows through a material. If water flows quickly through sand, the sand is said to have high permeability. Cat litter contains a large amount of clay. Since the litter was the least permeable material you tested, clay is not as permeable as sand or soil. Some soils contain clay, but usually not in the amount that is in the cat litter. So the soil was medium in permeability as compared to the cat litter and the sand.

133. Splat!

Purpose To model the way that raindrops affect rocks.

Materials 1 teaspoon (5 mL) flour
sheet of black construction paper
eyedropper
tap water
ruler

Procedure

1. Place the flour in a mound in the center of the paper.
2. Fill the eyedropper with water.
3. Hold the dropper about 12 inches (30 cm) above the center of the flour.
4. Squeeze two drops of water onto the mound of flour.
5. Observe the paper.

Results You see a burst of tiny specks of flour on the paper.

Why? The impact of the falling water forces particles of flour outward. Raindrops hitting the surface of rocks behave similarly to the water drops hitting the flour. Raindrops may fall thousands of yards (thousands of meters) before hitting the ground. The force of the raindrops striking a rock can

move loosened rock particles. Rain is one of the agents by which rock is **weathered** (process by which rocks are broken into small pieces).

134. Mudflow

Purpose To demonstrate a mudflow.

Materials cookie sheet
ruler
soil
empty 1-gallon (4-L) plastic milk jug
tap water

Procedure

1. Lay the cookie sheet on the ground and raise one end about 2 inches (5 cm) by putting soil under the end of the cookie sheet.
2. Cover the cookie sheet with a layer of soil.
3. Fill the jug with water.
4. Tilt the jug of water so that its mouth is about 6 inches (15 cm) above the raised end of the cookie sheet and let the water pour out. Observe any movement of the soil.

Results The soil becomes wet and moves down and off the lower end of the cookie sheet.

Why? **Mudflows** are fast-moving **mud** (a thick mixture of soil and water). Mudflows usually occur in dry areas where weathering has formed loose layers of **sediment** (loose materials such as particles of soil and rock). When heavy rains come, the water and sediment mix forming mud. Gravity causes mud to slide downhill as it did on the cookie sheet. If there is enough mud flowing, it is strong enough to move large objects in its path, including cars

and houses. **Erosion** is the process by which sediments are moved by agents or erosion, such as gravity, wind, water, and ice.

135. Compact

Purpose To model compaction of sediments.

Materials waste papers
wastebasket
yardstick (meterstick)

Procedure

1. Loosely wad one sheet of paper and place it in the wastebasket.
2. Continue wadding sheets of paper and placing them in the wastebasket until the wastebasket is full.
3. Use the measuring stick to measure the height of the paper wads in the wastebasket.
4. Use your foot to press the paper wads down in the wastebasket.
5. Repeat step 3.
6. Compare the initial and final heights of the paper wads.

Results The initial height of the paper wads is greater than the final height.

Why? Placing the paper wads in the wastebasket represents **deposition,** which is the buildup of sediments. Stepping on the paper wads represents **compaction** (the process by which particles are pressed together). Your weight presses the pieces of paper together so that they take up less volume. This happens to sediments in water. Newly deposited sediments, like the wads of paper, have spaces between them. Water fills these spaces. But when more sediments are deposited, the weight of the new layers presses on underlying layers of sediments. This squeezes the water out and packs the particles tightly together.

136. Cemented

Purpose To determine how sediments in sedimentary rock are held together.

Materials school glue
three 4-inch (10-cm) square pieces of corrugated cardboard

Procedure

1. Squeeze a zigzag pattern of glue over the surface of one of the cardboard square pieces.
2. Place the second piece of cardboard over the glue-covered surface of the first. Turn the top piece so that the "tunnels" running through the cardboard are perpendicular to the tunnels in the other piece of cardboard, as shown.
3. Repeat steps 1 and 2, squeezing glue on top of the second piece of cardboard and placing the third piece of cardboard on top.
4. Hold the cardboard pieces between your hands and as you press the pieces together try to slide one piece over the other.
5. Allow the glue to dry, then repeat step 4.

Results Before the glue dried, the cardboard pieces could move around. After the glue dried, the cardboard pieces were bound together into one solid mass that would not move.

Why? In this experiment, the cardboard pieces represent layers of sediments and the glue represents the minerals in water that **cement** (glue together) the sediments. **Sedimentary rock** forms when the layers of sediments are compacted and cemented by the substances in water. During compaction the water is squeezed out of the spaces between the particles, but substances dissolved in the water may be left behind. These substances form a thin layer around the particles and bind them together, just as the glue bound the cardboard pieces together in this experiment.

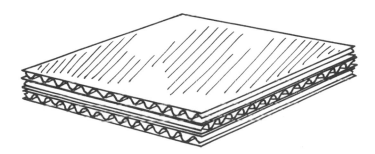

137. Recycled Rock

Purpose To model the formation of metamorphic rock.

Materials 3 different-colored golf ball–size pieces of modeling clay
ruler
plastic knife

Procedure

1. Shape each piece of clay into a roll about 3 inches (7.5 cm) long.
2. Stack the three clay rolls one on top of the other. Observe the top surface and the edges of the clay stack.
3. Hold the clay stack in your hands and twist the right end about half a turn away from you. As you twist the clay, press on it to prevent it from breaking apart.
4. Use the plastic knife to cut the clay stack in half from one end to the other along the longest part.

5. Observe the top surface and the cut edge of each clay half.

Results The cut edge shows how the different colors of clay are blended when layers of clay are twisted and pressed into one piece.

Why? The three original different-colored rolls of clay represent three layers of sedimentary rock. When pressure was applied to the model by twisting and pressing, the layers became mixed together. This represents **metamorphic rock** (rock that forms from other types of rock by pressure and heat). The process of changing from one form to another is called **metamorphism**.

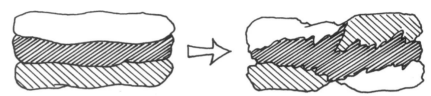

138. Fire Rocks

Purpose To model the difference between types of igneous rocks.

Materials 4 walnut-size pieces of modeling clay—
2 blue, 2 red

Procedure

1. Break one red clay piece into four relatively equal-size pieces.
2. Roll the four small pieces into balls.
3. Repeat steps 1 and 2 with one blue clay piece.
4. Lay the eight small balls in two rows next to each other, alternating the colors of the balls in the rows.
5. Gently press the clay balls just enough so that they stick together but retain as much of their shape as possible.
6. Break the other large red clay piece in half. From one half, shape two relatively equal-size balls, and from the other half, shape four relatively equal-size balls.
7. Repeat step 6 with the remaining large blue clay piece.
8. Lay the 12 small balls in two rows next to each other, alternating the colors and sizes in the rows.
9. Repeat step 5.
10. Compare the appearance of the two clay models.

Results One of the clay models has equal-size balls of clay pressed together. The second has large and small balls.

Why? Rocks produced by the cooling and **solidifying** (changing to a solid) of **molten** (liquid) rock are called

igneous rocks. Magma (molten rock under the Earth's surface) at great depths cools slowly, and during this cooling process, large mineral crystals form. Igneous rocks that form within the **crust** (the outer layer of Earth) and contain large crystals are called **intrusive igneous rocks.** In this experiment, the clay model made with equal-size clay balls represents a coarse-grained intrusive igneous rock.

In **porphyritic rock,** like other types of intrusive igneous rock, large crystals form from magma cooling at great depths beneath the Earth's surface. However, during the formation of this type of rock, the magma is pushed to the surface before it completely solidifies. There the final cooling occurs rapidly, producing small crystals. Thus, porphyritic rock contains two or more different sizes of interlocking crystals and can be said to have varied grain sizes. The clay model with the large and small clay balls represents a porphyritic rock.

139. Hot Spot

Purpose To determine why temperature varies around the Earth.

Materials masking tape
2 rulers
flashlight
graph paper

Procedure

1. Tape one of the rulers to the flashlight so that 6 inches (15 cm) of the ruler extends past the lamp end of the flashlight.
2. Lay the graph paper on a table.
3. Hold the flashlight perpendicular to the paper so that the free end of the ruler is on the edge of the paper and the flashlight is over the paper.
4. Darken the room and turn on the flashlight.
5. Observe the number of squares on the paper covered by the inner bright circle of light.
6. Without lifting the ruler off the paper, tilt the ruler so that the back end of the flashlight is about 6 inches (15 cm) above the table.
7. Again, observe the number of squares covered by the inner bright circle of light.

Results The number of squares covered by the circle of light depends on the scale of the graph paper and the size of the flashlight. Generally, more squares are illuminated when the flashlight is held at an angle than when it is held perpendicular to the paper.

Why? Roughly the same amount of light struck the paper each time, but when it was more direct—perpendicular—the light was more concentrated and therefore covered fewer squares. When the light was less direct—at an angle—it was spread across more squares. The Earth's surface and its atmosphere are heated by solar energy. The rays of the Sun traveling toward Earth are parallel to each other. But, because the Earth is a sphere, the Sun's rays hit different regions of the Earth at different angles. Like the perpendicular flashlight beam, the Sun's radiant energy is more concentrated at and near the equator and less so nearer the North and South Poles. The surface of the Earth in the equatorial region is therefore heated more by direct sunlight than are the polar regions because the Sun's rays are more angled at the Poles.

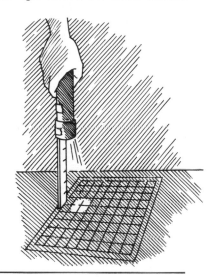

140. Turn Aside

Purpose To demonstrate how Earth's rotation affects wind and ocean currents.

Materials drawing compass
ruler
10-inch (25-cm) square poster board
scissors
paper brad
ruler with a hole in the center
transparent tape
2 felt-tipped pens—1 black, 1 red
adult helper

Procedure

1. Use the compass to draw a circle with an 8-inch (20-cm) diameter on the poster board. Cut out the circle.
2. Ask an adult to use the point of the compass to make a hole in the center of the paper circle.
3. Insert the paper brad through the hole in the center of the ruler and the hole in the paper circle. Turn the paper circle a few times to hollow out the hole in the paper so that the circle turns easily.
4. Lay the paper circle on a table with the ruler on top. Secure the ruler with tape.
5. Position the point of the pen at the top of the paper and to one side of the ruler as shown. Draw a line on the paper along the edge of the ruler.

6. Repeat step 5 using the red pen and asking a helper to slowly rotate the paper circle counterclockwise as you draw the line.

Results The black line you made when the circle was still is straight, and the red line you made when the circle was moving is curved.

Why? The Earth rotates in a counterclockwise direction as viewed from above the North Pole. The Earth's rotation affects the direction of wind and **ocean currents** (large streams of ocean water that move continuously in the same direction) that move freely across the Earth by causing them to **deflect** (turn aside from a straight path) and move in curved paths. This deflection of wind and ocean currents as a result of the Earth's rotation is called the **Coriolis effect**. In this experiment, the straight line models the path of a fluid in the absence of the Coriolis effect, and the curved line models the path of a fluid in the presence of the Coriolis effect.

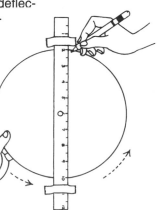

141. Fly Away

Purpose To determine wind direction.

Materials grass clippings (small leaves will work)
directional compass

Procedure

1. Gather together a handful of grass clippings.
2. Stand in an open area outdoors without grass and away from buildings, shrubs, or trees that could block the wind.
3. Throw the clippings straight up into the air.
4. Observe the motion of the clippings.
5. Face the direction of any horizontal motion of the clippings and use the compass to determine this direction.

Results The clippings may fall straight down or blow away from you as they fall. The direction of motion will vary with the presence and direction of wind.

Why? Gravity pulls the clippings down (vertically), but any wind will move the clippings horizontally at the same time. So the clippings move in an arc before hitting the ground. The direction of horizontal motion depends on the direction of the wind. If the clippings move toward the north, the wind is moving south to north. The direction of wind is identified as the direction it is coming from, so a south-to-north wind would be called a south wind.

142. Eye of the Storm

Purpose To demonstrate the calmness in the eye of a hurricane.

Materials 12-inch (30-cm) piece of sewing thread
paper clip
washer with the same circumference as the mouth of the bottles
two 2-L soda bottles
scissors
duct tape
tap water
spoon
helper

Procedure

1. Tie one end of the thread to the paper clip. Set the threaded paper clip aside until you reach step 8.
2. Place the washer over the mouth of one of the bottles.
3. Cut off the bottom of the second bottle.
4. Place the second bottle upside down on top of the first bottle and secure the bottles together with tape.
5. Stand the bottles in a sink with the open end up.
6. Fill the top bottle with water.
7. Ask your helper to stir the water with the spoon in a circular direction a few times.
8. While the water is swirling, quickly suspend the paper clip in the funnel of air in the center of the swirling water, making every effort not to allow the clip to touch the water.

Results As long as it remains suspended in the funnel of air surrounded by the swirling water, the paper clip is unaffected by the water's movement. If it touches the water, the paper clip swirls with it.

Why? A **hurricane** is a storm with winds of 74 miles (118 km) per hour or more rotating around a relatively calm center called the **eye**. The funnel of air in the center of the swirling water running down a drain, simulates the eye of a hurricane. The eye of a hurricane is about 20 miles (32 km) across in the middle of the storm, with few if any clouds. It is a long tube of calm all the way to the surface of the Earth, with high-speed winds spinning around it. Like the air in a hurricane's eye, the air in the center of the swirling water in the bottle is calm, as indicated by the paper clip's lack of movement.

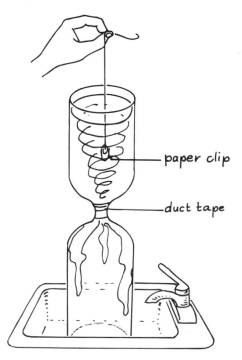

paper clip

duct tape

143. Cloud Maker

Purpose To model how a cloud forms.

Materials scissors
ruler
rubber dishwashing glove
1-quart (1-L) glass jar
tap water
match (to be used only by an adult)
2 wide, medium-size rubber bands
desk lamp
sheet of black construction paper
helper
adult helper

Procedure

1. Cut a 5-inch (12.5-cm) square from the glove.
2. Rinse the inside of the jar with water. Pour most of the water out of the jar, leaving only enough to cover the bottom of the jar.
3. Ask an adult helper to light the match and allow it to burn for about 3 seconds. Then blow out the match and have your adult helper hold the smoking end inside the jar for 2 seconds.
4. Immediately stretch the rubber square over the mouth of the jar and ask your helper to place the rubber bands over the rubber square and around the neck of the jar to hold the rubber square in place.
5. Hold the jar in front of the lamp so that the lamp illuminates the jar from behind.

6. Ask your helper to hold the sheet of black construction paper about 12 inches (30 cm) behind the lamp.
7. With your fingers push the center of the rubber square down into the jar about 1 inch (2.5 cm).
8. Observe the contents of the jar.
9. Pull the center of the rubber square upward.
10. Observe the jar's contents with the rubber square stretched upward, and continue to observe as you release the rubber square.

Results The contents of the jar look clear when the rubber square is pushed down and cloudy when the square is pulled up.

Why? Pushing the rubber square into the jar increases the pressure in the jar, causing an increase in temperature. This temperature rise causes the tiny water molecules to evaporate, forming invisible water vapor. When the rubber square is pulled up, the pressure inside the jar decreases, resulting in a decrease in temperature. This decrease in temperature causes the water vapor to condense, forming tiny water molecules again. The smoke particles provide a surface in the air to which the water molecules can cling. As more water molecules stick together, droplets of water are formed. These droplets are large enough to scatter the light, forming a white **cloud** (water particles that scatter light and float in the air).

144. Raindrops

Purpose To determine the shape of raindrops.

Materials 12-inch (30-cm) square waxed paper
3-ounce (90-mL) paper cup
tap water
drinking straw

Procedure

1. Place the waxed paper on a table.
2. Fill the cup with water.
3. Stand the straw in the cup of water.
4. With your finger over the top end of the straw, lift the straw out of the water.
5. Hold the straw about ½ inch (1.25 cm) above the waxed paper.
6. Slightly release the downward pressure of your finger on the top of the straw so that a drop of water is slowly released from the straw. Observe the shape of the bottom of the drop while it is attached to the straw.
7. Observe the shape of the water drop after it lands on the waxed paper.

Results The water drop is rounded while attached to the straw, but has a rounded top and a flat bottom on the paper.

Why? In most diagrams, falling raindrops appear teardrop-shaped. However, falling raindrops are actually more round, with a slightly flattened bottom. In the presence of gravity, raindrops are stretched downward. But due to the upward pressure of air on the drops, their bottoms are flat instead of round. The drop of water hanging from the straw has a rounded bottom and takes on a more exaggerated length than an actual raindrop because the top is attached to the straw. The drop is being stretched by the downward force of gravity and the attraction between the water and the straw. On the waxed paper, the top of the drop is rounded due to the attractive forces of the water molecules, which pull each other toward the center of the drop. Like air pushing on a raindrop, but more exaggerated, the bottom of the drop is flat due to the upward pressure of the paper.

145. Water Cycle

Purpose To demonstrate the movement of water between the Earth's surface and the atmosphere.

Materials 1 cup (250 mL) soil
2-quart (2-L) glass bowl
½ cup (125 mL) tap water
sheet of transparent plastic food wrap large
  enough to cover the bowl
gooseneck desk lamp
ruler
timer
ice cube
resealable plastic bag

Procedure

1. Pour the soil into the bowl and make it as level as possible.
2. Pour the water over the surface of the soil.
3. Cover the bowl with the food wrap, making sure it is tightly sealed.
4. Place the bowl on a table near the lamp.
5. Position the lamp so that the light is about 6 inches (15 cm) away from the side of the bowl.
6. After 10 minutes, place the ice cube in the bag and gently rub it over the surface of the plastic cover. While doing this, observe the appearance of the cover.
7. Remove the bag of ice and gently run your finger across the surface of the cover.

Results Rubbing the plastic cover with the ice causes the cover to change from clear to cloudy. Running your finger over the cover reveals that it is dry on the outside. (The bag keeps the melting ice from wetting the cover, so you can prove it is dry.)

Why? The cover's cloudy appearance is due to the formation of moisture on the underside. The bowl of damp soil simulates the movement of water between the Earth's surface and the atmosphere. This movement of water is called the **water cycle.** One stage in the water cycle is the **evaporation** (the process of a liquid changing into a gas) of water from the land. This stage requires an increase in the liquid's temperature by the Sun, the lamp in this experiment. Not only does the liquid from bodies of water such as oceans, lakes, and streams evaporate, but so does the water in soil, laundry, and anything else that is wet.

In the air, the water vapor cools and changes back to a liquid. This process of changing from vapor to liquid is called **condensation.** It is what makes the cover appear cloudy. This stage requires a decrease in the vapor's temperature, such as at nightfall, simulated by the ice cube. In nature, clouds form when water condenses in the cooler upper atmosphere. The liquid water in the clouds returns to the Earth as **precipitation** (liquid or solid particles that form in the atmosphere and then fall to the Earth's surface), which can evaporate, starting the water cycle again.

146. Open and Closed

Purpose To observe the effect of air pressure on a liquid's surface pressure.

Materials pushpin
small plastic soda bottle
tap water
adult helper

Procedure

1. Ask an adult helper to use the pushpin to poke a hole in the side of the bottle near the bottom.
2. Fill the bottle by holding it under a faucet. Then set the bottle on the counter with the hole pointing toward the sink. Observe the hole in the bottle.
3. After a few seconds, cover the mouth of the bottle with your palm and again observe the hole in the bottle.

Results Water streamed out of the hole in the bottle when the bottle's mouth was open. When you covered the bottle's mouth with your palm, water continued to come out of the hole for a short time, then stopped.

Why? Air in Earth's atmosphere is made up of billions of molecules moving around in every direction and constantly bumping into everything around them. These collisions result in what is known as air pressure. **Air pressure** is also called **barometric pressure** or **atmospheric pressure.**

In the open bottle, air inside and above the bottle is pressing down on the surface of the water in the bottle. Air outside the bottles is also pressing against the water through the hole in the side of the bottle. But the air pressure on the water's surface, plus the weight of the water itself, creates a pressure greater than the air pressure outside the hole, so water streams out the hole. When the bottle is closed, water continues to stream out of the hole until the combined air pressure and water pressure inside the bottle is less than the air pressure outside. The water pressure decreases as water leaves the bottle, and the air pressure inside the bottle decreases as the air inside the bottle spreads out, thus the water stops pouring out of the hole.

147. Holder

Purpose To test the strength of air pressure.

Materials pencil
two 3-ounce (90-mL) paper cups
12-inch (30-cm) string
tap water
suction cup with hooks (used to secure hanging crafts to windows)
100 or more pennies or metal washers

Procedure

1. Use the pencil to make holes beneath the rim on opposite sides of one of the cups.
2. Thread the string through the holes and tie the ends to
make a handle.
3. Fill the other cup about half full with water.
4. Dampen the suction cup with water by dipping it in the
cup of water.
5. Press the suction cup against a flat, smooth, vertical
surface such as the side of a metal filing cabinet.
6. Hang the cup by placing the string handle over the
hook of the suction cup.
7. Add 5 to 10 coins at a time to the cup until the cup is
full or the suction cup pulls away from the surface.

Results The number of pennies the cup will hold varies
with the size of the suction cup and how well the cup is
secured.

Why? Pressing the suction cup against the surface forces
the air out of the space under the suction cup. The water
on the suction cup helps to form a seal around its edges,
preventing air from entering. The air pressure in the room
pushes the flattened suction cup and holds it against the
surface. You can probably add many pennies to the paper
cup before the suction cup falls. This shows how strong the
air pressure pushing against the suction cup is.

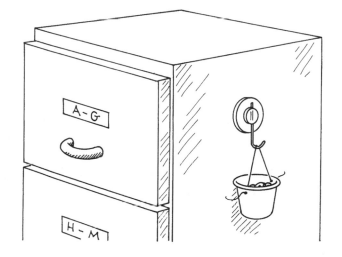

148. Pressed

Purpose To model air pressure at different heights
above Earth's surface.

Materials 4 paper towels

Procedure

1. Fold each of the towels in half twice.
2. Lay one of the folded towels on a table and observe
the thickness of the towel.
3. Stack another folded towel on the first one. Observe
the thickness of both towels.
4. Repeat step 3 two times using the two remaining
folded towels.

Results The thickness of each towel
decreases with the number of towels
stacked on top. The bottom towel is the
thinnest and the top towel is the thickest.

Why? The folded towels represent a section of the atmosphere from Earth's surface
to space. The layers of air in the section do
not have definite boundaries but differ from
each other in temperature and gas content.
The layers support one another, and the
bottom layer must support the weight of all
the layers above it. Gravity pulls the layers down, causing
the lowest layer to be more tightly **compressed** (pressed
tightly together) than the upper layers. Thus the air near
the Earth has a greater density and greater pressure than
air that is higher above Earth. Near the Earth's surface,
where the density of air is greatest, atmospheric pressure
is about 14.6 psi (pounds per square inch) (100,000 Pa
[pascals]). At 3.4 miles (5.5 km) above Earth's surface, the
pressure is about half that at the Earth's surface, and at
6.8 miles (11 km) the pressure is about one-fourth that at
Earth's surface.

149. Reducer

Purpose To detect changes in air pressure.

Materials 16-ounce (480-mL) glass soda bottle
tap water
ruler
red food coloring
drinking straw
scissors
modeling clay
marking pen
helper

Procedure

1. Make a barometer by following these steps.

   - Fill the bottle with water to about 1 inch (2.5 cm) below the mouth.

   - Add enough food coloring to make the water a dark red. Swirl the bottle to thoroughly mix the water and coloring.

   - At a point 2 inches (5 cm) from one end of the straw, cut three-fourths of the way through the straw with the scissors. Bend the short end over.

   - Insert about 3 inches (7.5 cm) of the straw into the soda bottle with the bent end up.

   - Mold a piece of clay around the straw and seal the mouth of the bottle.

   - Press down on the clay until the water rises to about ½ inch (1.25 cm) below the cut in the straw.

   - With the pen, mark the water level in the straw.

2. Ask your helper to hold the bent end of the straw at a right angle to the rest of the straw and blow hard through the bent end.

3. Observe the height of the water in the straw as your helper blows through the straw.

Results The water level in the straw rises.

Why? The **barometer** (an instrument used to measure air pressure) made in this experiment can be used to detect changes in air pressure. Air inside the bottle pushes down on the surface of the water with a constant amount of pressure. At the same time, air pushes down on the water inside the straw. When you blow across the straw, the moving stream of air reduces the pressure on the water inside the straw. The change in pressure means that the air pressure inside the bottle is greater than the air pressure inside the straw, so the water is pushed up the straw.

150. Down Under

Purpose To make a model of the features of the ocean floor.

Materials scissors
medium-size cardboard box
ruler
aluminum foil
papier-mâché (available where craft supplies are sold)
tap water
large bowl
¼ cup (63 mL) flour
adult helper

Procedure

1. Ask an adult to cut the box down to a height of about 2 inches (5 cm), then line the box with aluminum foil.

2. Follow the instructions on the papier-mâché, mixing it with the indicated amount of water in the bowl.

3. Pour the prepared papier-mâché into the foil-lined box and mold the papier-mâché to form these ocean features:

   - **continental shelf** The area of ocean floor starting at the shoreline and ending at the continental slope.

   - **continental slope** The steep slanted area between the continental shelf and the abyss.

   - **abyss** The great depths of the ocean floor, generally with an average depth of 15,000 feet (4,500 m).

   - **abyssal plain** The flat surface of the abyss.

   - **seamount** An underwater mountain.

   - **island** A seamount that extends above the ocean's surface.

   - **guyot** A flat-topped seamount.

   - **trench** An underwater valley that is V-shaped, narrow, and deep.

4. Let the papier-mâché dry.

5. Pour the flour over the abyssal plain.

Results You have made a model of the features of the ocean floor.

Why? The only structure extending above the surface (top of the box) is the island. The flour represents the **ooze deposits,** which are sediments consisting of dust particles from space, volcanic ash, dust blown seaward by winds, and particles of dead organisms that drift down from the upper levels of water to the abyssal plain.

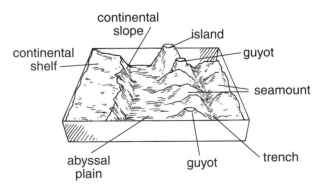

151. Streamers

Purpose To observe currents caused by differences in salt content.

Materials 2 tablespoons (30 mL) table salt
3-ounce (90-mL) paper cup
tap water
green food coloring
spoon
serrated knife (to be used only by an adult)
clean, empty 2-L plastic soda bottle
scissors
masking tape
pencil
adult helper

Procedure

1. Pour the salt into the paper cup.
2. Fill the cup with water and add five or more drops of food coloring to the cup. Stir.
3. Ask an adult to use the knife to cut off the top third of the bottle. To do this, make a small slit in the bottle with the knife and then use the scissors to cut around the bottle. Keep the bottom section and cover the cut edges with tape.
4. Fill the bottom section of the soda bottle about three-fourths full with water.
5. Hold the cup so that its bottom is just below the surface of the water in the bottle. Use the pencil to punch a small hole in the bottom of the cup.
6. Observe what happens in the water below the cup

Results A stream of green water flows out of the cup and down toward the bottom of the bottle.

Why? The density of the salt water is greater than that of fresh water. Thus, the salt water in the cup is heavier than the fresh (unsalted) water in the jar, causing the salt water to sink. Differences in density of ocean water create ocean currents called **density currents.** In oceans, denser water sinks and less dense water rises. The density of ocean water is also affected by temperature. As water gets colder, it contracts and its density increases. Thus the colder, denser water at the North and South Poles sinks and moves along the ocean floor toward the equator. At the same time, the warmer, less dense water at the equator rises and moves along the surface toward the Poles. If salt water freezes, some of the salt is left behind in the water just below the ice, making this water more dense. Evaporation of surface ocean water can also cause water at the surface to have a higher concentration of salt.

152. Rise and Fall

Purpose To demonstrate the two points of a water wave.

Materials 1 cup (250 mL) tap water
1-gallon (4-L) resealable plastic bag
blue food coloring

Procedure

1. Pour the water into the bag.
2. Add two to three drops of food coloring and seal the bag.
3. Hold the bag at eye level with your hands level with each other. Observe the surface of the water.
4. Raise one side of the bag then lower it to its original position. Observe the surface of the water.
5. Repeat step 4 raising the opposite side.
6. Repeat steps 4 and 5 several times.
7. Compare what you see on the surface of the water to the shapes in the diagram.

Results When your hands are level with each other, the water's surface is level. Raising and lowering the sides of the bag causes the water's surface to rise and fall in repeated shapes that can be identified.

Why? **Water waves** are disturbances on the surface of water consisting of high points called **crests** and low points called **troughs.** In this experiment, the bag is raised and lowered in order to disturb the surface of the water and produce waves. In the ocean, wind is the primary source of water disturbance. As the wind blows across the water, waves are produced.

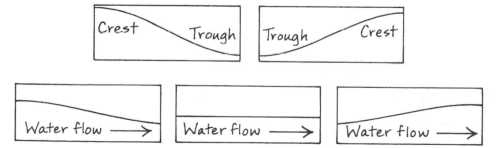

153. Washout

Purpose   To simulate erosion of a beach by water waves.

Materials   paint roller pan
4 cups (1,000 mL) sand
2 quarts (2 L) tap water
pencil

Procedure

1. Cover the bottom of the pan with 4 cups (1,000 mL) of sand. Make a thicker layer at the shallow end of the pan. This thicker layer is the beach.
2. Pour the water into the deep end of the pan.
3. Make a mental note of the appearance of the beach.
4. Make waves by laying the pencil in the deep end of the pan and quickly moving the pencil up and down with your fingertips.
5. Repeat step 3.

Results   Some of the sand is washed from the beach by the waves.

Why?   The area where the water meets the sand represents a **shoreline** (an area where the ocean and the land meet). The **shore** is the land at the shoreline, and a shore with a smooth stretch of sand and/or pebbles is called a **beach.** If the beach is mostly sand, as in the model in this experiment, it is called a sandy beach.

Tapping the water with the pencil causes water waves. Water waves that wash over a sandy beach cause erosion (the movement of sediments by wind, water, or ice) of the beach as some of the sand is pulled into the water.

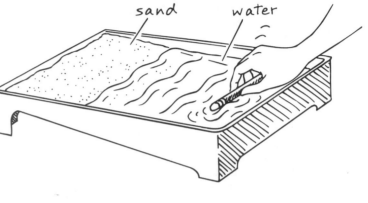

---

154. Overflow?

Purpose   To determine whether melting icebergs affect water level.

Materials   paper towel
saucer
9-ounce (270-mL) plastic cup
4 or more ice cubes
1 cup (250 mL) cold tap water
blue food coloring

Procedure

1. Fold the paper towel in half twice and place it in the bottom of the saucer.
2. Set the cup on the paper towel.
3. Place the ice cubes in the cup.
4. Fill the cup with water just short of overflowing. Then add two drops of food coloring. If the colored water spills out, you need to replace the paper towel and refill the cup.
5. Allow the cup to sit undisturbed until all the ice melts. Observe the paper towel for any signs of colored water spilling out.

Results   The level of the water in the cup remains the same.

Why?   The weight of the water displaced by the floating ice is exactly equal to the weight of the ice. Ice takes up more space than

water, so when the ice melts it shrinks and fits exactly into the space equal to the volume of water that it displaced. The same is true for **icebergs,** which are pieces of **glaciers** (large masses of ice and snow that move very slowly down a mountain or across land) that break off at the shoreline and fall into the ocean.

155. Below the Surface

Purpose To construct a topographic map of the undersea mountains.

Materials modeling clay
2-quart (2-L) glass baking dish 3 inch (7.6 cm) deep
masking tape
marking pen
2-quart (2-L) pitcher
tap water
spoon
blue food coloring
clear plastic report folder

Procedure

1. Use the modeling clay to mold the shape of two mountains in the bottom of the baking dish. They must not be taller than the dish.
2. Place a strip of masking tape down one end of the dish.
3. Mark off a ½-inch (1.3-cm) scale on the tape from the bottom up.
4. Fill the pitcher with tap water and stir in drops of food coloring until the water is dark blue.
5. Lay the folder over the top of the dish.
6. Standing so that you are looking straight down into the dish, draw the outline of the top of the dish on the folder.
7. Remove the folder and add the colored water up to the first ½-inch (1.3-cm) mark.
8. Put the folder back over the dish and draw the outline of the water line around the clay on the folder.
9. Remove the folder and add more colored water up to the next ½-inch (1.3-cm) mark.
10. Again, draw the outline of the water on the folder.
11. Continue this procedure until the water reaches the top measurement on the tape.

Results The tracing you have made is a topographic map of the mountains in the dish.

Why? A **topographic map** is a flat map that shows the shapes and heights of land areas. To do this, it uses lines to connect points on the Earth that have the same elevation. **Elevation** is the height something is raised and is often compared to sea level, which has an elevation of zero. The lines connecting the points are called **contour lines.** Each line on the folder is a contour line connecting points of equal depth on the clay mountains. The contour interval, or the elevation change between the contour lines, is ½ inch (1.3 cm).

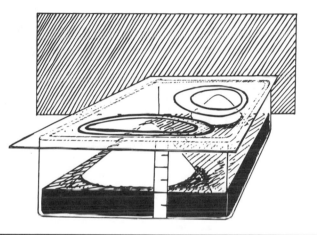

156. Coming Up!

Purpose To demonstrate how ballast tanks affect the density of ocean craft.

Materials masking tape
2 pennies
small narrow-mouthed plastic bottle
scissors
flexible drinking straw
modeling clay
large bowl
tap water
adult helper

Procedure

1. Tape the pennies side by side to the outside bottom of the bottle.
2. Ask an adult to use the point of the scissors to make a row of three holes down one side of the bottle.
3. Place the short end of the straw into the mouth of the bottle and secure the straw with clay.
4. Fill the bowl with water.
5. Place the bottle in the bowl, holes down.
6. Hold the bottle beneath the water until it fills with water and remains on the bottom of the bowl. If the bottle does not sink, add more coins.
7. Blow into the straw.

Results The bottle rises to the surface.

Why? **Submersibles** are ocean craft capable of going underwater and can be used to study the ocean. Some submersibles, including **submarines,** have ballast tanks. **Ballast tanks** are used to make a submarine rise or sink in the water by changing the craft's density. When seawater is pumped into the tanks, the submarine's density increases and it sinks, as did the bottle in this experiment. When air is used to force the water out of the tanks, the craft's density decreases and the craft rises.

157. Percolate

Purpose To model percolation of groundwater.

Materials large spoon
2 cups (500 mL) sand
2 cups (500 mL) aquarium gravel or small pebbles
2-quart (2-L) plastic or metal bowl
1-quart (1-L) widemouthed transparent plastic jar
½ cup (125 mL) tap water

Procedure

1. Use the spoon to mix the sand and gravel together in the bowl.
2. Spoon the sand and gravel mixture into the jar.
3. Slowly pour the water into the jar.
4. Observe the movement of the water through the sand and gravel mixture.
5. Allow the jar to stand in a warm area, such as a window with direct sunlight, for 2 or 3 days.
6. Observe the sand and gravel mixture, making note of its wetness.

Results The water first wets the sand and fills the spaces between the sand and gravel in the upper part of the jar. As the water moves toward the bottom of the jar, it moves out of the spaces in the upper layer and fills the spaces in the lower layer. The upper layer becomes dry, with a wet layer below it.

Why? Water, such as rainfall, that sinks into the ground is known as **groundwater.** This water passes through permeable materials, like the sand used in this experiment. The passing or seeping of groundwater or any liquid through a permeable material is called **percolation.**

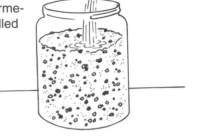

158. Sinker

Purpose To demonstrate how a volcanic caldera is formed.

Materials scissors
ruler
poster board
2-L soda bottle
2 cups (500 mL) soil
large bowl
tap water
1-teaspoon (5-mL) measuring spoon
adult helper

Procedure

1. Cut two 3-by-8-inch (7.5-by-20-cm) strips of poster board.
2. Ask an adult to cut the top off the soda bottle.
3. Ask the adult to cut two horizontal slits, one on each side, in the center of the bottle and large enough for the poster board strips to slide through.
4. Pour the soil into the bowl and add water, 1 teaspoon (5 mL) at a time, while mixing with your hands. Continue adding the water until the soil is slightly moist and begins to stick together.
5. Place half the moist soil inside the bottle.
6. Press the soil against the sides of the bottle up to the slits, leaving a large, empty cavity in the center.

7. Place the strips of poster board, one on top of the other, through the slits in the bottle.
8. Mound the remaining soil on top of the strips of poster board and mold it into the shape of a volcano top.
9. Hold the ends of the strips, one in each hand, and slowly pull the strips in opposite directions.
10. Observe the top of the volcano as the strips separate.

Results When the supporting strips are removed, the top of the volcano falls into the cavity below.

Why? The soil falling into the cavity below simulates the formation of a volcanic **caldera** (a large, roughly circular crater with steep walls that forms when the top of a volcano collapses). The rapid **ejection** (throwing out) of magma during a large volcanic **eruption** (the throwing forth of material) can leave the **magma chamber** (a pool of magma deep within the Earth) empty or partially empty. The unsupported roof of the empty chamber can slowly sink under its own weight, forming a caldera.

159. Erupting Volcano

Purpose To model an erupting volcano.

Materials 16-ounce (480-mL) soda bottle
large baking pan
two 1-cup (250-mL) measuring cups
spoon
1 tablespoon (15 mL) flour
1 tablespoon (15 mL) baking soda
funnel
red food coloring
1 cup (250 mL) white vinegar
tap water

Procedure

1. Place the soda bottle in the pan.
2. In one of the measuring cups, mix together the flour and baking soda.
3. Pour the flour and baking soda mixture through the funnel into the soda bottle.
4. Add 20 drops of red food coloring to the bottle.
5. Pour about half the vinegar into the bottle.
6. When the foaming stops, pour the remaining vinegar into the bottle.

Results Red foam bubbles out the top and then runs down the side of the bottle.

Why? The baking soda reacts with the vinegar, producing carbon dioxide gas. As the gas forms, it expands quickly, pushing the liquid and the flour particles out the top of the bottle. The mixture of the gas, flour, red food coloring, and liquid produces the foam, which simulates the foamy magma during a volcanic eruption.

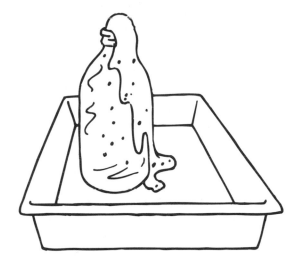

160. Magma Flow

Purpose To demonstrate how temperature affects the movement of magma.

Materials 1-teaspoon (5-mL) measuring spoon
soft margarine
baby food jar
cereal bowl
warm tap water
timer

Procedure

1. Fill the measuring spoon with the margarine.
2. Using your finger, push the margarine out of the spoon and into the baby food jar so that the glob of margarine is centered in the bottom of the jar.
3. Hold the jar in your hand and turn it on its side.
4. Observe any movement of the margarine.
5. Fill the bowl halfway with warm tap water.
6. Set the jar in the warm water.
7. After 3 minutes, pick up the jar and turn it on its side.
8. Again, observe any movement of the margarine.

Results At first the margarine inside the tilted jar does not move much, but heating the margarine causes it to move more freely.

Why? As the temperature of the margarine increased, it became thinner and moved more easily. Molecules in colder materials have less energy, are closer together, and move more slowly than warmer molecules with more energy. These warm, energized molecules move away from each other, causing solids to melt and liquids to thin. Just as the temperature of the margarine affected the way it moved across the surface of the jar, the temperature of magma affects the way it moves up the volcano's **vent** (the channel of a volcano that connects the source of magma to the volcano's opening). Hot magma is thin and moves easily and quickly up the vent, while cooler magma is thick and sluggish.

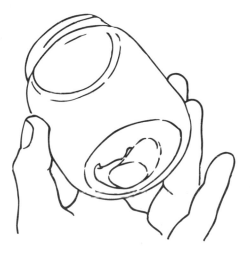

161. Shaker

Purpose To determine why some buildings are more damaged by earthquakes than others.

Materials   scissors
ruler
sheet of copy paper
transparent tape
4-by-8-inch (5-by-20-cm) piece of corrugated
cardboard

Procedure

1. Cut two 1-inch (2.5-cm) strips from the paper. One strip should be 10 inches (25 cm) long, and the other 8 inches (20 cm) long.
2. Tape the ends of each strip together to form two rings.
3. Tape the rings to the center of the piece of cardboard so that they are about 1 inch (2.5 cm) apart and stand side by side like the wheels of a car. The openings of the two rings should face the short ends of the cardboard.
4. Shake the cardboard from side to side, starting with a slow back-and-forth movement and gradually increasing the speed of the movements.

Results The large ring moves when the cardboard is shaken slowly, and the small ring moves when the cardboard is shaken quickly.

Why? Every object has its own natural frequency, or rate of vibrations. The larger ring's natural frequency is lower than the smaller ring's, so it vibrates at a lower frequency (has a slower back-and-forth motion) than the smaller ring. This is because it is less stiff and more massive. When an outside force of the same frequency causes an object to vibrate, this action is called **resonance** or **sympathetic vibration.** So when the cardboard is shaken at the frequency of the large ring, it vibrates or resonates, but the small ring does not. The opposite is true if the cardboard is shaken at the frequency of the small ring. During an **earthquake** (violent shaking of the Earth caused by sudden movement of rock beneath its surface), buildings of different sizes respond differently to the shaking of the Earth. One reason is their natural frequencies. If the earthquake's frequency matches a building's natural frequency, the building resonates, meaning it shakes more violently.

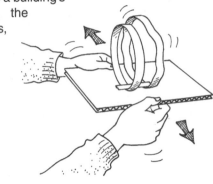

---

162. Fill 'Er Up

Purpose To demonstrate how different materials change in a landfill.

Materials   scissors
plastic trash bag
2 shoe boxes
masking tape
enough soil to fill both shoe boxes
large bowl
large spoon
tap water
ruler
2 sets of test materials: newspaper, orange
peel, aluminum foil, plastic lid

Procedure

1. Cut two pieces from the trash bag large enough to line each shoe box. Secure the plastic lining with tape.
2. Place the soil in the bowl and stir in enough water to moisten it.
3. Place about 2 inches (5 cm) of moistened soil in each box. On the surface of the soil in each box, place one of each test material. Spread the materials so that they do not touch each other.
4. Fill each box with soil to cover the test materials.
5. Place the boxes in a sunny place. For the next 28 days, keep the soil in each box moist by adding equal amounts of water to each. Treat the boxes exactly the same.

6. After the first 14 days, use the spoon to carefully uncover the test materials of one box. Observe any decaying of the materials.
7. After 14 more days, repeat step 6 using the second box.

Results After 14 days, the aluminum foil and plastic lid remain unchanged. The newspaper and orange peel show some signs of decay. After 28 days, the aluminum foil and plastic lid still remain unchanged, and the newspaper and orange peel show more signs of decay.

Why? When garbage is thrown into a landfill, it is hoped that **microorganisms** (microscopic organisms) in the soil will cause the materials to decompose. Some materials take longer than others to decompose. Things like paper and food substances can take only a few days, while plastics and aluminum cans may take hundreds of years, if they decompose at all. Materials that are easily broken down by microorganisms are called biodegradable.

In this experiment, each box is lined with plastic. This is similar to the clay and/or thick man-made plastic used to line sanitary landfills. Just as the plastic inside the box prevents the box from being damaged by the moist soil, the landfill liner prevents harmful fluids from leaking into groundwater.

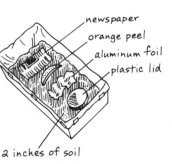

newspaper
orange peel
aluminum foil
plastic lid

2 inches of soil

163. Pollution Dilution

Purpose To show how pollution is affected by dilution.

Materials coffee cup
1-quart (1-L) jar
1-gallon (4-L) jug, with lid
tap water
red food coloring
spoon
adult helper

Procedure

1. Fill the cup, jar, and jug three-fourths full with water.
2. Add two drops of food coloring to the water in the cup and stir.
3. Pour all but a small amount of the water from the cup into the jar and stir.
4. Pour all but a small amount of the water from the jar into the jug.
5. Ask an adult to place the lid on the jug and shake the jug back and forth to mix thoroughly.
6. Compare the color of the water left in the cup and jar with the color of the water in the jug.

Results The water is dark red in the cup, pale red in the jar, and pale pink to colorless in the jug.

Why? The red color is deepest in the cup because the molecules of red coloring are close together and reflect more red light to your eyes. When this colored water is added to clean water, the color molecules spread evenly throughout the water. By the time the color molecules are added to the clean water in the jug, they are far enough apart to become very pale to invisible because of their small size.

This is what happens with some water **pollutants** (substances that destroy the purity of air, water, or land). The material may be visible where it is initially dumped into a river, but as it flows downstream and becomes mixed with more water, it can no longer be seen with the naked eye. This does not mean that the pollutant is gone. Animal and plant life in a stream is affected by pollutants many miles (kilometers) from the source. The degree of harm to the animal depends on the type of pollutant and how much water has been added in order to **dilute** (lessen the concentration of a solute by mixing more solvent, usually water, into the solution) the pollutant.

164. Runoff

Purpose To simulate how pollutants move from the land into the ocean.

Materials

long, shallow baking pan	grass
cookie sheet	red food coloring
soil	tap water
ruler	2-quart (2-L)
trowel	pitcher

Procedure

1. Place the baking pan on the ground.
2. Place one end of the cookie sheet on the rim of one long edge of the baking pan, and use a mound of soil to raise the other end of the cookie sheet about 4 inches (10 cm) above the rim of the pan.
3. Cover the surface of the cookie sheet with soil.
4. With permission, use the trowel to dig up five or six small clumps of grass. Then set these on the soil-covered sheet.

NOTE: Grass clumps can be replaced in the ground when the experiment is completed.

5. Squeeze five to six drops of food coloring near the base of each clump of grass.
6. Fill the baking pan half full with water.
7. Fill the pitcher with water.
8. Hold the pitcher at the raised end of the cookie sheet and slowly pour the water across the soil at the raised end of the cookie sheet.
9. Observe the color and contents of the water as it washes into the pan.

Results Water from the pitcher, along with bits of soil and red food coloring, wash into the pan.

Why? Sources of pollution such as trash and oil spills are very visible and publicized, but one source that is very damaging to some coastal areas is polluted **runoff** (the part of precipitation that washes from the land into bodies of water). Runoff becomes polluted when rainwater runs across farmland, highways, city streets, lawns, mining areas, or any polluted place on the land. Fertilizers, pesticides, salt, oil, and all kinds of chemicals dissolve or float in the water and are carried to their final dumping place: the ocean. In this experiment, the red food coloring represents the pollutant.

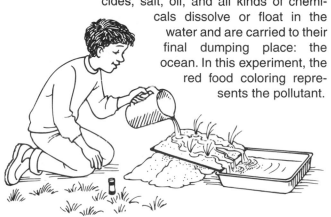

V
Physics

object

focal length

virtual
image

165. Unreal

Purpose To demonstrate that a plane mirror has a virtual image.

Materials   pencil
ruler
sheet of copy paper
walnut-size piece of modeling clay
paper clip
small flat mirror
index card

Procedure

1. Use the pencil and the ruler to draw a 6-inch (15-cm) line in the center of the paper. Mark a dot in the center of the line.
2. Use a small piece of clay to stand the paper clip upright at one end of the line.
3. Use the remaining clay to stand the mirror upright on the dot on the line so that the mirror faces the paper clip.
4. Look in the mirror and determine how far behind the mirror the image of the paper clip appears to be.
5. Look behind the mirror at the end of the line where the image appears to be. Hold the index card at this spot and look at the card for signs of the image of the paper clip.

Results The image of the paper clip appears to be the same distance behind the mirror as the paper clip is in front of the mirror, which is 3 inches (7.5 cm). But the image, which appears behind the mirror, cannot be projected onto a card held at this spot.

Why? A **plane mirror** is a mirror with a flat surface. The image of an object in a plane mirror appears to be as far behind the mirror as the object is in front of the mirror. Since the image cannot be projected onto a screen in the place where it appears to be, the image is called a **virtual image.**

166. Backward

Purpose To demonstrate that an image in a plane mirror is reversed.

Materials   mirror
index card
pencil

Procedure

1. Stand so that you can see your face in the mirror.
2. Hold the card on your forehead and while looking into the mirror, use the pencil to print your name on the card.
3. Turn the card around and look at what you wrote.

Results Your name is correct when read in the mirror, but reads backward without the mirror.

Why? The image seen in a plane mirror is **laterally reversed,** which means it is reversed from left to right. Since a mirror image is always laterally reversed, any laterally reversed image is called a **mirror image.**

167. Outward

Purpose To determine the type of image seen in a convex mirror.

Materials large metal serving spoon
ruler
pencil

Procedure
1. In one hand, hold the spoon vertically with the back side of the spoon's bowl about 1 foot (30 cm) from your face.
2. With your other hand, hold the pencil upright in front of, but not touching, your face. Then slowly move the pencil toward the spoon until it touches the spoon's bowl. As the spoon is being moved, observe the pencil's image in the spoon's bowl.

Results The image of the pencil is upright and smaller than the pencil regardless of its distance from the spoon. But the image is larger when the pencil is held closer to the spoon than when held at a distance.

Why? Surfaces that curve outward, such as the backside of the spoon, are said to be **convex**. Convex mirrors cause the light hitting them to bend so that the image is virtual, upright, and smaller than the object.

Because convex mirrors cause a large area to appear small, they are sometimes used in stores to allow clerks to watch large areas.

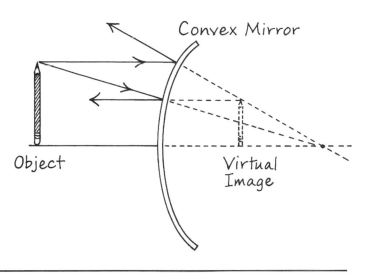

168. Inward

Purpose To determine the type of image seen in a concave mirror.

Materials large metal serving spoon
ruler
pencil

Procedure
1. In one hand, hold the spoon vertically with the inside of the spoon's bowl about 1 foot (30 cm) from your face.
2. With your other hand, hold the pencil upright in front of, but not touching, your face. Then slowly move the pencil toward the spoon until it touches the spoon's bowl. As the spoon is being moved, observe the pencil's image in the spoon's bowl.

Results When the pencil is held at a distance from the spoon, its image is smaller than the pencil's actual size and inverted. When the pencil is close to the spoon, its image is upright and larger than the pencil's actual size.

Why? Surfaces that curve inward, such as the inside of the spoon's bowl, are said to be **concave**. Concave mirrors cause the light hitting them to bend so that you see a small, upside-down image of an object that is distant from the mirror. This image is a **real image,** which means it could be projected onto a screen. If the object is close to the mirror, you see an enlarged upright virtual image. Concave mirrors are used for shaving or applying makeup.

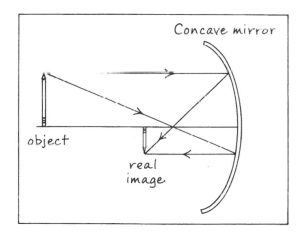

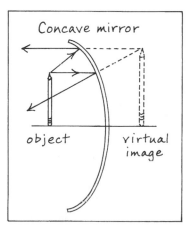

169. To the Point

Purpose To determine the focal length of a convex lens.

Materials white unruled index card
magnifying lens
ruler
helper

Procedure

1. Stand outdoors in a sunny area.
2. With your back toward the Sun, hold the index card in one hand and the magnifying lens in the other.
3. Point one side of the magnifying lens toward the Sun and the other side toward the index card.

CAUTION: Do not look directly at the Sun because it can permanently damage your eyes.

4. Separate the lens and the card until the brightest light spot falls on the card.
5. Ask your helper to measure the distance between the lens and the card.

CAUTION: Do not focus sunlight on the card for more than a few seconds because the card can get hot enough to burn.

NOTE: Keep the magnifying lens and index card for the next experiment.

Results The focal length of a magnifying lens is determined. The focal length will vary depending on the lens used. The lens used by the author had a 16-cm focal length.

Why? A magnifying lens is a convex lens. The **focal length** of a convex lens is the distance from the lens to the **focal point,** the point where light rays passing through the lens **converge** (come together). Light rays from a distant object, such as the Sun in this experiment, are parallel. The spot of light on the card is the focal point of the lens.

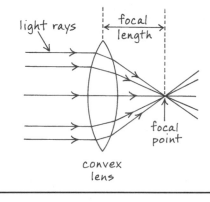

170. Beyond

Purpose To determine the type of image produced when an object is beyond the focal length of a convex lens.

Materials transparent tape
yardstick (meterstick)
magnifying lens and index card from Experiment 169, "To the Point"

Procedure

1. Tape the index card to the zero end of the measuring stick so that the card is perpendicular to and even with the end of the stick.
2. Hold the magnifying lens with your writing hand.
3. Support the card and measuring stick with your other hand and lay the free end of the measuring stick on the shoulder of your writing hand.
4. During the daytime, stand in a darkened room with your back to an uncovered window.
5. Hold the magnifying lens on the measuring stick and move it toward and away from the index card until the brightest and clearest picture of the scene outside appears on the paper.
6. Note the size of the image and whether it is upright or inverted.

NOTE: Keep the magnifying lens for the next experiment.

Results The image is smaller than the object and inverted.

Why? The focal length of the lens used was determined in Experiment 169, but even if it is not known, the distance from the lens to an object outside the window is much greater than the focal length of any small magnifying lens. When an object is beyond the focal length of the lens, the lens will produce a real image that is smaller than the object and inverted.

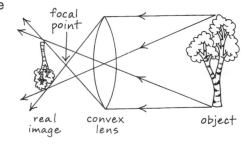

171. Within

Purpose To determine the type of image produced when an object is within the focal length of a convex lens.

Materials pencil
ruler
sheet of copy paper
magnifying lens from Experiment 169, "To the Point"
helper

Procedure

1. Use the pencil and ruler to draw a 1-cm-long arrow on the paper.
2. Lay the lens on top of the arrow.
3. With one eye closed, look through the lens with the other eye. Then slowly raise the lens until the largest, clearest image of the arrow is visible through the lens.
4. With the lens in this position, ask your helper to measure the distance from the arrow to the lens. Compare this distance to the focal length of the lens as determined in Experiment 169, "To the Point."

Results The distance from the arrow to the lens is less than the focal length of the lens.

Why? When the distance from an object to a convex lens is less than the focal length of the lens, the lens will produce a magnified image of the object on the same side of the lens as the object. The image will be virtual and upright. To view the arrow, you have to look through the lens toward the object.

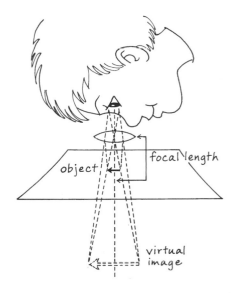

172. Stored

Purpose To demonstrate the change from potential energy to kinetic energy.

Materials 1-yard (1-m) piece of thread
paper clip
disk magnet or bar magnet
masking tape
scissors

Procedure

1. Tie one end of the thread to the paper clip.
2. If you are using a disk magnet, tape the magnet to the side of a tabletop. If you are using a bar magnet, lay the magnet on the table so that one end extends over the edge of the table.
3. Attach the free end of the paper clip to the lower edge of the magnet.
4. Tape the free end of the thread to the floor so that the thread is at an angle to the table as shown.
5. Slowly pull the end of the thread (it will slide under the tape) until the paper clip separates from the magnet but remains suspended in midair. Then cut the thread and observe the motion of the paper clip.

Results The paper clip moves up and sticks to the magnet when the thread is cut.

Why? Energy causes things to move. **Potential energy** is energy of an object at rest that has the potential to cause the object to move. There is a magnetic force of attraction between the paper clip and the magnet. So when held away from the magnet by the thread, the paper clip has magnetic potential energy. When the thread was cut and the paper clip started to move, the paper clip's potential energy was **converted** (changed) to **kinetic energy** (energy of moving objects).

173. Cooling

Purpose To demonstrate how ice acts as a refrigerant.

Materials 5-ounce (150-mL) paper cup
tap water
outdoor thermometer
timer

Procedure

1. Fill the cup half full with water.
2. Stand the thermometer in the cup.
3. Place the cup in the freezer for 2 hours or until the water in the cup freezes.
4. Remove the cup from the freezer and read the temperature on the thermometer.
5. Read the temperature every 30 minutes until the ice melts.

Results The temperature of the ice and the ice water remains at or below 32°F (0°C) until all or most of the ice melts.

Why? **Melting** is a change in phase of matter from a solid to a liquid. The temperature at which a substance melts is called its **melting point.** Freezing is also a change from a liquid to a solid, and the temperature at which a substance freezes is called its freezing point. The melting point and freezing point of a substance are the same. Ice acts as an efficient **refrigerant** (a cooling substance used in refrigeration) because the temperature of melting ice remains at or below its melting point of 32°F (0°C) until the ice is entirely melted. Ice absorbs heat from warmer surroundings, thereby cooling them while not itself becoming warmer. Ice water will remain at the melting point as long as there is enough ice to keep the water chilled, but as the ice melts, the water like the ice absorbs energy and becomes warmer.

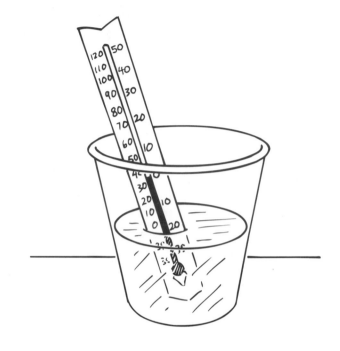

---

174. Cold Skin

Purpose To compare the thermal conductivity of metal and paper.

Materials paper towel
penny

Procedure

1. Fold the paper towel in half twice and lay it on a table.
2. Place the coin in the center of the folded towel.
3. Lay your hand across the paper towel so that part of your hand touches the coin.
4. Observe any difference you feel between the temperature of the coin and the temperature of the paper towel.

Results The coin feels colder than the towel.

Why? Energy that flows from one object to the other because of a difference in their temperature is called heat. Things feel cold to the touch when heat energy is drawn away from your skin; things feel warm when heat energy is trans-ferred to your skin. The coin feels colder than the paper towel because metal has a greater thermal conductivity than paper. **Thermal conductivity** is a measure of how rapidly heat flows through a material that is exposed to a difference in temperature.

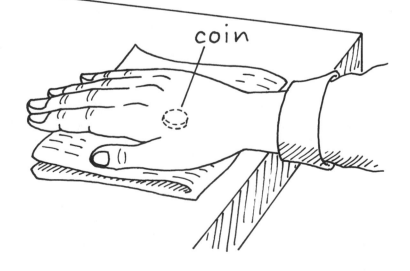

coin

175. Thermometer

Purpose To make a model of a gas thermometer.

Materials ruler
tap water
1-quart (1-L) jar
red food coloring
drinking straw
glass soda bottle
golf ball–size piece of modeling clay
timer

Procedure

1. Pour about 2 inches (5 cm) of water into the jar.
2. Add enough drops of food coloring to the water to make the water a deep red color.
3. Insert about 2 inches (5 cm) of one end of the straw into the mouth of the soda bottle.
4. Mold a piece of clay around the straw to seal the mouth of the bottle.
5. Turn the bottle upside down and stand it in the jar. The jar should support the bottle with the open end of the straw just above the bottom of the jar. If necessary, adjust the length of the straw outside the bottle.
6. Remove the bottle and hold it in your hands. Wrap your hands around the sides of the bottle. Press as much of the palms of your hands as possible against the glass, but do not press hard enough to break the glass.
7. At the end of 1 minute, turn the bottle upside down and stand it straw side down in the jar of colored water. The straw should extend below the surface of the water.
8. Observe the straw for 2 or more minutes.

Results The colored water rises in the straw and flows into the bottle.

Why? **Temperature** is a measure of how cold or hot an object is. Temperature is measured by an instrument called a **thermometer.** Modern thermometers measure temperature numerically, but the thermometer you made in this experiment is a simple model of a thermoscope, which was invented by Galileo (1564–1642) to indicate changes in the temperature of materials. Thermoscopes, as well as some modern thermometers, use the fact that a fluid expands when heated and **contracts** (draws together) when cooled to indicate a change in temperature. The bottle and straw in the thermoscope in this experiment are filled with air. Holding the bottle in your hand causes the gas inside to be heated. The heated gas molecules move faster and farther apart. The expanded molecules escape through the open end of the straw. As the bottle cools, the gas molecules move slower and closer together. Since there are now fewer gas molecules in the bottle, the contracted molecules take up less space, and a partial **vacuum** (an empty space) is created. The air pressure inside the bottle is less than that inside the jar above the water. Thus, air pushing on the surface of the water forces the water into the straw.

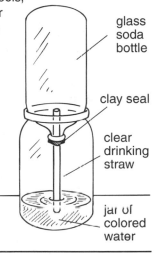

glass soda bottle

clay seal

clear drinking straw

jar of colored water

176. Gravity

Purpose To demonstrate that falling objects accelerate.

Materials timer
helper
two 10-ounce (300-mL) transparent plastic cups

Procedure

1. Turn on the faucet so that the thinnest possible straight stream of water falls.
2. Place one of the cups under the wider part of the stream of water near the faucet (point A on the diagram). Ask your helper to immediately turn on the timer.
3. After 10 seconds, remove the cup.
4. Without changing the stream of water, place the second cup under a narrow part of the stream farther away from the faucet (point B on the diagram). Ask your helper to immediately turn on the timer.
5. Again, remove the cup after 10 seconds.
6. Set the cups side by side and compare the amount of water in each.

Results The amount of water in the cups is equal or nearly equal.

Why? The same amount of water was collected at points A and B over the same amount of time. Thus, it can be stated that the same volume of water per second flows past points A and B in the stream of falling water. Since the stream of water is narrower at point B than at point A, the speed of the water at point B must be faster. (**Speed** is a measure of distance traveled per unit of time. **Acceleration** is the rate of increase of speed.) The stream of water narrows from top to bottom, so it can be concluded that the water accelerates (increases in speed with each second that it falls). While Galileo was the first to discover that falling objects accelerate, Sir Isaac Newton (1642–1727) determined that falling objects accelerate at a rate of 32 feet (9.8 m) per second per second. This means that the speed of a falling object increases 32 feet (9.8 m) per second for every second the object is falling. For example, if the object falls for 2 seconds, then it reaches a speed of 64 feet (19.6 m) per second.

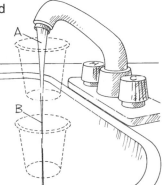

177. Weightless?

Purpose   To demonstrate apparent changes in weight.

Materials   bathroom scale
elevator

Procedure
1. Place the scale on the floor of the elevator car. When the car is stationary, observe your weight measurement on the scale. This is your true weight.
2. As the elevator moves upward, again observe your weight measurement on the scale.
3. Repeat step 2 as the elevator moves down.

Results   Your weight measurement is greater when the elevator is moving upward and less when it is moving down.

Why?   **Weight** is a measure of the pull of gravity on an object. Your weight depends on your mass. **True weight** is due only to the force of gravity. **Apparent weight** is the weight an object appears to be and may be more than, less than, or equal to the object's true weight depending on the direction of the forces acting on the object. In this experiment, your true weight is measured when the elevator is stationary. At that time, the force of gravity is pulling you down against the scale and the scale is pushing back with an equal force. The reading on the scale is the measure of your true weight, which is equal to the gravitational force of Earth where you are located. When the elevator car moves upward, the scale measures not only your true weight but the force of the scale against your feet because the elevator is pushing the scale upward. So your apparent weight is greater when the car moves up. Your apparent weight decreases when the elevator moves down. Even though your true weight does not change, the scale shows a lower measurement because it is moving away from you. Only if you were **free-falling** (falling with gravity as the only acting force on it) would the scale show a zero reading. This is because the scale and you would be moving at the same rate and you would not be applying a force on the scale.

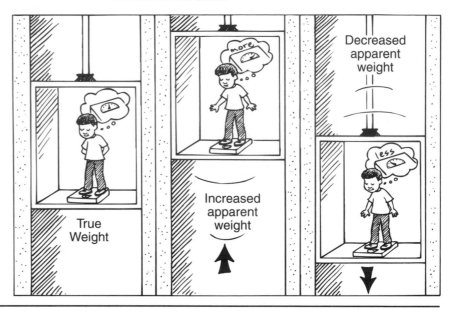

---

178. Roller

Purpose   To demonstrate a turning force.

Materials   ruler
empty cardboard toilet paper tube
pencil
transparent tape
1 foot (30 cm) of ribbon ½ inch (1.25 cm) to ⅛ inch (0.3 cm) wide

Procedure
1. Use the ruler to measure the length of the tube. Divide this length in half. Then use the pencil to mark the center of the tube.
2. Tape one end of the ribbon to the center mark on the tube.
3. Wrap the ribbon one and a half turns around the tube.
4. Lay the tube on a table with the free end of the ribbon extending from the underside of the tube and lying on the table.
5. Hold the free end of the ribbon at an angle of about 45° or less. Then gently pull on the ribbon. Notice how the tube moves.

6. Repeat steps 4 and 5 holding the ribbon at an angle greater than 45° but less than 90°. Again notice how the tube moves.

Results   When the ribbon is at a smaller angle, the tube does not roll and is instead dragged forward. When the ribbon is at a greater angle, the tube rolls backward.

Why?   Pulling on the ribbon at an angle results in a vertical force on the tube that tends to make it rotate backward and a horizontal force that tends to pull the tube forward. As the angle increases, the vertical force increases and the horizontal force decreases. Thus at the greater angle the tube tends to rotate backward, and at the smaller angle it is pulled forward.

179. Balancing Act

Purpose To determine why a heavy person and a lighter person can balance on a seesaw.

Materials 1 foot (30 cm) of ribbon ¼ inch (0.63 cm) wide (Thick cord will do.)
ruler with a hole in the center
transparent tape
3 spring-type clothespins

Procedure

1. Thread the ribbon through the hole in the ruler and tie the ends together to make a loop. The loop supports the ruler at its center, at the 6-inch (15-cm) mark.
2. Tape the knotted end of the loop to the edge of a table so the ruler hangs freely.
3. Clip a clothespin to the ruler at the 4-inch (10-cm) mark. Clip another clothespin at the 8-inch (20-cm) mark. The ruler should hang parallel with the floor. Reposition the clothespins if the ruler is not balanced.
4. Clip the remaining clothespin to the end of the first or second clothespin. Then move the single clothespin to a place on the ruler that causes the ruler to be balanced.

Results The ruler is balanced when two single clothespins are at equal distances from its center. The single clothespin balances the other two when it is placed twice the distance from the center of the ruler as the two joined clothespins.

Why? The point about which an object can rotate if supported there is called the **fulcrum**. The ruler's fulcrum is its center point where the ribbon supports it. The ruler balanced when the **torque** (turning effect of a force) on one side of the fulcrum equaled the torque on the other side. The torque on each side is determined by multiplying the weight of the clothespins times their distance from the fulcrum. It will be assumed that the clothespins have equal weights. The single clothespin had to be placed at twice the distance to balance the other two. Thus, a heavier person and a lighter one can balance on a seesaw if the lighter person is a greater distance from the seesaw's fulcrum—where it rotates.

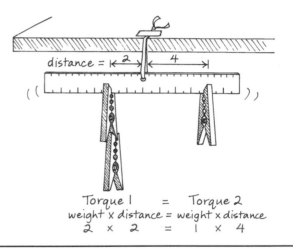

180. Equal Arms

Purpose To compare the mass of two objects.

Materials pencil
two 5-ounce (150-mL) paper cups
three 12-inch (30-cm) pipe cleaners
wire clothes hanger
transparent tape
walnut-size ball of modeling clay
12 or more pennies

Procedure

1. Use the pencil point to punch two holes beneath the rim and on opposite sides of one of the cups.
2. Wrap the center of one of the pipe cleaners around the clothes hanger near one end of the lower bar. Thread the ends of the pipe cleaner through the holes in the cup and twist them to secure them. The cup should hang level.
3. Repeat steps 1 and 2 attaching the second cup near the other end of the lower bar.
4. Bend the remaining pipe cleaner into a loop and tape the ends to the edge of a table.
5. Support the hanger on the loop and adjust the position of the cups so that they balance and the hanger's lower bar is parallel with the floor. The hook of the hanger may have to be adjusted to achieve this.
6. When the cups are balanced, secure the cups to the hanger with tape.

7. Place the clay ball in one of the cups. Then add pennies to the other cup until the hanger is again parallel with the floor.

Results The number of pennies needed to balance the clay ball will vary with the size of the ball. The author's clay ball balanced with eight pennies.

Why? The device in this experiment is called an **equal arm balance**, which is used to compare the mass of the contents of the cups on each side of the balance. The bigger the size of the ball, the greater the mass. When the balance is level, parallel with the floor, the mass of the contents of the cups is the same. Pennies are used to measure the mass of the clay ball. The author's ball is equal to the mass of eight pennies.

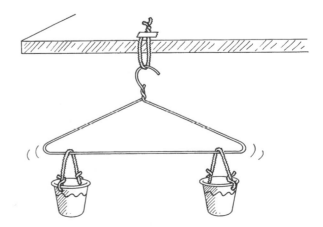

181. Stable

Purpose To determine how the center of gravity affects the stability of a building.

Materials masking tape
eight 9-ounce (270-mL) or larger paper cups
20 pennies

Procedure

1. Use tape to connect two of the cups together at their rims.
2. Place 10 coins in the third cup, and use tape to connect a fourth cup to the cup of coins at their rims. Set this combination of cups on top of the set made in step 1. Secure the cups with tape.
3. Repeat steps 1 and 2 with the remaining cups, but place the cup of coins on the bottom.
4. Place the cup structures side by side near the edge of a table.
5. Kneel next to the table so that your face is about 1 foot (0.3 m) from the cups.
6. Gently blow on the middle of one of the cup structures. If neither structure falls, blow harder.
7. Repeat step 6. Which structure is easier to blow over?

Results The structure with the coins lower to the table is harder to blow over.

Why? The lower the center of gravity of a structure, the more stable it is. This means that the closer the bulk of the weight of a structure is to the ground, the harder it is to make the structure fall. It took much more force to blow over the cups with the coins in the bottom than to blow over the cups with the coins in the center.

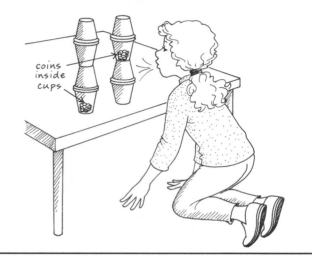

coins inside cups

---

182. Contact

Purpose To compare sliding and rolling friction.

Materials your hands

Procedure

1. Make a fist with one of your hands.
2. Rub your fist back and forth across the palm of your other hand several times (see Figure A). Observe any sound or heat felt by this motion.

(A)

3. Now roll your fist back and forth across your palm several times (see Figure B). What do you hear and feel?

Results You hear sound and feel heat when you rub your fist across your palm, but not when you roll your fist across it.

Why? Friction is a force that resists motion. It involves objects that are in contact with each other. Rubbing your fist back and forth across your palm is an example of slid-

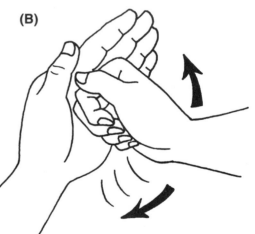

(B)

ing friction (friction produced when objects are sliding with respect to one another). **Work** is the product of the force needed to move an object times the distance the object moves. Work done by sliding is changed into thermal energy (energy that affects the temperature of an object). Thus, your skin feels warmer due to an increase of thermal energy. The jerking of the skin as your fist and palm slide past each other causes the skin to vibrate and strike air molecules, thus producing sound.

Rolling your fist across your palm is an example of **rolling friction** (friction produced when one object rolls over another). It takes more force to move one object across another by sliding than by rolling. Thus with the low rolling friction between your fist and palm, any thermal energy produced is not noticeable. Generally when the fist rolls there is not enough vibration of the skin to produce an audible sound.

183. **Bumpy**

Purpose To determine how surfaces affect friction.

Materials quarter or other coin
4-by-12-inch (10-by-30-cm) piece of cardboard
ruler
4-by-12-inch (10-by-30-cm) testing papers—
sandpaper and waxed paper
paper clip

Procedure

1. Place the coin at one end of the cardboard.
2. Hold the ruler upright at the coin end of the cardboard.
3. Raise the coin end of the cardboard until the coin slides to the bottom. Note the height to which the cardboard is raised.
4. Lay the first testing paper on the cardboard and secure it with the paper clip. Repeat steps 1 to 3 using the first testing paper over the cardboard.
5. Repeat steps 1–4 using the other testing paper.

Results The rougher the surface, the higher the cardboard must be held for the coin to slide to the bottom.

Why? Friction is a force that opposes the motion of two surfaces that are in contact with each other. No matter how smooth a surface may seem to the naked eye, it has some irregularities. The irregularities on surfaces that are rubbing against each other interlock and offer resistance to motion. In this experiment, the most friction was between the rough sandpaper and the coin and the least friction was between the smooth waxed paper and the coin. Thus it took more force to move the coin on the sandpaper, indicated by the need to raise the cardboard higher. As the cardboard was raised, the gravitational force pulling the coin down the cardboard increased.

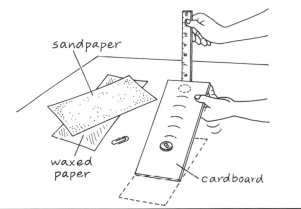

184. **Slider**

Purpose To demonstrate how friction stops a moving object.

Materials 2 feet (60 cm) of aluminum foil
pencil with sharpened point
transparent tape
2 feet (60 cm) of string

Procedure

1. Wad the aluminum foil into a ball about the size of a tennis ball.
2. Set the foil ball on a table and use the pencil to poke a hole straight through the center of the ball.
3. Wrap a small piece of tape around one end of the string to make it stiff. Then thread the stiff end of the string through the tunnel in the ball.
4. Position the ball in the center of the string. Hold the ends of the string in your hands. Pull the string taut and turn it so that it is vertical. Observe any motion of the ball. Turn the string from top to bottom and again observe any motion of the ball.
5. Take the string out of the ball. Use the pencil to poke another hole in the ball at an angle to the first hole. Hollow the hole enough so that you can pull the string through it, then thread the string through the L-shaped tunnel. Squeeze the ball around the string slightly to reduce the width of the tunnel. Pull the string back and forth through the ball several times to make sure the ball will move easily.
6. As before, position the ball in the center of the string, then hold the ends of the string in your hands and pull

it taut. Observe any motion of the ball. Relax the tension on the string, then pull hard on both ends. Again, observe any motion.

Results When the string is straight through the ball, the ball slides down the string without stopping. When the string follows an L-shaped path through the ball, the ball slides down the string but it can be stopped by pulling hard on the ends of the string.

Why? When the tunnel through the ball is straight, there is little friction between the string and the ball, so the ball slides easily down the string whether the string is relaxed or taut. When the string follows an L-shaped path through the ball and the string is pulled taut, there is more friction between the string and the ball. The string pushes against the sides of the tunnel in the bend of the L, acting like brakes to stop the motion of the ball. When the string is relaxed, there is less friction in the bend and the ball slides easily down the string.

185. No Rubbing

Purpose To determine how lubricants affect motion.

Materials two 4-inch (10-cm) squares of rough
              sandpaper
              craft stick
              petroleum jelly

Procedure

1. Place the rough sides of the sandpaper together.
2. Slide the two pieces of paper back and forth against each other. Observe how easy or difficult it is to move the sandpaper pieces.
3. Separate the sandpaper pieces and use the craft stick to spread a thick layer of petroleum jelly over the rough surface of one of the pieces.
4. Repeat steps 1 and 2.

Results It's hard to move the sandpaper pieces when their rough sides are rubbing against each other. The sandpaper pieces move more easily when one of them is covered with petroleum jelly.

Why? The ridges on the sandpaper catch against each other and stop motion. The surfaces of all materials have some rough spots. So when two surfaces are rubbed together, these rough areas catch and stop or slow motion. The petroleum jelly, like all **lubricants** (slippery substances that are placed between two moving surfaces to make them move more smoothly), fills the low places in surfaces it covers. When the petroleum jelly was sandwiched between the two sandpaper pieces, the jelly filled the low places in each piece. This smoothed out the rough spots on the sandpaper pieces, so there was less friction.

186. Stand Up

Purpose To produce a standing wave.

Materials 6 feet (1.8 m) of cord

Procedure

1. Tie one end of the cord to an object, such as the door handle of a refrigerator. You want the cord to be secure at one end, but with no restriction on the movement of the cord.
2. Holding the free end of the cord, walk away from the refrigerator until the cord is taut.
3. Facing the refrigerator, slowly move the cord back and forth from left to right to produce waves in the cord. Continue this motion at a constant rhythm six or more times so that a uniform number of waves are produced in the cord. Make note of the number of waves produced.
4. Move the cord faster and observe the number of waves produced.

Results The number of waves increases as the speed with which you move the cord back and forth increases.

Why? To make a wave, there must be a source of vibrations. Your hand movement vibrates the cord and produces waves. Each back-and-forth motion of your hand produces one wave. When the wave reaches the tied end of the cord, the wave is reflected back. If you continue to produce waves, there will be waves moving in both directions along the cord. Two series of waves are produced: one by vibrating the cord and the other by the reflection of waves from the tied end of the cord. If the cord is moved at the right speed, the waves combine forming a pattern such as the one shown. The cord appears to be vibrating in segments. A wave pattern produced when two identical waves traveling in opposite directions combine is called a **standing wave.** The points in a standing wave that are relatively stationary are called **nodes.** The points of maximum vibration are called **antinodes.**

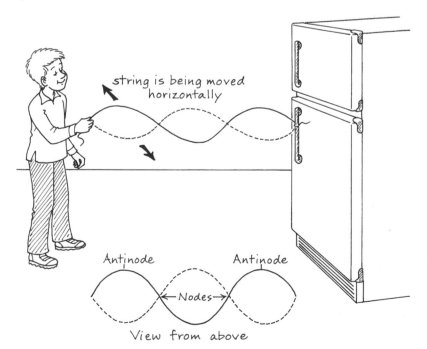

187. Twang

Purpose To determine how a string vibrates.

Materials about 36 inches (1 m) of white string
2 chairs with straight legs
ruler
marking pen
4 metal paper clips

Procedure

1. Tie one end of the string to a chair leg and the other end to the leg of a second chair. The string should be at least 6 inches above the floor.
2. Move the chairs apart so that the string is as taut as possible.
3. Use the pen to make a mark on the string about 6 inches (15 cm) from one end.
4. Clip the paper clips to the string so that they hang freely and are able to spin around the string.
5. Position the paper clips at the end opposite the mark and about 1 inch (2.5 cm) apart.
6. Pluck the string where it is marked and observe the motion of the paper clips. Repeat this step two or more times.
7. Move the paper clips to different places along the string. Then repeat step 6.

Results Some of the paper clips vibrate so much that they spin around the string. Some paper clips spin at greater speeds than others, and some vibrate a small amount and continue to hang without spinning.

Why? When the string is plucked, a standing wave with nodes and antinodes is produced in the string. The position of a paper clip in relation to the nodes and antinodes determines how much the paper clip vibrates. At the nodes, the paper clip vibrates the least and remains relatively stationary. At the peak of an antinode, it vibrates the most and spins around the string. The faster the string itself vibrates, the shorter the waves and the closer the nodes.

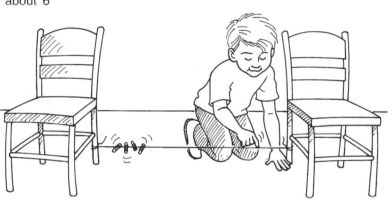

188. Bounce Back

Purpose To capture an echo.

Materials 2 empty paper towel tubes
watch that ticks
book
helper

Procedure

1. Lay the tubes on a table with their ends together and at about a 45° angle to each other.
2. Hold the watch in your hand at the end of one of the tubes and position one of your ears at the end of the other tube. Cover your other ear with your free hand. Make note of the loudness of the ticking of the watch.
3. Ask your helper to hold the book in front of the open ends of the tubes. Again make note of the loudness of the ticking of the watch.

Results When you first listened through the tubes, you could not hear the ticking of the watch. However, with the book at the end of the tubes, you did hear the ticking of the watch.

Why? Sound travels through air in waves. Sound from the watch travels through the tube. Without the book at the open end, the ticking sound exits the tube and spreads out in all directions. The loudness of sound depends on the energy of its waves—the more the energy, the louder. The more the sound is scattered, the less energy it has, so the more difficult it is to hear. With the book, some of the sound waves spread in all directions but a great deal of them are reflected off the book and some enter the tube leading to your ear. This sound is less spread out and thus has more energy, so it is louder. An **echo** is a reflected sound wave. In other words, like the ticking sound, an echo bounces back off a surface.

189. Louder

Purpose To determine how to make sound louder.

Materials metal fork
metal spoon
10-ounce (300-mL) plastic cup

Procedure

1. Firmly grasp the lower end of the fork's handle between the thumb and index finger of one hand and hold the fork in midair.
2. Strike the prongs of the fork three or more times with the outside bowl of the spoon. Make note of the sound produced.
3. Turn the cup upside down on a table.
4. Repeat steps 1 and 2 standing the handle end of the fork on the bottom of the upturned cup.

Results Standing the fork on the cup makes the sound louder.

Why? Generally, the larger the vibrating surface, the louder the sound. Because the cup is hollow, its sides can easily vibrate. When the vibrating fork is standing on the cup, the cup also vibrates, creating a louder sound. The cup in this activity acts like the **sounding board** (a part of a musical instrument that increases the loudness and quality of sound) of some musical instruments, such as a guitar. The sounding board of a guitar is its hollow part, which is usually made of thin wood that easily vibrates.

190. High or Low?

Purpose To determine how the thickness of the strings of a musical instrument affects the sound.

Materials 2 rubber bands of different thicknesses
empty cardboard box with the lid on (A greeting card box works well.)
pencil

Procedure

1. Close the box. Then stretch the rubber bands around the box.
2. Place the pencil under the rubber bands near one edge of the box as shown. This is your music box.
3. Pluck each rubber band and compare the sounds they produce.

NOTE: Keep the music box for the next experiment.

Results The thin rubber band produces a higher tone.

Why? The faster an object vibrates, the higher its **pitch** (the high or low quality of a sound). Generally, the smaller the vibrating surface, the faster the surface vibrates and the higher its pitch. The thinner the strings of musical instruments such as guitars, violins, and pianos, the higher the pitch of the sound they produce.

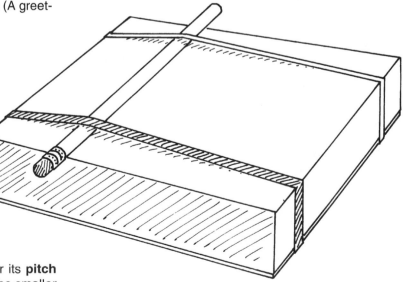

191. Shorter

Purpose To determine how the length of the strings of a musical instrument affects pitch.

Material   music box from Experiment 190, "High or Low?"

Procedure
1. While holding the music box in place with the fingers of one hand, pluck the thin rubber band several times with the thumb of the same hand. Pluck the rubber band at the end opposite the pencil. Note the pitch of the sound.
2. While plucking the thin rubber band, use your free hand to slowly move the pencil toward your plucking hand, noting any change in the pitch of the sound produced.
3. Repeat steps 1 and 2, plucking the thick rubber band.

Results As the pencil moves toward your hand, the pitch of the sound gets higher for both rubber bands.

Why? The pitch of a string on a musical instrument is affected by the length and tautness of the string. The shorter and more taut the string, the higher the pitch. Moving the pencil not only reduced the length of the vibrating section of the rubber band but also tightened the rubber band. So the pitch got higher as the pencil was moved.

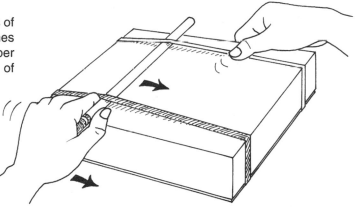

---

192. Spread Out

Purpose To determine the best shape for supporting weight.

Materials   2 large uncooked potatoes (Any object of comparable weight will work.)
plastic grocery bag with handles
yardstick (meterstick)

Procedure
1. Place the potatoes inside the plastic bag.
2. Slip the handles of the bag over one end of the measuring stick.
3. Hold the free end of the measuring stick in both hands with the numbered side facing up. (See Figure A.) Note the thickness of the stick.

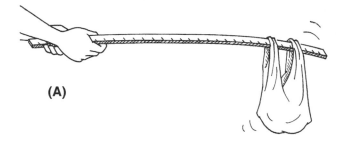

(A)

4. Lift the sack of potatoes. Observe any bending in the measuring stick.
5. Turn the measuring stick so that its narrow edge faces up (the numbered side will face sideways). (See Figure B.) Again note the thickness of the stick and any change in the bending of the stick.

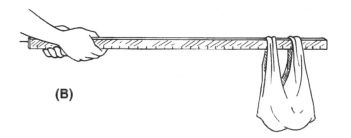

(B)

Results The stick is thicker when it is turned with its narrow edge facing up and bends less or not at all in this position.

Why? The weight of the potatoes creates tension and compression forces on the measuring stick. **Tension** is a pulling force that causes a separation of molecules, thus an increase in the length of an object. **Compression** is a pressing force that causes molecules to be pushed together, decreasing the volume of the object where compression is applied. The weight of the potatoes causes the measuring stick to bend, even if not noticeably, thus creating both tension and compression on the measuring stick. When the stick bends down, its top side is stretched due to tension, and the under side shortens due to compression. The thicker an object, the more tension required to cause it to stretch the same amount as when stretched by a thinner object of the same material. In this experiment, turning the measuring stick so that its narrow edge faces up increases the stick's thickness below the weight and makes it less likely to bend under the weight.

193. Flipper

Purpose To demonstrate Bernoulli's principle.

Material   penny

Procedure
1. Place the coin next to the edge of a table.
2. Squat down next to the table's edge so that your mouth is in line with the coin.
3. Pucker your lips and hold them as close to the coin as possible without touching it.
4. Blow as hard as possible across the top of the coin. If the coin does not lift and flip in the air, move your head slightly up or down. Then repeat this step. The air must move across the top of the coin.

Results The coin lifts and flips in the air.

Why? Before blowing across the coin, the air pressure above and below the coin is the same, thus the downward pressure of air on the top of the coin is equal to the upward pressure of air on the bottom of the coin. As air increases in speed, it exerts less pressure on the material that it flows across. This is known as **Bernoulli's principle.** The air moving across the top of the coin produces a low-pressure area above the coin as compared to the pressure of the air beneath the coin. This difference in pressure lifts the coin, and since the pressure on the upper surface is not the same over the entire surface, the coin tends to flip over.

194. Riser

Purpose To demonstrate buoyant force.

Materials   large bowl
tap water
9-inch (22.5-cm) round balloon

Procedure
1. Fill the bowl about half-full with water.
2. Partially inflate the balloon and tie it.
3. Try to push the balloon into the water.
4. Release the balloon and note any movement of the balloon.

Results It is difficult to push the balloon into the water, and when released, the balloon quickly moves out of the water and floats on the water's surface.

Why? The force required to push the balloon beneath the water is equal to the weight of the water displaced, which is equal to the **buoyant force** (upward force of a fluid on an object floating in it) on the submerged balloon.

When the balloon is released, this buoyant force pushes the balloon to the surface. Since the balloon's density is so much less than that of the water, the balloon floats on the water's surface.

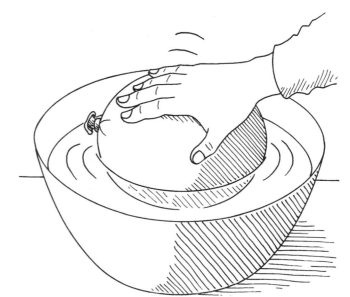

195. Pull Away

Purpose To test the adhesive strength of tape.

Materials sharpened pencil
9-ounce (270-mL) paper cup
12-inch (300-cm) pipe cleaner
transparent tape
plastic ruler with one flat side
one-hole paper punch
large paper clip
spoon
9 ounces (270 mL) sand or salt

Procedure

1. Use the pencil to make two holes beneath the rim on opposite sides of the cup.
2. Thread the ends of the pipe cleaner through the holes in the cup. Twist the ends to secure them in the holes.
3. Tape the ruler to the edge of a table so that about 2 inches (5 cm) of the ruler sticks out over the edge. The flat side of the ruler should be against the table.
4. Tear off about 3 inches (7.5 cm) of tape. Stick 1 inch (2.5 cm) of the tape on the underside of the ruler. Fold the excess tape over two times. Then use the paper punch to make a hole in the center of the folded tape.
5. Unbend the paper clip to make a hook. Slip the hook through the hole in the tape.
6. Slip the pipe cleaner handle of the cup onto the hook.
7. Use the spoon to add sand to the cup, one spoonful at a time. Continue adding sand until the tape just begins to pull away from the ruler.

Results The amount of sand needed will vary depending on several things, such as the tape used and how clean the ruler is.

Why? An **adhesive** is a substance used to stick surfaces together. The sticky side of tape is covered with an adhesive. The force of attraction between unlike molecules, such as the adhesive and the object it sticks to, is called **adhesion**. The greater the adhesion between the adhesive substance and the material it is stuck to, the more effort it takes to separate them. The weight of the sand in the cup pulls down on the tape, thus pulling the tape away from the ruler. The amount of sand needed to pull the tape off the ruler indicates the strength of the adhesion between the sticky (adhesive) side of the tape and the plastic.

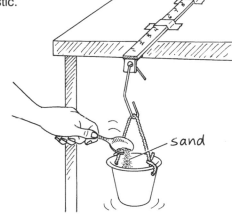

sand

---

196. Same Kind

Purpose To test the cohesion of water.

Materials 3-ounce (90-L) paper cup
tap water
ruler

Procedure

1. Fill the cup about half-full with water.
2. Dip the index finger of one hand in the water in the cup.
3. Press your wet index finger against the thumb of one hand.
4. Slowly separate your finger and thumb and observe how the water stretches between them. Measure how far apart your fingers are when the water breaks. Repeat this step several times.

Results The distance varies but it averages about ¼ inch (0.63 cm).

Why? The tiny molecules that make up water are attracted to each other, so they stick together. The force of attraction between molecules of the same kind within an object that cause them to stick together is called **cohesion**.

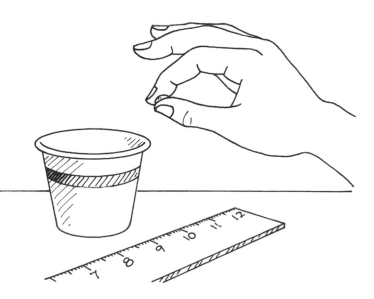

197. Thin Skin

Purpose To demonstrate the surface tension of water.

Materials cereal bowl
tap water
2 small paper clips
scissors
paper towel
pencil

Procedure
1. Fill the bowl with water.
2. Hold one of the paper clips vertically above the water's surface, then drop it. Observe the movement of the paper clip
3. Cut a rectangle from the paper towel, slightly larger than the other paper clip.
4. Carefully lay the paper rectangle on the surface of the water.
5. Quickly and gently lay the paper clip on the paper.
6. With the pencil, push down slightly on the edges of the paper until the paper sinks.

Results The paper clip that is dropped into the water sinks and remains on the bottom of the bowl. When you push down on the paper, it gets wet and sinks, but the paper clip laid on the paper continues to float on the water's surface.

Why? Dropping the paper clip into the water shows that paper clips are not buoyant, which means they are not naturally able to float. A paper clip can be made to float on water not because of buoyancy but because of the surface tension of water. **Surface tension** is the result of the cohesion of molecules on the surface of a liquid, which causes the surface to act as if it is covered with a thin skin. The paper was used to position the paper clip on the water's surface. In time the paper would have absorbed water and sunk on its own. Pushing it underwater with the pencil speeded up this process. The paper clip is spread out enough that it doesn't break through the water's surface tension, so it floats on the surface. Some insects can walk on water because of surface tension. Dropping the paper clip broke the surface tension, and the paper clip sank.

198. Surface Film

Purpose To compare the surface tension of water to that of alcohol.

Materials 1-tablespoon (15-mL) measuring spoon
tap water
plate
red, blue, or green food coloring
spoon
rubbing alcohol

Procedure
1. Pour water into the plate, covering its surface with the thinnest possible layer of water.
2. Add 2 drops of food coloring to the water and stir.
3. Pour 1 tablespoon (15 mL) of alcohol in the center of the colored water.

CAUTION: Keep alcohol away from your eyes, nose, and mouth because it can damage these tissues.

Results The colored water moves away from the alcohol, and the edge of the water touching the alcohol trembles.

Why? The attraction between like molecules, such as water to water and alcohol to alcohol, is called cohesion. The attraction between unlike molecules, such as between water and alcohol, is called adhesion. The cohesion of water molecules is greater than the cohesion of alcohol molecules. The cohesion of water is also greater than the adhesive force between the two liquids. The competition between the cohesive and adhesive forces results in a type of tug-of-war between the water and alcohol molecules, causing the pulling away of water from alcohol and a trembling motion where the two liquids meet.

199. Wetter

Purpose To determine why raincoats do not get wet.

Materials craft stick
petroleum jelly
sheet of copy paper
3-ounce (90-mL) paper cup
tap water

Procedure

1. Use the craft stick to rub a thin layer of petroleum jelly over the surface of about one-fourth of the paper.
2. Fill the paper cup about half-full with water.
3. Dip your index finger into the water in the cup. Hold your finger over the petroleum-covered surface of the paper and allow a drop of water to fall onto the paper. Then observe the shape of the water drop on the paper.
4. Repeat step 3 dropping water on an area of the paper not covered by petroleum jelly.
5. Compare the shape of the water drops produced in steps 3 and 4.
6. Repeat steps 3 to 5 four or more times.

Results The water drops appear smaller and more spherical on the petroleum jelly–covered paper.

Why? The greater the adhesion between water and the surface it is on, the more the water spreads out and wets the surface. There is less adhesion between the molecules in water and those in petroleum jelly, so the molecules do not spread out and wet the petroleum jelly. Raincoats are treated with a substance that, like petroleum jelly, doesn't get wet. There is little adhesion between water and the materials in rainwear. These materials, like the petroleum jelly–covered paper, are said to be water resistant.

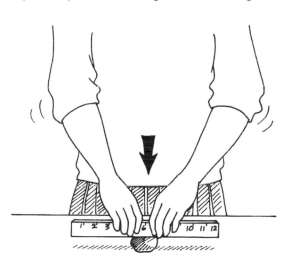

200. Spread

Purpose To demonstrate the effect of pressure.

Materials Walnut-size piece of modeling clay
ruler

Procedure

1. Shape the clay into a ball.
2. Lay the ruler face up on top of the clay.
3. Firmly push down on the ruler, then lift the ruler and observe the shape of the clay ball.

4. Repeat steps 1 to 3 turning the ruler on edge.

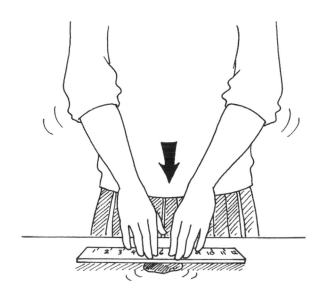

Results The clay ball is flattened when the wider surface of the ruler is against the clay. But the edge of the ruler cuts the clay in half.

Why? Pressure is a force spread over an area. When the same force is spread over a larger area, the pressure is not as great as when it is spread over a smaller area. In this experiment, the pressure spread over the larger surface of the ruler flattened the clay ball but was not great enough to cut it. Sharp objects, such as scissors or a knife, cut through things because the surfaces of their cutting edges are very thin. More of the force is concentrated in a smaller area, so these surfaces push against a material with more pressure.

201. Speedy

Purpose   To demonstrate the method used by early sailors to determine the speed of ships.

Materials   scissors
yardstick (meterstick)
11-foot (3.3-m) cord
pencil
stopwatch
helper

Procedure

1. Cut 9 feet (2.7 m) of cord and tie a knot in each end.
2. Cut eight 3-inch (7.5-cm) pieces of cord.
3. Tie one short piece of cord at each 12-inch (30-cm) interval along the long piece of cord.

NOTE: Tie the short pieces tight enough so they do not slide along the string.

4. Wind the long piece of cord around the center of the pencil.
5. Hold the pencil in both hands and position the wound cord loosely between the thumb and index finger of one hand.
6. Ask your helper to hold the free end of the cord and start the stopwatch.
7. When your helper says, "Go," slowly walk away backward from your helper, allowing the cord to unwind and counting the knots on the cord as they pass between your thumb and index finger.
8. Stop when your helper informs you that 2 seconds have passed.
9. Rewind the cord onto the pencil and repeat steps 5 to 8, but this time walk as fast as you can.

10. Compare the amount of cord unwound each time.

Results   The number of knots passing through your fingers is fewer when you walk slow than when you walk fast.

Why?   In this experiment, counting the knots as you moved at different speeds is similar to the method that sailors in the past used to determine the speed of ships. Knots were tied at regular intervals along the rope, and a log was tied to one end of the rope. When the rope was thrown overboard, the floating log and rope trailed behind the moving ship. A sailor counted the number of knots that passed through his hands in a given time. As with the number of knots that passed through your hands as you walked faster, the more knots that passed through the sailor's hands, the greater the speed of the ship. Sailors used the word *knot* to measure the speed of the ship. The word is still used today. A **knot** is 1 nautical mile per hour. A **nautical mile** equals 6,076 feet (1,823 m).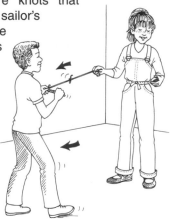

202. Stop!

Purpose   To demonstrate Newton's first law of motion.

Materials   marker
2 eggs about the same size—one raw and one hard-boiled (Have an adult boil the egg in water for about 4 minutes, then allow the egg to cool)
helper

CAUTION: After handling raw eggs, wash your hands and any materials touched by the eggs. Raw eggs can contain harmful bacteria. Discard eggs after completing the experiment.

Procedure

1. Use the marker to label the raw egg "Raw" and the boiled egg "Boiled."
2. Place one of the eggs on a table. Ask your helper to place the second egg on the table.
3. Instruct your helper to start spinning his or her egg when you've counted to three. At the same time, spin your own egg. Observe the motion of the eggs until they stop spinning.
4. Repeat step 3 stopping the eggs from spinning after a few spins by touching them with your hands. Then quickly release the eggs and observe any motion.

Results   The raw egg wobbles and stops spinning more quickly than does the boiled egg. The raw egg will start spinning again after it has been stopped.

Why?   Newton's first law of motion states that an object in motion will continue to move or continue to be at rest unless some force stops or starts it. The eggs continue to spin after they have been released because they have inertia. Friction between the egg and the table causes the eggs to stop spinning. The raw egg has liquid inside the shell but the hard-boiled egg has a solid inside. The shell and liquid of the raw egg do not move together as do the shell and solid of the hard-boiled egg. The liquid inside sloshes around, causing the egg to wobble. When the eggs are stopped by touching them, the motion of the shell and the solid inside the boiled egg is stopped. But the raw egg starts to spin again because even though the shell is stopped, the liquid inside continues to spin, and this motion starts the shell spinning again.

203. Constant

Purpose To demonstrate Newton's second law of motion.

Materials book 1 inch (2.5 cm) or more thick
ruler with a groove down its center
scissors
5-ounce (150-mL) paper cup
2 equal-size marbles

Procedure

1. Place the book on a flat surface, such as a table or the floor.
2. Raise one end of the ruler and rest it on the edge of the book.
3. Cut a 1-inch (2.5-cm) square out of the side of the paper cup near the bottom.
4. Stand the paper cup at the low end of the ruler so that ½ inch (1.25 cm) of the ruler extends inside the cup through the cut-out section.
5. Place a marble in the ruler's groove at its elevated end.
6. Release the marble and observe how far the cup moves when the marble strikes its back side.
7. Repeat steps 4 to 6 placing the two marbles one behind the other.

Results The cup moves farther when struck by two marbles than when struck by one marble.

Why? **Newton's second law of motion** states that an object acted on by a constant force will move with a constant acceleration. The set of two marbles has twice as much mass as the single marble. Both the single and the pair of marbles roll down the incline because of gravity, and thus they have the same acceleration. The force of gravity acting on the marbles is equal to the weight of the marbles, so the force on the two marbles is twice that on the single marble. Since it takes twice as much force to move the two marbles at the same acceleration as the single marble, it takes twice as much force to **decelerate** (decrease the speed of) them until they have stopped. The cup was pushing against the marbles with the same force, so to stop the two marbles it had to push for a longer time. During this time the cup was pushed farther away from the ruler and more frictional force from the flat surface helped to stop their motion.

---

204. Hero's Engine

Purpose To demonstrate Newton's third law of motion.

Materials scissors
ruler
2 flexible drinking straws
pencil
10-ounce (300-mL) paper cup
petroleum jelly
24-inch (60-cm) piece of string
16-ounce (480-mL) plastic cup (A small pitcher will do)
tap water

Procedure

1. Cut two 2-inch (5-cm) sections from each straw with the flexible part of the straw in the center of each section.
2. Use the pencil to make two holes with a diameter a little smaller than the diameter of the straw sections on opposite sides near the bottom of the small cup.
3. Insert one end of a straw section in each hole leaving the flexible part on the outside of the cup. Make an effort not to make the hole any bigger than the straw. Put petroleum jelly around the straw on the inside of the cup to form a seal.
4. Use the pencil to make two small holes on opposite sides below the rim of the small cup.

5. Thread one end of the string through both holes and tie the string so the cup hangs from a long straight string.
6. Bend the flexible part of the straw sections so that they point in the same clockwise direction.
7. Fill the large cup with water.
8. In an outdoor area, hold the small cup by the string and fill it with water from the large cup. Continue to pour water into the cup as you observe the motion of the cup in relation to the direction the straw sections are pointing.

Results The cup spins in a counterclockwise direction, opposite the direction the straw sections are pointing.

Why? **Newton's third law of motion** states that for every action there is an equal reaction in the opposite direction. The spinning cup is an example of this law. The water in the cup is forced out of the straws in the cup due to the pull of gravity. This is the action. The reaction is the movement of the cup in the opposite direction.

Gravity is the force that pulls things toward the center of Earth. The water in the cup is being pulled down and out the straws. The rotating cup was originally called Hero's engine after its inventor, Hero of Alexandria (c. A.D. 60).

Glossary

abscission layer A layer of cells holding the petiole of a leaf to the stem.

absorb (1) To take in. (2) To soak up.

abyss The great depths of the ocean floor, generally with an average depth of 15,000 feet (4,500 m).

abyssal plain The flat surface of the abyss.

acceleration The rate of increase of speed.

acid A substance that reacts with baking soda to produce carbon dioxide gas.

activate To cause to function.

adhesion The force of attraction between unlike molecules, such as an adhesive and the object it sticks to.

adhesive A substance used to stick surfaces together.

air pressure Force caused by the impact of moving air molecules on an area of Earth or objects on Earth. Also called **atmospheric pressure** or **barometric pressure.**

altitude The angular distance of the Sun or other celestial body above the horizon.

angiosperm A plant whose flowers produce seeds.

angular diameter Angle of an apparent diameter expressed in degrees.

annually Each year.

Antarctic Circle Latitude 66.5°S.

Antarctic region The region of Earth south of the Antarctic Circle.

antinode A point of maximum vibration in a standing wave.

apparent diameter How large an object's diameter appears to be at a given distance.

apparent size How large an object appears to be at a given distance.

apparent weight The weight an object appears to be, which may be more than, less than, or equal to the object's true weight depending on the direction of the forces acting on the object.

arc A segment of a circle

Arctic Circle Latitude 66.5°N.

Arctic region The region of Earth north of the Arctic Circle.

artificial satellite A man-made object that is launched into orbit around Earth.

asteroid A relatively small, irregular, rocky chunk of matter that orbits the Sun; also called a **minor planet.**

astronomer A scientist who studies the Sun and other celestial bodies.

atmosphere The gaseous area that surrounds the Sun, Earth, and some other celestial bodies.

atmospheric pressure See **air pressure.**

atom A building block of matter.

autumnal equinox The first day of autumn, on or about September 23 in the Northern Hemisphere.

axis (plural **axes**) (1) An imaginary line through the center of an object about which the object rotates. (2) A line about which a three-dimensional object is symmetrical.

bacterium (plural **bacteria**) Microscopic one-celled organisms.

ballast tanks Tanks in a submersible that change the density of the submersible and so allow the submersible to rise or sink.

barometer An instrument used to measure air pressure.

barometric pressure See **air pressure.**

barycenter The point about which binary bodies revolve.

beach A shore with a smooth stretch of sand and/or pebbles.

Bernoulli's principle A natural law stating that faster-moving fluids, such as air, exert less pressure than slower-moving fluids.

bilateral symmetry A design with one line of symmetry.

binary bodies Two celestial bodies held together by their mutual gravity.

blade The main part of a broad leaf.

blood A liquid that circulates in blood vessels, transporting oxygen to cells and removing waste.

blood clot A solid mass made of fibrin and blood that plugs a hole in the skin, preventing blood from passing through.

blood vessels Pathways in the body through which blood flows.

bond To link together, as atoms of a molecule or monomers of a polymer; the link between atoms.

broad leaf A leaf that is broad and basically flat and that is found on broadleaf plants.

broadleaf plants Plants with broad leaves.

bromelin An enzyme in fresh pineapples that digests gelatin.

buoyant force The upward force of a fluid on an object floating in it that is equal to the weight of the fluid displaced by the object.

caldera A large, roughly circular crater with steep walls that forms when the top of a volcano collapses.

calendar A system for showing the length and divisions of a year.

canine teeth The pointy, fang-shaped teeth of some animals that are used for tearing food. In dogs, the canine teeth lock together.

Cassini's division Dark spaces between Saturn's rings.

catalyst A chemical that changes the speed of a chemical reaction without being changed itself.

celestial bodies Natural objects in the sky, such as stars, suns, moons, and planets.

cells The building blocks of organisms.

cement To glue together.

center of gravity The point at which the weight of a body seems to be concentrated. Same point as the **center of mass.**

center of mass The point at which the mass of a body seems to be concentrated. Same point as the **center of gravity.**

chemical change See **chemical reaction.**

chemical reaction The process by which one or more new chemicals are formed; also called a **chemical change.**

chemistry The study of the composition, structure, properties, and interactions of matter.

chitin The hard but flexible material that an insect's exoskeleton is made of.

chlorophyll A green pigment that enables plants to use solar energy to make food.

chromatography A method of separating a mixture into its different substances.

circulatory system A group of body parts that carry materials to and from cells.

cloud A group of water particles that scatter light and float in the air.

cohesion The force of attraction between like molecules within an object that holds them together.

colorant Pigment.

combination chemical reaction When two or more molecules combine to form one or more different molecules.

compaction The process by which particles are pressed together.

composites Plants with flowers that look like a single flower but are actually a cluster of many separate flowers.

compress To press tightly together.

compression A pressing force that causes molecules to be pushed together, decreasing the volume of an object.

concave Curved inward.

concentrated (1) Gathered closely together. (2) Drawn toward a common center.

concentration The amount of one substance in another substance, such as the amount of a dissolved solute in a solution.

concentric Having the same center point.

condensation The process of a vapor or gas changing into a liquid.

condense To change from a gas to a liquid.

cones Light-sensitive cells on the retina that send color visual messages to the brain.

conserve Not to waste.

constellation A group of stars that appear to make a pattern in the sky.

continent One of the seven major landmasses of the Earth: North America, South America, Africa, Australia, Antarctica, Europe, and Asia.

continental shelf The area of ocean floor starting at the shoreline and ending at the continental slope.

continental slope The steep slanted area between the continental shelf and the abyss.

contour lines Lines on a topographic map that connect points of the same elevation.

contracts Draws together.

convection zone The area above the radiation zone of the Sun made of circulating gas rising from the radiation zone.

converge To come together.

convert To change.

convex Curved outward.

core The center and hottest part of the Sun.

Coriolis effect The deflection of wind and ocean currents as a result of Earth's rotation.

crescent moon The phase of the Moon when the lighted area of the Moon resembles a ring segment with pointed ends.

crest The high point of a wave.

crust The outer layer of Earth.

crystal A solid made up of atoms arranged in an orderly, regular pattern of flat faces.

cuticle The dead skin around the base and sides of a fingernail.

daylight saving time (DST) The time from late spring to early autumn when clocks are set forward 1 hour so that there are more usable hours of daylight in the evening.

deactivate To cause something not to function.

decelerate To decrease the speed.

deciduous A plant that loses its leaves annually.

decompose To break apart into basic substances.

decomposition reaction A chemical reaction in which a substance decomposes.

deflect To turn aside from a straight path.

deliquescent Being a hygroscopic material that absorbs so much water that it dissolves and passes into a solution.

denaturing The process by which a protein changes from its natural form.

density The mass of a substance divided by its volume.

density current Ocean currents created by differences in water density.

deposition A buildup of sediments.

diffuse To spread freely and scatter.

digest To change food into smaller parts that the body can use.

digestive system A group of body parts that digests food.

dilute To lessen the concentration of a solute by mixing more solvent, usually water, into the solution.

direct rotation Clockwise rotation that is arbitrarily determined to be normal.

disk (1) The center of the head of a composite flower made up of disk flowers. (2) A pad between the vertebrae of the backbone that keeps the vertebrae from rubbing against each other.

disk flowers Tube-shaped flowers in the head of a composite flower.

displace To push out of place.

dissolve To break into small particles and mix thoroughly with a liquid.

distribute To spread out.

dormant Alive but not growing as a seed in winter.

dough A mixture of flour and a liquid.

duodenum The upper part of the small intestine closest to the stomach.

ear canal A passage from the outer ear to the eardrum.

eardrum A thin, tight skin stretched inside the ear that vibrates when sound hits it.

earthquake A violent shaking of the Earth caused by a sudden movement of rock beneath its surface.

Eastern Hemisphere The half of Earth east of the prime meridian between longitude 0° and 180°.

echo A sound that is heard again when it bounces back off a surface.

eclipse The passing of one body in front of another, cutting off its light.

ecliptic The apparent yearly path of the Sun across the celestial sphere.

efflorescence The loss of water from a hydrate.

eject To throw out.

elevation The height something is raised; often compared to sea level which has an elevation of zero.

elongation The angle between the Sun and any planet as viewed from Earth.

embryo The undeveloped organism.

emulsifier A substance that prevents an emulsion from separating.

emulsion A mixture of two or more liquids that do not dissolve in each other, such as oil and water.

energy The ability to cause things to move.

entire margin A smooth, unbroken leaf margin.

enzyme A catalyst found in living organisms.

equal arm balance A device that compares the weight of objects.

equator   An imaginary line at 0° latitude that divides Earth into the Northern and Southern Hemispheres, and the only parallel that is a great circle.

erosion   The movement of sediments by gravity, wind, water, or ice.

erupt   To throw forth, such as magma from a volcano.

evaporate   To change from a liquid to a gas.

evaporation   The process of a liquid changing into a gas.

evergreen   A plant that retains some or all of its leaves throughout the year, growing new leaves before the old ones fall off.

exoskeleton   The jointed outer covering of bodies of adult insects that is made of chitin and provides support and protection.

expand   To move farther apart.

eye   The relatively calm center of a hurricane.

eyepiece   The lens of a telescope that the user looks through.

faces   The flat sides of crystals.

fade   To get lighter in color.

fault   Movement along either side of a fracture in rock layers.

fault plane   The fracture line of a fault.

fermentation   A chemical reaction involving the breakdown of glucose.

fertilization   The joining of special male and female parts to produce seeds in plants.

fibrin   A threadlike fiber in blood clots.

fibrous root system   A root system consisting of a mass of many roots growing from a small central root.

fluctuates   Changes continuously.

fluid   A gas or a liquid.

focal length   The distance from a lens to the focal point.

focal point   The point where light rays passing through a lens converge.

footwall   The side of a fault below the fault plane.

force   A push or pull on things.

fracture   A break in rock layers.

free-fall   To fall with gravity as the only force acting.

freeze   To change a liquid to a solid.

freezing point   The temperature at which a liquid freezes.

frequency   The number of vibrations of a material in a specific time period.

friction   A force that tends to stop the motion of objects that are moving against each other.

fulcrum   The point about which an object can rotate if supported there.

Galilean satellites   The four largest moons of Jupiter: Io, Europa, Ganymede, and Callisto.

gelatin   A gummy protein obtained from animal tissues that is used in making jellylike desserts.

germination   The process by which a seed's embryo starts to grow.

glacier   A large mass of ice and snow that moves very slowly down a mountain or across land.

globular protein   A protein made up of compact, rounded, coiled chains of chemicals and found in egg white.

glucose   A type of sugar.

gluten   A tough, elastic protein in dough.

gravity   (1) The force of attraction that draws objects on or near the surface of a celestial body toward the center of the celestial body. (2) The force of attraction between two bodies.

great circle   A circle that has the same center point as the sphere it surrounds.

Gregorian calendar   A calendar system of 365 days plus a leap year every four years.

groundwater   Water, such as rainfall, that sinks into the ground.

guyot   A flat-topped seamount.

hanging wall   The side of a fault above the fault plane.

hard palate   The front part of the roof of your mouth.

hard water   Water that is rich in the minerals calcium, magnesium, and/or iron.

head   The flower cluster as a whole making up a composite flower.

heat   Energy that is transferred from a warm body to a cooler body, such as infrared radiation, because of the difference in termperature.

helioseismology   The study of the interior of the Sun by observing how its surface vibrates.

heterogeneous mixture   A mixture that is not the same throughout.

homogeneous mixture   A mixture, such as a solution, that is the same throughout.

horizon   An imaginary line where the sky and Earth appear to meet.

humus   An organic substance in soil made up of decayed animal and plant matter.

hurricane   A storm with winds of 74 miles (118 km) per hour or more rotating around a calm eye.

hydrate   A crystalline substance that contains water.

hygroscopic   Absorbing water vapor from the air.

iceberg   Piece of a glacier that breaks off at the shoreline and falls into the ocean.

igneous rock   Rock produced by the cooling and solidifying of molten rock.

illuminate   To light up.

image   The likeness of an object formed by a lens or mirror.

incisors   Front teeth in the upper and lower jaws of people, dogs, and other animals that are relatively flat and have sharp edges used to cut food.

inertia   The tendency of an object at rest to remain at rest, and an object in motion to remain in motion, unless acted on by an outside force.

inferior planet   A planet whose orbit lies between Earth and the Sun.

infrared radiation   Heat transferred by radiation; also called **radiant energy.**

insulator   A material that does not easily transfer heat.

intrusive igneous rock   A large-grained igneous rock formed beneath the Earth's surface when magma cools slowly.

irregular flower   A flower whose petals have bilateral symmetry.

island   A seamount that extends above the ocean's surface.

keratin   A tough protein that makes up hair, nails, and the outer layers of skin.

kinetic energy   Energy of moving objects.

knot   A unit of speed equal to 1 nautical mile per hour.

laterally reversed   Reversed from left to right.

latitude   Distance in degrees north or south of the equator.

law of conservation of matter   A natural law which states that in a chemical reaction, matter is neither created nor destroyed but remains the same.

leaf   The main food-producing part of a plant.

leaf margin   The edge of a broad leaf.

leap year   A year of 366 days occuring every fourth year in the Gregorian calendar.

leavening agent   A substance that produces gases in baked dough and some other foods.

lens A clear material, often glass, that changes the direction of light passing through it.

linear Having the characteristics of a straight line.

line of symmetry A line that divides a figure into two identical parts that match if folded along the line.

lines of latitude See **parallels.**

lines of longitude See **meridians.**

lobed margin A leaf margin with an extension that sometimes looks like an earlobe.

longitude Distance in degrees east or west of the prime meridian.

lubricant A slippery substance that is placed between two moving surfaces to make them move more smoothly.

luminous Giving off light.

lunar calendar A calendar based on a lunar month.

lunar month The time it takes the Earth's Moon to pass through its phases—29½ days.

lunula The whitish, half-moon-shaped area at the base of fingernails.

magma Molten rock under the Earth's surface.

magma chamber A pool of magma deep within the Earth.

mammals Animals that have hair and feed their young on milk.

mass The amount of matter in a material.

mass ratio As used in this book, it is a number indicating how many times as massive an object is as compared to another object, such as how many times as massive as Earth a planet is.

materials Physical things that you can touch, taste, feel, see, or smell.

matter Anything that has mass and takes up space.

melanin A pigment that causes skin to darken, especially when the skin is exposed to sunlight.

melt To change in phase of matter from a solid to a liquid.

melting point The temperature at which a substance melts.

meridians Imaginary lines from the North Pole to the South Pole; also called **lines of longitude.**

metamorphic rock Rock that forms from other types of rock due to pressure and heat.

metamorphism The process of changing from one form to another, such as the changing of one rock type to another.

microorganisms Microscopic organisms.

mineral A solid substance that was never an animal or a plant and that was formed in the earth by nature.

minor planet See **asteriod.**

mirror image A laterally reversed image.

mixture A combination of two or more substances that retain their physical characteristics.

molecule A particle made up of two or more atoms bonded together.

molt In an insect, to shed the exoskeleton and grow a new one.

molten Liquid.

monomer A single molecule in a polymer.

mucus A thick, slimy liquid that coats and protects the inside of the nose and other body parts.

mud A thick mixture of soil and water.

mudflow Fast-moving mud.

nail bed The pink, fleshy area beneath the nail that provides a smooth surface for the growing nail to glide across.

natural satellite A celestial body revolving around another body, such as a moon around a planet.

nautical mile A unit of distance equal to 6,076 feet (1,823 m).

near point The distance of distinct vision.

needle leaf A narrow, needlelike leaf; commonly called a **needle.**

needles See **needle leaf.**

nerves Fibers that carry messages to and from the brain.

Newton's first law of motion A natural law that describes inertia.

Newton's second law of motion A natural law that states that an object acted on by a constant force will move with a constant acceleration.

Newton's third law of motion A natural law that states that if one object pushes on another (action), the second object pushes back with an equal force but in the opposite direction (reaction).

night vision The ability to see in dim light.

node A point on a standing wave that is relatively stationary.

non-Newtonian fluid A fluid that acts like a solid when pressure is applied, which is different from the way that Sir Isaac Newton described the behavior of fluids.

normal fault Vertical movement of areas along a fault plane in which the footwall moves up and the hanging wall moves down.

Northern Hemisphere The region between the equator and the North Pole of Earth or another celestial body.

north pole The end of a planet's axis on the same side of its orbital plane as the Sun's northern hemisphere.

North Pole The north end of Earth's axis, at latitude 90°N.

nuclear fusion The joining of the nuclei of atoms.

nucleus (plural **nuclei**) The positively charged central part of an atom.

nutrients Substances needed for the life and growth of organisms.

objective lens The lens of a telescope that is pointed toward an object and gathers the light from that object.

ocean current A large stream of ocean water that moves continuously in the same direction.

odor The property of a substance that activates smell dectors in the nose.

ooze deposits Sediments on the abyss consisting of dust particles from space, volcanic ash, dust blown seaward by winds, and particles of dead organisms that have drifted down from the upper levels of water.

opaque Not allowing light to pass through.

opposable Capable of being positioned opposite something, as an opposable thumb can be positioned opposite the fingers.

optical illusion Something that appears to be different from what is really there.

optic nerve The main nerve connecting the eye to the brain.

orbit The curved path of one celestial body about another.

organisms Living things, such as plants and animals.

oxidation A chemical reaction in which oxygen combines with other materials.

oxygen A gas in the air that combines with other chemicals to produce a new molecule.

Pangaea The name given to the large, single landmass believed to have existed before it broke apart into separate landmasses.

Panthalassa The name given to the large, single ocean believed to have existed before Pangaea broke.

parallax An apparent change in the position of an object when viewed from two different points.

parallels Imaginary parallel lines circling Earth perpendicular to the meridians; also called **lines of latitude.**

penumbra The outer, lighter part of a shadow.

percolation The passing or seeping of groundwater or any liquid through a permeable material.

perimeter   The measurement of a boundary.

period of revolution   The time it takes an object such as a celestial body to make one revolution about another.

period of rotation   The time it takes an object to make one turn on its axis.

permeability   A measure of how easily water flows through a material.

persistence of vision   The tendency of an image of an object to remain on the retina after the object has moved or is removed.

petiole   A stalklike structure that attaches a leaf blade to a stem and serves as a passageway for the transport of water and nutrients.

phases of matter   Solid, liquid, and gas.

phases of the Moon   The changes in the shape of the sunlit surface of the Moon facing Earth.

pheromones   Scented chemicals produced by organisms, which are used in communication between members of the same species.

phloem tubes   Tubelike structures in some plants that transport nutrients made in the leaves throughout the plant.

photometer   An instrument that measures the brightness of light.

photosphere   The layer of the Sun above the convection zone and the first layer of the Sun's atmosphere.

physical properties   Characteristics of a material such as how it looks, feels, or tastes, its size, and its phase of matter.

pigment   Any substance that gives color to a material.

pitch   The high or low quality of a sound.

plane mirror   A mirror with a flat surface.

planet   A celestial body that orbits a sun and shines only by the light it reflects.

Polaris   The North Star.

pollination   A process of plant fertilization.

pollutants   Substances that destroy the purity of air, water, or land.

polymer   A very long chainlike molecule.

porphyritic rock   A fine-grained igneous rock formed beneath the Earth's surface when magma cools rapidly.

potential energy   Energy of an object at rest that could cause the object to move.

precipitation   Liquid or solid particles that form in the atmosphere and then fall to the Earth's surface.

pressure   Force spread over an area.

primates   A category of mammals including people, monkeys, apes, and chimpanzees in which most have opposable thumbs.

prime meridian   The meridian at 0° longitude running through Greenwich, England, that divides the Earth into Eastern and Western Hemispheres.

proboscis   A sucking mouthpart of some animals.

product   A final material produced in a chemical reaction.

propagate   To produce a new organism.

proteins   Large molecules necessary for life and growth.

radial symmetry   A design in which the parts branch out from the center in all directions and if folded across the middle from any direction, each fold forms a line of symmetry.

radiant energy   Energy that can travel through space.

radiant heat   See **infrared radiation.**

radiation   Radiant energy as well as the transmission of radiant energy.

radiation zone   The area above the core of the Sun through which energy from the core is transmitted.

ray flowers   Flowers that radiate from the center of the head of a composite flower.

reactant   A starting material in a chemical reaction.

real image   An image that can be projected onto a screen.

reflect   To bounce back, as light off a surface.

refracting telescope   An instrument that uses only lenses to make distant objects appear closer.

refrigerant   A cooling substance used in refrigeration.

regular flower   A flower whose petals have radial symmetry.

resonance   When an outside force causes an object to vibrate at its own natural frequency; also called **sympathetic vibration.**

retina   The light-sensitive layer on the back of the inside of the eyeball where light is received.

retrograde   Clockwise, which is backward motion.

revolve   To move about a central point, as planets about the Sun or celestial bodies about their barycenter.

rods   Light-sensitive cells on the retina that respond to dim light and send black-and-white visual messages to the brain.

rolling friction   Friction produced when one object rolls over another.

root   (1) The part of a plant that grows into the ground to anchor the plant. (2) The part of a nail beneath the lunula where growth takes place.

rootlet   One of the small hairlike roots that branch from a taproot.

rotate   To turn about an axis.

runoff   The part of precipitation that washes from the land into bodies of water.

rusting   A chemical reaction in which a material (usually iron) combines with oxygen in the air.

saliva   A watery liquid in the mouth that helps digest food.

satellite   See **artificial satellite, Galilean satellites,** and **natural satellite.**

scab   A hardened blood clot covering a cut in the skin.

scale model   A replica made in proportion to the object it represents.

seamount   An underwater mountain.

secrete   To produce and give off.

sediment   Loose materials, such as particles of soil and rock.

sedimentary rock   Rock formed when layers of sediment are compacted and cemented together.

seed   The part of a flowering plant that is able to grow into a new plant.

seed leaves   For some seeds, such as beans, it is the two parts that make up the seed, which provide food for the growing embryo inside the seed.

shore   The land at the shoreline.

shoreline   An area where the ocean and the land meet.

shortening   A fat added to dough that shortens gluten molecules.

silk   A fine, soft fiber made by some insects.

sliding friction   Friction produced when objects are sliding with respect to one another.

small intestine   A long tube in the digestive system where food goes when it leaves the stomach.

smell detectors   Special cells in the nose that respond to smells by sending a message to your brain, which then identifies the smell.

soap scum   A waxy material that doesn't dissolve in water and is formed from the combination of soap and any of the minerals in hard water.

soft water   Water that has little if any calcium, magnesium, or iron.

soil   A mixture of particles of rock, humus, air, and water.

solar eclipse   An eclipse in which the Moon passes in front of the Sun.

solar energy   Radiant energy from the Sun.

solar noon   The time at or near 12:00 P.M. standard time, when the Sun is at its highest altitude.

solar system   A group of celestial bodies that move in a curved path about a star called a sun.

solar year   The full cycle of seasons—365¼ days.

solidify   To change to a solid.

solute   A substance that is dissolved in a solution.

solution   A homogeneous mixture of two or more substances; the combination of a solute and a solvent.

solvent   A substance that dissolves a solute.

sounding board   A part of a musical instrument that increases the loudness and quality of sound.

Southern Hemisphere   The region between the equator and the South Pole of Earth or another celestial body.

South Pole   The south end of Earth's axis, at latitude 90°S.

species   A group of similar organisms.

speed   A measure of distance traveled per unit of time.

sphincter   A muscle that opens and closes the opening between the stomach and the duodenum.

spinal cord   A large bundle of nerves running down through the backbone.

spine   Backbone.

spinneret   A body part on the hind end of a spider that spins liquid silk from inside the spider's body.

sprout   To begin to grow.

standard time (ST)   The time when it isn't daylight saving time.

standing wave   A wave pattern produced when two identical waves traveling in opposite directions combine, forming stationary points called nodes between points of maximum vibration called antinodes.

starch   A nutrient; a large molecule made up of many smaller sugar molecules bonded together.

stem   The part of a plant that supports the plant.

stomach   Where food goes when it is swallowed.

submarine   A submersible with ballast tanks.

submersible   An ocean craft capable of going underwater.

summer solstice   The day of the year, on or about June 21 in the Northern Hemisphere, when Earth's North Pole is tilted closest to the Sun.

sunrise   The apparent rising of the Sun above the eastern horizon.

sunset   The apparent setting of the Sun below the western horizon.

surface tension   The result of cohesion of molecules on the surface of a liquid, which creates a skinlike film over the surface of the liquid.

sympathetic vibration   See **resonance.**

tapetum   The mirrorlike reflective surface on the retina of most night animals.

taproot   The main root that grows straight down in a taproot system.

taproot system   A root system consisting of a taproot and rootlets branching from it.

temperature   A measure of how cold or hot an object is.

tension   A pulling force that causes a separation of molecules, thus an increase in the length of an object.

texture   How large the grain size of a material is.

thermal conductivity   A measure of how rapidly heat flows through a material that is exposed to a difference in temperature.

thermometer   An instrument that measures temperature.

three-dimensional   Having length, width, and height.

tissue   A group of cells that perform a special job.

toothed margin   A leaf margin that is either large and blunt or small and sharp.

topographic map   A flat map that shows the shapes and heights of land areas, using lines to connect points on the Earth that have the same elevation.

torque   The turning effect of a force.

total solar eclipse   A solar eclipse in which the shadow of the Moon reaches Earth and the entire photosphere of the Sun is blocked to observers in the Moon's shadow.

transmission   Act of being sent from one place to another.

trench   An underwater valley that is V-shaped, narrow, and deep.

trough   The low point of a wave.

true weight   Weight due only to gravity.

umbra   The inner, darker part of a shadow.

universe   All the matter and energy in space.

vacuum   An empty space.

vapor   A gas formed from a substance that is usually a solid or a liquid at room temperature.

vaporize   To change to a vapor.

vein   The phloem and xylem tubes that transport nutrients and provide support for the leaves.

vent   The channel of a volcano that connects the source of magma to the volcano's opening.

vernal equinox   The first day of spring, on or about March 21 in the Northern Hemisphere.

vertebra (plural **vertebrae**)   One of the bones that makes up the backbone.

vibrate   To move quickly back and forth.

vibration   A single back-and-forth movement.

virtual image   An image that cannot be projected onto a screen.

viscosity   A measure of how viscous a substance is.

viscous   Having a relatively high resistance to flow.

vocal cords   Tissues stretched across the windpipe that vibrate when air from the lungs flows past them.

volume   The amount of space a material occupies.

water cycle   The cycle of evaporation of water from the surface of the Earth and the return of that water to the Earth in solid or liquid form.

water wave   A disturbance on the surface of water consisting of a crest and a trough.

waxing   Growing larger.

weather   Process by which rocks are broken into small pieces by natural agents such as falling rain.

weight   A measure of the pull of gravity on an object.

Western Hemisphere   The half of Earth west of the prime meridian between longitudes 0° and 180°.

windpipe   A breathing tube from the mouth to the lungs.

winter solstice   The day of the year, on or about December 22 in the Northern Hemisphere, when Earth's axis is tilted farthest away from the Sun.

work   The product of the force needed to move an object times the distance the object is moved.

xylem tubes   Tubelike structures in some plants that transport nutrients from the soil throughout the plant.

zenith   The highest point in the sky, which is directly overhead.

zodiac   The band of zodiac constellations along the ecliptic.

zodiac constellations   The 12 constellations along the zodiac.

Index

abscission layer, 31, 114
absorb, 28, 114
abyss, 84, 114
abyssal plain, 84, 114
acceleration, 99, 113, 114
acid, 57, 69, 114
activate, 43, 114
adhesion, 109, 110, 111, 114
adhesive, 109, 111, 114
air pressure, 82, 114
altitude
    definition of, 5, 114
angiosperm, 26, 114
angular diameter, 21, 114
annually, 31, 114
Antarctic Circle, 14, 114
Antarctic region, 14, 114
antinode, 104, 105, 114
apparent diameter, 21, 114
apparent size, 21, 114
arc, 7, 117
Arctic Circle, 14, 114
Arctic region, 14, 114.
artificial satellite, 19, 114
asteroid
    Ceres, 18
    definition of, 18, 114
    shape of, 18
astronomer, 4, 114
atmosphere, 8, 114
atmospheric pressure, 82, 114
atom, 8, 114
autumnal equinox, 13, 114
axis
    crystal, 59
    definition of, 4, 59, 114
    Earth's, 4

bacteria, 41, 114
ballast tank, 87, 114
barometer, 84, 114
barometric pressure, 82, 114
barycenter, 23, 114
beach, 86, 114
Bernoulli's principal, 108, 114
bilateral symmetry, 30, 114
binary body, 23, 114
blade, 30, 114

blood, 40, 114
blood clot, 40, 114
blood vessel, 40, 114
bond, 52, 114
broad leaf, 26, 114
broadleaf plants, 26, 114
bromelin, 56, 114
buoyant force, 108, 114

caldera, 88, 114
calendar, 18, 114
canine teeth, 38, 114
Cassini's division, 16, 114
catalyst, 55, 114
celestial bodies, 4, 114
cell, 28, 114
cement, 77, 114
center of gravity, 23, 102, 114
center of mass, 23, 114
Ceres, 18
chemical change, 52, 114
chemical reaction, 52, 114
chemistry, 50, 114
chitin, 32, 114
chlorophyll, 56, 114
chromatography, 66, 114
circulatory system, 40, 115
cloud, 81, 115
cohesion, 109, 110, 115
colorant, 66, 115
combination chemical reac-
    tion, 52, 115
communication, 37
compaction, 77, 114
compass, 7
composites, 26, 115
compress, 83, 115
compression, 107, 115
concave, 95, 115
concentrated, 13, 23, 115
concentration, 62, 115
concentric, 15, 115
condensation, 82, 115
condense, 41, 115
cone, 45, 115
conserve, 61, 115
constellation, 5, 115
continent, 73, 115

continental shelf, 84, 115
continental slope, 84, 115
contour lines, 87, 115
contracts, 99, 115
convection zone, 8, 115
converge, 96, 115
convert, 97, 115
convex, 95, 115
core, 8, 115
Coriolis effect, 79, 115
crescent moon, 18, 115
crest, 85, 115
crust, 78, 115
crystal, 59, 115
cuticle, 38, 115

daylight saving time (DST), 6,
    115
deactivate, 56, 115
deceleration, 113, 115
deciduous, 31, 115
decompose, 54, 115
decomposition reaction, 54,
    115
deflect, 79, 115
deliquescent, 65, 115
denaturing, 58, 115
density, 50, 51, 115
density current, 85, 115
deposition, 77, 115
diffuse, 56, 115
digest, 34, 115
digestive system, 39, 115
dilute, 91, 115
direct rotation, 11, 115
disk
    definition of, 26, 39, 115
    flower, 26
    spine, 39
disk flowers, 26, 115
displaced, 50, 115
dissolve, 36, 115
dormant, 28, 115
dough, 57, 115
duodenum, 39, 115

ear canal, 44, 115
eardrum, 44, 115

earthquake, 90, 115
Eastern Hemisphere, 72, 115
echo, 105, 115
eclipse, 9, 115
ecliptic, 5, 9, 115
efflorescence, 64, 115
eject, 88, 115
elevation, 87, 115
elongation, 15, 115
embryo, 27, 115
emulsifier, 64, 115
emulsion, 64, 115
energy
    definition of, 7, 8, 97, 115
    kinetic, 97, 116
    magnetic potential energy,
    97
    potential, 97, 118
entire margin, 31, 115
enzyme
    bromelin, 56, 114
    catalyst, 55, 114
    definition of, 55, 115
    fermentation, 68
equal arm balance, 101, 115
equator, 7, 72, 116
erosion
    agents of, 76
    definitions, 76, 86, 116
erupt, 88, 116
evaporate, 41, 116
evaporation, 82, 116
evergreen, 26, 116
exoskeleton, 32, 116
expand, 8, 99, 116
eye, 80, 116
eyepiece, 20, 116

faces, 59, 116
fade, 41, 116
fault, 74, 116
fault plane, 74, 116
fermentation, 68, 116
fertilization, 26, 116
fribrin, 40, 116
fibrous root system, 29, 116
flatfish, 35
fluctuates, 19, 116

fluid, 62, 116
focal length, 96, 116
focal point, 96, 116
footwall, 74, 116
force, 54, 116
fracture, 74, 116
free-fall, 100, 116
freeze, 66, 116
freezing point, 66, 116
frequency, 8, 116
friction, 112
  definition of, 102, 103, 116
  rolling, 102, 118
  sliding, 102, 118
fulcrum, 101, 116

Galilean satellites, 16, 116
gelatin, 56, 116
germination, 27, 116
glacier, 86, 116
globular protein, 58, 116
glucose, 68, 116
gluten, 58, 116
gravity, 14, 116
great circle, 72, 116
Gregorian calendar, 18, 116
groundwater, 88, 116
guyot, 84, 116

hanging wall, 74, 116
hard palate, 44, 116
hard water, 69, 116
head, 26, 116
heat, 7, 98, 116
heat telescope, 20
helioseismology, 8, 116
Hero's engine, 113
heterogeneous mixture, 63, 116
homogeneous mixture, 63, 116
horizon
  definition, 4, 116
hummingbirds, 35
humus, 75, 116
hurricane, 80, 116
hydrate, 64, 116
hygroscopic, 65, 116

iceberg, 86, 116
igneous rock, 78, 116
illuminate, 13, 116
Image
  definition of, 20, 116
  mirror, 94
  real, 95, 96, 118

virtual, 94, 97, 119
incisors, 38, 116
inertia, 19, 116
inferior planet, 15, 116
infrared radiation, 7, 116
insects, 32–34
insulator, 67, 116
International Astronomical Union (IAU), 10
intrusive igneous rock, 78, 116
irregular flowers, 30, 116
island, 84, 116

keratin, 38, 116
kinetic energy, 97, 116
knot, 112, 116

laterally reversed, 94, 116
latitude, 7, 116
law of conservation of matter, 52, 116
leaf, 26, 30, 31, 116
leaf margin, 31, 116
leap year, 18, 116
leavening agent, 57, 116
lens
  definitions, 20, 117
  eyepiece, 20, 116
  magnifying, 96, 97
  objective lens, 16, 117
linear, 19, 116
line of symmetry, 30, 116
lines of latitude, 7, 22, 72, 117
lines of longitude, 72, 117
lobed margin, 31, 117
longitude, 72, 117
lubricant, 104, 117
luminous, 17, 117
lunar calendar, 18, 117
lunar month, 18, 117
lunula, 38, 117

magma, 78, 117
magma chamber, 88, 117
mammals, 37, 117
mass, 4, 117
mass ratio, 4, 117
matter, 4, 117
melanin, 41, 117
melt, 98, 117
melting point, 98, 117
meridians, 72, 117
metamorphic rock, 78, 117
metamorphism, 78, 117

microorganisms, 90, 117
mineral, 69, 117
minor planets, 18, 117
mirror
  concave, 95
  convex, 95
  image, 94
  plane, 94, 119
mirror image, 94, 117
mixture, 53, 117
model
  Earth, 10, 11
  solar eclipse, 9
  Sun, 8
  Venus, 11
molecule, 52, 117
molt, 32, 117
molten, 78, 117
monomer
  definition of, 60, 117
  ethylene, 60
mucus, 36, 117
mud, 76, 117
mudflow, 76, 117

nail bed, 38, 117
natural satellite, 16, 117
nautical mile, 112, 117
near point, 47, 117
needle leaf, 26, 117
nerves, 43, 117
Newton's first law of motion, 19, 112, 117
Newton's second law of motion, 113, 117
Newton's third law of motion, 113, 117
night vision, 45, 117
nodes, 104, 105, 117
nomenclature, 10
non-Newtonian fluid, 62, 117
normal fault, 74, 117
Northern Hemisphere, 7, 117
north pole, 10, 117
North Pole, 10, 117
nuclear fusion, 8, 117
nucleus (pl nuclei), 8, 117
nutrients, 29, 117

objective lens, 20, 117
ocean current, 79, 117
odor, 43, 117
ooze deposits, 84, 117
opaque, 41, 117
opposable, 37, 117

optical illusion, 46, 117
optic nerve, 45, 117
orbit
  definition of, 4, 117
  Earth's, 5
organisms, 27, 117
oxidation, 53, 117
oxygen, 28, 117

Pangaea, 73, 117
Panthalassa, 73, 117
parallax, 22, 117
parallels, 72, 117
penumbra, 9, 117
percolation, 88, 117
perimeter, 27, 118
period of revolution, 17, 118
period of rotation, 17, 118
permeability, 75, 118
persistence of vision, 46, 118
petiole, 30, 118
phases of matter, 50, 118
phases of the Moon, 18, 118
pheromones, 33, 118
phloem tubes, 29, 31, 118
photometer, 17, 118
photosphere, 8, 9, 118
physical properties, 57, 118
pigment, 41, 117
pitch, 106, 118
plane mirror, 94, 118
planet
  definition of, 4, 118
  list of, 4
Polaris, 22, 118
pollination, 26, 118
pollutants, 91, 118
polymer, 60, 118
porphyritic rock, 78, 118
potential energy, 97, 118
precipitation, 82, 118
pressure, 62, 111, 118
primate, 37, 118
prime meridian, 72, 118
proboscis, 34, 118
product, 52, 118
propagate, 27, 118
protein, 56, 118

radial symmetry, 30, 118
radiant energy, 7, 118
radiant heat, 7, 118
radiation, 7, 20, 118
radiation zone, 8, 118
ray flower, 26, 118
reactant, 52, 118

real image, 95, 118
reflect, 17, 118
refracting telescope, 20, 118
refrigerant, 98, 118
regular flower, 30, 118
resonance, 90, 118
retina, 45, 46, 118
retrograde, 11, 118
revolve
  definition, 5, 118
  Earth, 13, 22
  Venus, 15
rods, 45, 118
rolling friction, 102, 119
root
  definition of, 29, 38, 118
  fingernail, 38
  plant, 29
rootlets, 29, 118
rotate
  definition of, 4, 118
  Earth, 4, 9, 11, 12
  Venus, 11
runoff, 91, 118
rusting, 53, 118

saliva, 34, 118
satellite, 19, 118
Saturn, rings of, 16
scab, 40, 118
scale model
  definition of, 10, 118
  Earth, 10
seamount, 84, 118
seasons, 12
secrete, 33, 118
sediment, 76, 118
sedimentary rock, 77, 118
seed, 26, 118
seed leaves, 28, 118
shadows
  Moon's, 9

penumbra, 9, 117
umbra, 9, 119
Sun, 5, 6
shore, 86, 118
shoreline, 86, 118
shortening, 58, 118
silk, 34, 118
sliding friction, 102, 118
small intestine, 39, 118
smell dectectors, 43, 118
soap scum, 69, 118
soft water, 69, 118
soil, 75, 118
solar eclipse, 9, 119
solar energy, 7, 8, 119
solar noon, 6, 119
solar system, 4, 119
solar year, 18, 119
solidify, 78, 119
solute, 62, 119
solution, 62, 119
solvent, 62, 119
sound, 105, 106
sounding board, 106, 119
Southern Hemisphere, 7, 119
South Pole, 7, 119
species, 33, 119
speed, 99, 119
sphincter, 39, 119
spinal cord, 39, 119
spine, 39, 119
spinneret, 34, 119
sprout, 27, 119
standard time, 6, 119
standing wave
  antinode, 104, 114
  definition of, 104, 119
  node, 104, 117
starch, 57, 67, 119
stem, 28, 119
stomach, 39, 119
submarine, 87, 119

submersible, 87, 119
summer solstice, 12, 13, 119
Sun
  apparent motion of, 4, 5, 12
  eclipse, 9
  model, 8
  time, 5, 6
  vibration, 8
sunrise, 4, 6, 119
sunset, 4, 119
surface tension, 110, 119
sweat, 41
sympathetic vibration, 90,
  119

tapetum, 45, 119
tap root, 29, 119
tap root system, 29, 119
temperature, 99, 119
tension, 107, 119
texture, 75, 119
thermal conductivity, 98, 119
thermometer, 99, 119
thermoscope, 99
three-dimensional, 59, 119
time, 5, 6
time zone, 5
tissue, 445, 119
toothed margin, 31, 119
topographic map, 87, 119
torque, 101, 119
total solar eclipse, 9, 119
transmission, 7, 119
trench, 84, 119
trough, 85, 119
true weight, 100, 119

umbra, 9, 119
universe, 4, 7, 119

vacuum, 99, 119
vapor, 41, 119

vaporize, 43, 119
vein, 30, 119
vent, 89, 119
Venus
  model of, 11
  rotation of, 11
vernal equinox, 13, 119
vertebra, 39, 119
vibrate, 8, 119
vibration, 8, 119
virtual image, 94, 119
viscosity, 61, 119
viscous, 58, 119
vocal cords, 44, 119
volcano, 88, 89
volume, 50, 119

water cycle, 82, 119
water resistant, 111
water wave, 85, 119
waxing, 15, 119
weathered, 76, 119
weight
  apparent, 100, 114
  definition of, 14, 100, 119
  true, 100, 119
Western Hemisphere, 72,
  119
wetting, 111
windpipe, 44, 119
winter solstice, 12, 13, 14,
  119
work, 102, 119

xylem tubes, 29, 31, 119

zenith, 7, 119
zodiac, 5, 119
zodiac constellations, 5, 119